Mometrix
TEST PREPARATION

I0878455

Secrets of the

National Board Certification®

Library Media: Early Childhood through Young Adulthood Exam Study Guide

DEAR FUTURE EXAM SUCCESS STORY

First of all, **THANK YOU** for purchasing Mometrix study materials!

Second, congratulations! You are one of the few determined test-takers who are committed to doing whatever it takes to excel on your exam. **You have come to the right place.** We developed these study materials with one goal in mind: to deliver you the information you need in a format that's concise and easy to use.

In addition to optimizing your guide for the content of the test, we've outlined our recommended steps for breaking down the preparation process into small, attainable goals so you can make sure you stay on track.

We've also analyzed the entire test-taking process, identifying the most common pitfalls and showing how you can overcome them and be ready for any curveball the test throws you.

Standardized testing is one of the biggest obstacles on your road to success, which only increases the importance of doing well in the high-pressure, high-stakes environment of test day. Your results on this test could have a significant impact on your future, and this guide provides the information and practical advice to help you achieve your full potential on test day.

Your success is our success

We would love to hear from you! If you would like to share the story of your exam success or if you have any questions or comments in regard to our products, please contact us at **800-673-8175** or **support@mometrix.com**.

Thanks again for your business and we wish you continued success!

Sincerely,
The Mometrix Test Preparation Team

Written and edited by the Mometrix Exam Secrets Test Prep Team
Printed in the United States of America

TABLE OF CONTENTS

Introduction

Thank you for purchasing this resource! You have made the choice to prepare yourself for a test that could have a huge impact on your future, and this guide is designed to help you be fully ready for test day. Obviously, it's important to have a solid understanding of the test material, but you also need to be prepared for the unique environment and stressors of the test, so that you can perform to the best of your abilities.

For this purpose, the first section that appears in this guide is the **Secret Keys**. We've devoted countless hours to meticulously researching what works and what doesn't, and we've boiled down our findings to the five most impactful steps you can take to improve your performance on the test. We start at the beginning with study planning and move through the preparation process, all the way to the testing strategies that will help you get the most out of what you know when you're finally sitting in front of the test.

We recommend that you start preparing for your test as far in advance as possible. However, if you've bought this guide as a last-minute study resource and only have a few days before your test, we recommend that you skip over the first two Secret Keys since they address a long-term study plan.

If you struggle with **test anxiety**, we strongly encourage you to check out our recommendations for how you can overcome it. Test anxiety is a formidable foe, but it can be beaten, and we want to make sure you have the tools you need to defeat it.

Secret Key #1 – Plan Big, Study Small

There's a lot riding on your performance. If you want to ace this test, you're going to need to keep your skills sharp and the material fresh in your mind. You need a plan that lets you review everything you need to know while still fitting in your schedule. We'll break this strategy down into three categories.

Information Organization

Start with the information you already have: the official test outline. From this, you can make a complete list of all the concepts you need to cover before the test. Organize these concepts into groups that can be studied together, and create a list of any related vocabulary you need to learn so you can brush up on any difficult terms. You'll want to keep this vocabulary list handy once you actually start studying since you may need to add to it along the way.

Time Management

Once you have your set of study concepts, decide how to spread them out over the time you have left before the test. Break your study plan into small, clear goals so you have a manageable task for each day and know exactly what you're doing. Then just focus on one small step at a time. When you manage your time this way, you don't need to spend hours at a time studying. Studying a small block of content for a short period each day helps you retain information better and avoid stressing over how much you have left to do. You can relax knowing that you have a plan to cover everything in time. In order for this strategy to be effective though, you have to start studying early and stick to your schedule. Avoid the exhaustion and futility that comes from last-minute cramming!

Study Environment

The environment you study in has a big impact on your learning. Studying in a coffee shop, while probably more enjoyable, is not likely to be as fruitful as studying in a quiet room. It's important to keep distractions to a minimum. You're only planning to study for a short block of time, so make the most of it. Don't pause to check your phone or get up to find a snack. It's also important to **avoid multitasking**. Research has consistently shown that multitasking will make your studying dramatically less effective. Your study area should also be comfortable and well-lit so you don't have the distraction of straining your eyes or sitting on an uncomfortable chair.

The time of day you study is also important. You want to be rested and alert. Don't wait until just before bedtime. Study when you'll be most likely to comprehend and remember. Even better, if you know what time of day your test will be, set that time aside for study. That way your brain will be used to working on that subject at that specific time and you'll have a better chance of recalling information.

Finally, it can be helpful to team up with others who are studying for the same test. Your actual studying should be done in as isolated an environment as possible, but the work of organizing the information and setting up the study plan can be divided up. In between study sessions, you can discuss with your teammates the concepts that you're all studying and quiz each other on the details. Just be sure that your teammates are as serious about the test as you are. If you find that your study time is being replaced with social time, you might need to find a new team.

Secret Key #2 – Make Your Studying Count

You're devoting a lot of time and effort to preparing for this test, so you want to be absolutely certain it will pay off. This means doing more than just reading the content and hoping you can remember it on test day. It's important to make every minute of study count. There are two main areas you can focus on to make your studying count.

Retention

It doesn't matter how much time you study if you can't remember the material. You need to make sure you are retaining the concepts. To check your retention of the information you're learning, try recalling it at later times with minimal prompting. Try carrying around flashcards and glance at one or two from time to time or ask a friend who's also studying for the test to quiz you.

To enhance your retention, look for ways to put the information into practice so that you can apply it rather than simply recalling it. If you're using the information in practical ways, it will be much easier to remember. Similarly, it helps to solidify a concept in your mind if you're not only reading it to yourself but also explaining it to someone else. Ask a friend to let you teach them about a concept you're a little shaky on (or speak aloud to an imaginary audience if necessary). As you try to summarize, define, give examples, and answer your friend's questions, you'll understand the concepts better and they will stay with you longer. Finally, step back for a big picture view and ask yourself how each piece of information fits with the whole subject. When you link the different concepts together and see them working together as a whole, it's easier to remember the individual components.

Finally, practice showing your work on any multi-step problems, even if you're just studying. Writing out each step you take to solve a problem will help solidify the process in your mind, and you'll be more likely to remember it during the test.

Modality

Modality simply refers to the means or method by which you study. Choosing a study modality that fits your own individual learning style is crucial. No two people learn best in exactly the same way, so it's important to know your strengths and use them to your advantage.

For example, if you learn best by visualization, focus on visualizing a concept in your mind and draw an image or a diagram. Try color-coding your notes, illustrating them, or creating symbols that will trigger your mind to recall a learned concept. If you learn best by hearing or discussing information, find a study partner who learns the same way or read aloud to yourself. Think about how to put the information in your own words. Imagine that you are giving a lecture on the topic and record yourself so you can listen to it later.

For any learning style, flashcards can be helpful. Organize the information so you can take advantage of spare moments to review. Underline key words or phrases. Use different colors for different categories. Mnemonic devices (such as creating a short list in which every item starts with the same letter) can also help with retention. Find what works best for you and use it to store the information in your mind most effectively and easily.

Secret Key #3 – Practice the Right Way

Your success on test day depends not only on how many hours you put into preparing, but also on whether you prepared the right way. It's good to check along the way to see if your studying is paying off. One of the most effective ways to do this is by taking practice tests to evaluate your progress. Practice tests are useful because they show exactly where you need to improve. Every time you take a practice test, pay special attention to these three groups of questions:

- The questions you got wrong
- The questions you had to guess on, even if you guessed right
- The questions you found difficult or slow to work through

This will show you exactly what your weak areas are, and where you need to devote more study time. Ask yourself why each of these questions gave you trouble. Was it because you didn't understand the material? Was it because you didn't remember the vocabulary? Do you need more repetitions on this type of question to build speed and confidence? Dig into those questions and figure out how you can strengthen your weak areas as you go back to review the material.

Additionally, many practice tests have a section explaining the answer choices. It can be tempting to read the explanation and think that you now have a good understanding of the concept. However, an explanation likely only covers part of the question's broader context. Even if the explanation makes perfect sense, **go back and investigate** every concept related to the question until you're positive you have a thorough understanding.

As you go along, keep in mind that the practice test is just that: practice. Memorizing these questions and answers will not be very helpful on the actual test because it is unlikely to have any of the same exact questions. If you only know the right answers to the sample questions, you won't be prepared for the real thing. **Study the concepts** until you understand them fully, and then you'll be able to answer any question that shows up on the test.

It's important to wait on the practice tests until you're ready. If you take a test on your first day of study, you may be overwhelmed by the amount of material covered and how much you need to learn. Work up to it gradually.

On test day, you'll need to be prepared for answering questions, managing your time, and using the test-taking strategies you've learned. It's a lot to balance, like a mental marathon that will have a big impact on your future. Like training for a marathon, you'll need to start slowly and work your way up. When test day arrives, you'll be ready.

Start with the strategies you've read in the first two Secret Keys—plan your course and study in the way that works best for you. If you have time, consider using multiple study resources to get different approaches to the same concepts. It can be helpful to see difficult concepts from more than one angle. Then find a good source for practice tests. Many times, the test website will suggest potential study resources or provide sample tests.

Practice Test Strategy

If you're able to find at least three practice tests, we recommend this strategy:

Untimed and Open-Book Practice

Take the first test with no time constraints and with your notes and study guide handy. Take your time and focus on applying the strategies you've learned.

Timed and Open-Book Practice

Take the second practice test open-book as well, but set a timer and practice pacing yourself to finish in time.

Timed and Closed-Book Practice

Take any other practice tests as if it were test day. Set a timer and put away your study materials. Sit at a table or desk in a quiet room, imagine yourself at the testing center, and answer questions as quickly and accurately as possible.

Keep repeating timed and closed-book tests on a regular basis until you run out of practice tests or it's time for the actual test. Your mind will be ready for the schedule and stress of test day, and you'll be able to focus on recalling the material you've learned.

Secret Key #4 – Pace Yourself

Once you're fully prepared for the material on the test, your biggest challenge on test day will be managing your time. Just knowing that the clock is ticking can make you panic even if you have plenty of time left. Work on pacing yourself so you can build confidence against the time constraints of the exam. Pacing is a difficult skill to master, especially in a high-pressure environment, so **practice is vital**.

Set time expectations for your pace based on how much time is available. For example, if a section has 60 questions and the time limit is 30 minutes, you know you have to average 30 seconds or less per question in order to answer them all. Although 30 seconds is the hard limit, set 25 seconds per question as your goal, so you reserve extra time to spend on harder questions. When you budget extra time for the harder questions, you no longer have any reason to stress when those questions take longer to answer.

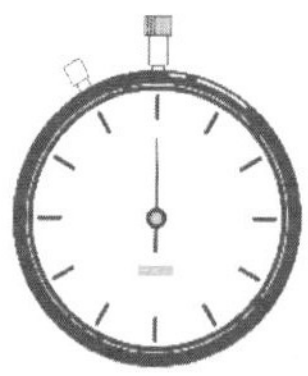

Don't let this time expectation distract you from working through the test at a calm, steady pace, but keep it in mind so you don't spend too much time on any one question. Recognize that taking extra time on one question you don't understand may keep you from answering two that you do understand later in the test. If your time limit for a question is up and you're still not sure of the answer, mark it and move on, and come back to it later if the time and the test format allow. If the testing format doesn't allow you to return to earlier questions, just make an educated guess; then put it out of your mind and move on.

On the easier questions, be careful not to rush. It may seem wise to hurry through them so you have more time for the challenging ones, but it's not worth missing one if you know the concept and just didn't take the time to read the question fully. Work efficiently but make sure you understand the question and have looked at all of the answer choices, since more than one may seem right at first.

Even if you're paying attention to the time, you may find yourself a little behind at some point. You should speed up to get back on track, but do so wisely. Don't panic; just take a few seconds less on each question until you're caught up. Don't guess without thinking, but do look through the answer choices and eliminate any you know are wrong. If you can get down to two choices, it is often worthwhile to guess from those. Once you've chosen an answer, move on and don't dwell on any that you skipped or had to hurry through. If a question was taking too long, chances are it was one of the harder ones, so you weren't as likely to get it right anyway.

On the other hand, if you find yourself getting ahead of schedule, it may be beneficial to slow down a little. The more quickly you work, the more likely you are to make a careless mistake that will affect your score. You've budgeted time for each question, so don't be afraid to spend that time. Practice an efficient but careful pace to get the most out of the time you have.

Secret Key #5 – Have a Plan for Guessing

When you're taking the test, you may find yourself stuck on a question. Some of the answer choices seem better than others, but you don't see the one answer choice that is obviously correct. What do you do?

The scenario described above is very common, yet most test takers have not effectively prepared for it. Developing and practicing a plan for guessing may be one of the single most effective uses of your time as you get ready for the exam.

In developing your plan for guessing, there are three questions to address:

- When should you start the guessing process?
- How should you narrow down the choices?
- Which answer should you choose?

When to Start the Guessing Process

Unless your plan for guessing is to select C every time (which, despite its merits, is not what we recommend), you need to leave yourself enough time to apply your answer elimination strategies. Since you have a limited amount of time for each question, that means that if you're going to give yourself the best shot at guessing correctly, you have to decide quickly whether or not you will guess.

Of course, the best-case scenario is that you don't have to guess at all, so first, see if you can answer the question based on your knowledge of the subject and basic reasoning skills. Focus on the key words in the question and try to jog your memory of related topics. Give yourself a chance to bring the knowledge to mind, but once you realize that you don't have (or you can't access) the knowledge you need to answer the question, it's time to start the guessing process.

It's almost always better to start the guessing process too early than too late. It only takes a few seconds to remember something and answer the question from knowledge. Carefully eliminating wrong answer choices takes longer. Plus, going through the process of eliminating answer choices can actually help jog your memory.

Summary: Start the guessing process as soon as you decide that you can't answer the question based on your knowledge.

How to Narrow Down the Choices

The next chapter in this book (**Test-Taking Strategies**) includes a wide range of strategies for how to approach questions and how to look for answer choices to eliminate. You will definitely want to read those carefully, practice them, and figure out which ones work best for you. Here though, we're going to address a mindset rather than a particular strategy.

Your odds of guessing an answer correctly depend on how many options you are choosing from.

Number of options left	5	4	3	2	1
Odds of guessing correctly	20%	25%	33%	50%	100%

You can see from this chart just how valuable it is to be able to eliminate incorrect answers and make an educated guess, but there are two things that many test takers do that cause them to miss out on the benefits of guessing:

- Accidentally eliminating the correct answer
- Selecting an answer based on an impression

We'll look at the first one here, and the second one in the next section.

To avoid accidentally eliminating the correct answer, we recommend a thought exercise called **the $5 challenge**. In this challenge, you only eliminate an answer choice from contention if you are willing to bet $5 on it being wrong. Why $5? Five dollars is a small but not insignificant amount of money. It's an amount you could afford to lose but wouldn't want to throw away. And while losing $5 once might not hurt too much, doing it twenty times will set you back $100. In the same way, each small decision you make—eliminating a choice here, guessing on a question there—won't by itself impact your score very much, but when you put them all together, they can make a big difference. By holding each answer choice elimination decision to a higher standard, you can reduce the risk of accidentally eliminating the correct answer.

The $5 challenge can also be applied in a positive sense: If you are willing to bet $5 that an answer choice *is* correct, go ahead and mark it as correct.

Summary: Only eliminate an answer choice if you are willing to bet $5 that it is wrong.

Which Answer to Choose

You're taking the test. You've run into a hard question and decided you'll have to guess. You've eliminated all the answer choices you're willing to bet $5 on. Now you have to pick an answer. Why do we even need to talk about this? Why can't you just pick whichever one you feel like when the time comes?

The answer to these questions is that if you don't come into the test with a plan, you'll rely on your impression to select an answer choice, and if you do that, you risk falling into a trap. The test writers know that everyone who takes their test will be guessing on some of the questions, so they intentionally write wrong answer choices to seem plausible. You still have to pick an answer though, and if the wrong answer choices are designed to look right, how can you ever be sure that you're not falling for their trap? The best solution we've found to this dilemma is to take the decision out of your hands entirely. Here is the process we recommend:

Once you've eliminated any choices that you are confident (willing to bet $5) are wrong, select the first remaining choice as your answer.

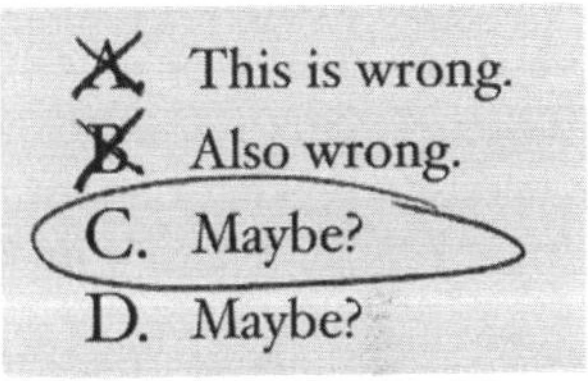

Whether you choose to select the first remaining choice, the second, or the last, the important thing is that you use some preselected standard. Using this approach guarantees that you will not be enticed into selecting an answer choice that looks right, because you are not basing your decision on how the answer choices look.

This is not meant to make you question your knowledge. Instead, it is to help you recognize the difference between your knowledge and your impressions. There's a huge difference between thinking an answer is right because of what you know, and thinking an answer is right because it looks or sounds like it should be right.

Summary: To ensure that your selection is appropriately random, make a predetermined selection from among all answer choices you have not eliminated.

Test-Taking Strategies

This section contains a list of test-taking strategies that you may find helpful as you work through the test. By taking what you know and applying logical thought, you can maximize your chances of answering any question correctly!

It is very important to realize that every question is different and every person is different: no single strategy will work on every question, and no single strategy will work for every person. That's why we've included all of them here, so you can try them out and determine which ones work best for different types of questions and which ones work best for you.

Question Strategies

✓ Read Carefully

Read the question and the answer choices carefully. Don't miss the question because you misread the terms. You have plenty of time to read each question thoroughly and make sure you understand what is being asked. Yet a happy medium must be attained, so don't waste too much time. You must read carefully and efficiently.

✓ Contextual Clues

Look for contextual clues. If the question includes a word you are not familiar with, look at the immediate context for some indication of what the word might mean. Contextual clues can often give you all the information you need to decipher the meaning of an unfamiliar word. Even if you can't determine the meaning, you may be able to narrow down the possibilities enough to make a solid guess at the answer to the question.

✓ Prefixes

If you're having trouble with a word in the question or answer choices, try dissecting it. Take advantage of every clue that the word might include. Prefixes can be a huge help. Usually, they allow you to determine a basic meaning. *Pre-* means before, *post-* means after, *pro-* is positive, *de-* is negative. From prefixes, you can get an idea of the general meaning of the word and try to put it into context.

✓ Hedge Words

Watch out for critical hedge words, such as *likely, may, can, often, almost, mostly, usually, generally, rarely,* and *sometimes*. Question writers insert these hedge phrases to cover every possibility. Often an answer choice will be wrong simply because it leaves no room for exception. Be on guard for answer choices that have definitive words such as *exactly* and *always*.

✓ Switchback Words

Stay alert for *switchbacks*. These are the words and phrases frequently used to alert you to shifts in thought. The most common switchback words are *but, although,* and *however*. Others include *nevertheless, on the other hand, even though, while, in spite of, despite,* and *regardless of*. Switchback words are important to catch because they can change the direction of the question or an answer choice.

⊘ Face Value

When in doubt, use common sense. Accept the situation in the problem at face value. Don't read too much into it. These problems will not require you to make wild assumptions. If you have to go beyond creativity and warp time or space in order to have an answer choice fit the question, then you should move on and consider the other answer choices. These are normal problems rooted in reality. The applicable relationship or explanation may not be readily apparent, but it is there for you to figure out. Use your common sense to interpret anything that isn't clear.

Answer Choice Strategies

⊘ Answer Selection

The most thorough way to pick an answer choice is to identify and eliminate wrong answers until only one is left, then confirm it is the correct answer. Sometimes an answer choice may immediately seem right, but be careful. The test writers will usually put more than one reasonable answer choice on each question, so take a second to read all of them and make sure that the other choices are not equally obvious. As long as you have time left, it is better to read every answer choice than to pick the first one that looks right without checking the others.

⊘ Answer Choice Families

An answer choice family consists of two (in rare cases, three) answer choices that are very similar in construction and cannot all be true at the same time. If you see two answer choices that are direct opposites or parallels, one of them is usually the correct answer. For instance, if one answer choice says that quantity *x* increases and another either says that quantity *x* decreases (opposite) or says that quantity *y* increases (parallel), then those answer choices would fall into the same family. An answer choice that doesn't match the construction of the answer choice family is more likely to be incorrect. Most questions will not have answer choice families, but when they do appear, you should be prepared to recognize them.

⊘ Eliminate Answers

Eliminate answer choices as soon as you realize they are wrong, but make sure you consider all possibilities. If you are eliminating answer choices and realize that the last one you are left with is also wrong, don't panic. Start over and consider each choice again. There may be something you missed the first time that you will realize on the second pass.

⊘ Avoid Fact Traps

Don't be distracted by an answer choice that is factually true but doesn't answer the question. You are looking for the choice that answers the question. Stay focused on what the question is asking for so you don't accidentally pick an answer that is true but incorrect. Always go back to the question and make sure the answer choice you've selected actually answers the question and is not merely a true statement.

⊘ Extreme Statements

In general, you should avoid answers that put forth extreme actions as standard practice or proclaim controversial ideas as established fact. An answer choice that states the "process should be used in certain situations, if..." is much more likely to be correct than one that states the "process should be discontinued completely." The first is a calm rational statement and doesn't even make a definitive, uncompromising stance, using a hedge word *if* to provide wiggle room, whereas the second choice is far more extreme.

⊘ Benchmark

As you read through the answer choices and you come across one that seems to answer the question well, mentally select that answer choice. This is not your final answer, but it's the one that will help you evaluate the other answer choices. The one that you selected is your benchmark or standard for judging each of the other answer choices. Every other answer choice must be compared to your benchmark. That choice is correct until proven otherwise by another answer choice beating it. If you find a better answer, then that one becomes your new benchmark. Once you've decided that no other choice answers the question as well as your benchmark, you have your final answer.

⊘ Predict the Answer

Before you even start looking at the answer choices, it is often best to try to predict the answer. When you come up with the answer on your own, it is easier to avoid distractions and traps because you will know exactly what to look for. The right answer choice is unlikely to be word-for-word what you came up with, but it should be a close match. Even if you are confident that you have the right answer, you should still take the time to read each option before moving on.

General Strategies

⊘ Tough Questions

If you are stumped on a problem or it appears too hard or too difficult, don't waste time. Move on! Remember though, if you can quickly check for obviously incorrect answer choices, your chances of guessing correctly are greatly improved. Before you completely give up, at least try to knock out a couple of possible answers. Eliminate what you can and then guess at the remaining answer choices before moving on.

⊘ Check Your Work

Since you will probably not know every term listed and the answer to every question, it is important that you get credit for the ones that you do know. Don't miss any questions through careless mistakes. If at all possible, try to take a second to look back over your answer selection and make sure you've selected the correct answer choice and haven't made a costly careless mistake (such as marking an answer choice that you didn't mean to mark). This quick double check should more than pay for itself in caught mistakes for the time it costs.

⊘ Pace Yourself

It's easy to be overwhelmed when you're looking at a page full of questions; your mind is confused and full of random thoughts, and the clock is ticking down faster than you would like. Calm down and maintain the pace that you have set for yourself. Especially as you get down to the last few minutes of the test, don't let the small numbers on the clock make you panic. As long as you are on track by monitoring your pace, you are guaranteed to have time for each question.

⊘ Don't Rush

It is very easy to make errors when you are in a hurry. Maintaining a fast pace in answering questions is pointless if it makes you miss questions that you would have gotten right otherwise. Test writers like to include distracting information and wrong answers that seem right. Taking a little extra time to avoid careless mistakes can make all the difference in your test score. Find a pace that allows you to be confident in the answers that you select.

⊘ KEEP MOVING

Panicking will not help you pass the test, so do your best to stay calm and keep moving. Taking deep breaths and going through the answer elimination steps you practiced can help to break through a stress barrier and keep your pace.

Final Notes

The combination of a solid foundation of content knowledge and the confidence that comes from practicing your plan for applying that knowledge is the key to maximizing your performance on test day. As your foundation of content knowledge is built up and strengthened, you'll find that the strategies included in this chapter become more and more effective in helping you quickly sift through the distractions and traps of the test to isolate the correct answer.

Now that you're preparing to move forward into the test content chapters of this book, be sure to keep your goal in mind. As you read, think about how you will be able to apply this information on the test. If you've already seen sample questions for the test and you have an idea of the question format and style, try to come up with questions of your own that you can answer based on what you're reading. This will give you valuable practice applying your knowledge in the same ways you can expect to on test day.

Good luck and good studying!

The NBPTS Certification Process

Eligibility Requirements

Earning your NBPTS certification is not a trivial task. Certification is earned through a rigorous assessment of your teaching skills. An NBPTS certification shows not just that you understand the material that you are teaching and relevant pedagogical practices, but also that you understand your students and how to most effectively teach those students and that you continually strive to improve by reflecting on your practices. Merely understanding the theory of how to teach is not enough—to earn your NBPTS certification, you must show that you are an outstanding teacher.

To be eligible for NBPTS certification, you must have the minimum of a bachelor's degree (except for the Career and Technical Education certificate), a valid teaching license, and at least three years of teaching experience (or serving as a school counselor for the ECYA/School Counseling certification).

For all certifications, you must have a class of at least 6 students, and more than half of the students must be in the age range of your desired certificate. This usually means your own class, but applicants in some specialty areas and situations may be able to "borrow" or guest-teach a class to meet certification criteria.

Everything in the NBPTS certification assessment is ultimately based on the Five Core Propositions. Your job in completing your application is to demonstrate that you apply these principles in everything you do. The five core propositions can be summarized as follows:

- Dedication to students and their learning
- Knowledge of the subject matter and how to teach it
- Assessment of student progress and how to adjust teaching to maximize student success
- Reflection on teaching practices and a commitment to constant improvement
- Collaboration with other teachers, families, and the community

Assessment Components

There are four components in the assessment that you must pass to earn NBPTS certification. The four components do not all have to be completed at once: you have up to 3 years to attempt all four at least once. If you do not earn a satisfactory score on a component on the first try, you may retake it once or twice; your highest score will count. You must complete all four components, including any retakes, within 5 years.

Multiple-Choice Test Components

Component 1 (Content Knowledge) is a computer-based assessment of your knowledge of the content area and the NBPTS standards for your teaching area and age group. The standards focus on how to understand your students, apply pedagogical theory to teaching those students, and use the instructional content to impart larger lessons about the world and your students' place in it. The test consists of approximately 45 multiple choice questions and 3 constructed response items.

Note: This study guide primarily relates to Component 1.

PORTFOLIO COMPONENTS

The remaining assessment components—Components 2, 3, and 4—comprise a portfolio of your work in the classroom that will be used to assess your ability to apply the standards in the real world. This portfolio contains evidence of your accomplishments in teaching, your students' work, and your commentary on your and your students' work. You are not expected to teach using a particular approach; rather, the assessment is based on the evidence that you provide to show your accomplishment with your chosen approach and your ability to adjust to fit your students' needs.

The exact contents of the portfolio will depend on the certification area and age group. NBPTS provides detailed instructions as to what these components must contain, including the format in which they must be submitted, along with suggestions for how to go about writing the commentaries. Be sure to follow the instructions *exactly*. Deviating from the instructions may mean that parts of your application will not be read by the assessors and that these sections will therefore be given a score of 0 or not scored at all.

Component 2 (Differentiation in Instruction) is a demonstration of your ability to adjust your approach to instruction based on your students' needs and strengths. This includes samples of student work and written commentaries about that work and how it reflects your support of your students.

Component 3 (Teaching Practice and Learning Environment) consists of videos of you teaching and interacting with students, along with written commentaries containing a description, analysis, and reflection about your teaching.

Component 4 (Effective and Reflective Practitioner) concerns your knowledge about the students you teach, how you gain information about your students, and how you apply that knowledge in the classroom. It also includes evidence about your involvement in the community, with students' families, and in professional learning communities. It consists of a profile of a group of your students, details about your generation and use of assessment data to develop and continually refine your classroom practices, and evidence of your participation in learning communities, along with your written commentary.

SCORING

The selected response portion of Component 1 contains 45 scored items. The number of correct responses is converted to a score between 0.75 and 4.25 using a proprietary formula.

The constructed response items and the three components of the portfolio are assessed by accomplished and teachers in your subject area. Each of the three constructed response items in Component 1 are given a score of 0.75 to 4.25 according to a rubric that is included in the instructions for each certificate area. Each of the portfolio items—Components 2,3, and 4—are given a single rubric-based score. Each of these scores is then multiplied by a scaling weight and they are added together to obtain a total weighted scaled score.

To earn your certification, you must score an unweighted average of at least 1.75 on Component 1, an unweighted average of 1.75 on the three portfolio components, *and* a total weighted scaled score of 110. For any components that earn a score below 3.75, your score report will also contain feedback comments that you may use to improve your materials for a retake and/or improve your teaching practices in general.

Knowledge of Students

Environmental Factors that Promote Learning

Impact of Environmental Factors on Student Learning

Environmental factors are any conditions within a school capable of impacting learning. There are both physical and emotional factors. Physical examples include space, temperature, seating arrangements, materials available, lighting, and noise level. Emotional factors include student relationships with adults and peers as well as their own feelings toward school and learning. Together, these factors create a **learning environment**. When these factors are positive, a positive learning environment will develop, which lends itself to positive learning experiences and students who are open to these learning experiences. Similarly, if these factors are negative, they will cultivate a negative learning environment. By meeting the physical and emotional needs of students, the LMS helps students learn, participate, and grow without disruption.

Safety

Maslow's hierarchy of needs places safety in the second level of basic needs, meaning safety must be met before individuals are able to learn and grow emotionally. Feelings of safety comprise both physical and emotional aspects. Ensuring physical safety means maintaining safe spaces free of hazards and having students participate in safety drills and emergency preparedness scenarios within the school. This provides students with a sense of readiness as well as security for their physical well-being. Emotional safety is more complex. It is described as a sense of safety when expressing oneself openly. This requires trust and relationship-building between librarians and students. Within the library, this will allow students to feel comfortable asking for resources to meet their own needs and suit their unique interests. Once students feel a general sense of safety, they can begin their journeys of growth in education and information-seeking.

Lighting and Sound

Lighting and sound are both examples of environmental factors that impact learning. Adequate lighting is necessary to be able to read and maneuver through the library, but it should be chosen and used thoughtfully. Where possible, use natural light to support brain function and circadian rhythms. Harsh lighting can cause glare and impact visibility, leading to difficulty processing information.

Sounds can be one of the most disruptive factors in a learning environment. Excessive noise interferes with both the students' and librarian's ability to concentrate. As such, it is important to prevent and control negative noise through classroom management skills. Additionally, any purposefully added sounds should be chosen with the proper thought given to their potential impact on the learning environment. For example, choosing white noise or instrumental music to drown out disruptive sounds helps students to remain calm and focused, while over-energetic, popular songs would probably create distractions. As with all environmental factors, it is important to consider the needs of diverse learners and how they will be impacted.

Signage

Signage is a key component in libraries. It provides direction, assists in organization, and aids patrons in fulfilling their needs. In order to create effective signage, one should begin with a purpose in mind. Some examples include instructions on circulation, steps to finding the right book, or indicators of kinds of media are in specific areas. Once a topic is selected, the next step is drafting the content, and after settling on the content, the librarian can create the sign. To create the most effective sign, the font should be easy to read and have high contrast with the background (e.g., black text on a white background). When creating signage, it is important to take into consideration the needs of visually impaired patrons. Additionally, images may be added to enhance clarity for patrons who need visual aids. The overall goal in creating signs is to promote independence and provide clear and easy-to-understand aids for patrons.

Decor

Regarding learning spaces, decor should be intentional and used to promote learning. Book displays are one key way to decorate that simultaneously promotes reading and the books available to students. These displays should be thematic in nature and well organized with promotional signage to draw attention. Typically, displays are used to promote awareness of causes or heritage months, thus lending themselves directly to developing students' cultural awareness. Outside of book displays, posters are commonly seen in school libraries. These usually promote specific books or authors. Signs are also helpful for guiding students in appropriate book selection. Key examples include suggestions for book levels and steps to selecting a good-fit book. Overdecorating and misusing colors and patterns should be avoided, as this can lead to distractions in learning, especially for those students with sensory concerns or attention disorders.

Developmental Characteristics of School-Age Children

Physical Development of School-Age Children

While students should have developed strong motor skills and coordination before starting school, there will inevitably be a variance in students' physical abilities across and within grade levels. Thus, strength, balance, coordination and related abilities will not be the same for every student. This is important to acknowledge when planning so there are realistic expectations for students and appropriate accommodations can be made. Before beginning kindergarten, children should have developed the abilities to walk, hop on one foot, climb stairs, turn pages in a book, dress and undress themselves, steadily hold thick writing utensils like large crayons and beginner pencils, and be able to feed themselves. Then, between ages five and six, students should be able to jump, skip, hop with both feet, steadily hold pencils, and begin writing letters. Overall physical coordination continues to develop between ages six and seven, as does hand-eye coordination, the ability to draw more complex shapes, and the ability to write sentences. Beyond this, children continue to develop these foundational skills and improve their coordination and mobility. By knowing and understanding the abilities of children in each age group, educators are better able to create developmentally appropriate plans for their students and maintain reasonable expectations.

Social Development of School-Age Children

Because social development is so deeply affected by many factors beyond a child's control, it is to be expected that children's social skills and ability to interact with others will vary highly among the students within a school. The variance will be more prominent in early years, but it tends to level out as students spend more time in formal learning environments. In ideal conditions, before a child begins kindergarten he or she will play with others, share toys and materials, and be aware of his or her own feelings and the feelings of others. After entering kindergarten, children will become more social and continue to show an ability to share and play collaboratively with others. Then, around second grade, a child's interest in social relationships deepens, and he or she begins to focus more on forming friendships. Overall, children will continue to develop their independence and their own moral standards throughout their years in school. When establishing expectations for children, educators must understand what children are capable of based on their expected development, and they should use that information to guide decision-making.

Cognitive Development of School-Age Children

Cognitive skills refer to the ability to think, learn, and reason. Their development in school-age children allows the children to access a multitude of new skills, like simple mathematical processes, sorting, and organizing. As they continue to age, students will mature, develop longer attention spans, a better understanding of logic and reasoning, and broader imaginations. First, when entering kindergarten, children can represent their thoughts with pictures or written words, but they lack the ability to reason and think logically. Then, during early school years, children begin to develop the ability to think in a less egocentric way and begin to consider the feelings of others, a crucial component of socialization in school. Between the ages of six and eleven, children develop the ability to think logically about concrete concepts, but it is not until age twelve and beyond that children develop the ability to think in a more abstract manner and use advanced reasoning. These stages of development should be considered in lesson planning to ensure the concepts being delivered are developmentally appropriate.

Emotional Development of School-Age Children

Upon entering school, most children begin to pursue friendships and develop relationships with classmates. This tests their ability to cooperate and consider the feelings of others, which are both still developing during this time. Compassionate understanding, self-regulation, and emotional control are also beginning to develop as students enter school. Across early elementary school years, children develop the ability to comfort their peers and consciously control their own behavior. Then, in late elementary years, children begin to develop the ability to see things through the lens of their peers. Their ability to provide support to peers continues to strengthen, and their ability to express their own emotions improves; however, they may still require assistance. Beyond elementary years, children's ability to self-regulate and express their feelings continues to develop and improve, and they begin to crave more independence from their parents and families. Through understanding these stages, school personnel are better able to support the emotional needs of students to ensure their success.

Basic Tenets of Predominant Learning Theories

Theory of Behaviorism

The theory of **behaviorism** suggests that learning is a product of one's interactions with his or her environment. As such, it is an educator's responsibility to create an environment that will produce the desired interactions and responses for students. The responses that individuals receive from their interactions will provide feedback, either positive or negative, that tells them whether what they have done is correct or incorrect. In a learning environment, positive reinforcement tools may look like recognition, awards, prizes, or praise. In some cases, negative consequences may be given to reduce behaviors that are not desirable. Test scores and grades can fall under both the positive and negative category depending upon the earned score. Positive scores let students know they are on the right track, while negative scores reflect a need for some type of change. These types of feedback are part of what is known as operant conditioning. In **operant conditioning,** positive consequences are given to reinforce desired behaviors and negative consequences are given to decrease negative behaviors.

Theory of Cognitivism

Cognitivism focuses on the processes of the mind and how the brain receives, organizes, and retrieves information. It highlights the role that thinking plays in learning and insists that learning takes place through the brain organizing information into concepts. A large portion of this theory focuses on **schemas**, units of already-understood concepts within the brain that are interconnected. Schemas are sometimes referred to as the building blocks of learning. They provide a framework for the brain to continue building new knowledge because it is easier for the brain to remember new concepts and information by connecting it to schemas of similar, already-learned concepts and information. In cognitivism, educators are responsible for **scaffolding** instruction, meaning to break it down into more manageable pieces so that learners are better able to use those pieces to make connections. Where students have no existing schema, it is important to help them build up knowledge and activate prior knowledge through discussion before beginning instruction.

Theory of Constructivism

As the name suggests, the theory of **constructivism** states that new knowledge is constructed on top of prior knowledge during a student's learning journey. As such, learning will be a personal experience, and the way each student learns will be unique. It also describes learning as an active event in which the learner must be engaging in some type of hands-on experience, discussion, reading, or other immersive activity in order to obtain new knowledge rather than a passive event, such as listening to a speaker or seeing something done. Because learning is so personal and unique to the individual student in this context, educators should act as facilitators or guides and provide opportunities for extensive engagement as opposed to providing direct instruction. This theory also calls for more group work opportunities and time to share learning among participants, which may require physical adjustments to the learning space.

Education Theorists

The following are education theorists that have impacted modern education:

- Jean Piaget: Piaget is most well-known for his **theory of cognitive development**, which explains the processes through which a child's mind learns and develops understanding. Through his work, Piaget was able to prove that children think and process differently than adults and need education catered to their unique way of learning.
- Lev Vygotsky: Vygotsky's **zone of proximal development** has been his most impactful work in the education field. It is viewed as the zone between what learners can do without assistance and what they can do when assisted by an adult or peer. Vygotsky established that it is within this zone that learning takes place.
- Abraham Maslow: Maslow's **hierarchy of needs** is a prioritized list of the needs humans must fulfill. It begins with the most basic needs for survival and becomes more abstract as it continues into self-actualization. Maslow's research suggests that students are not able to participate in learning until the needs lower in the hierarchy are all met.

Review Video: Piaget's Cognitive Development Theory
Visit mometrix.com/academy and enter code: 100376

Chapter Quiz

Ready to see how well you retained what you just read? Scan the QR code to go directly to the chapter quiz interface for this study guide. If you're using a computer, simply visit the online resources page at **mometrix.com/resources719/nbptslibmecya** and click the Chapter Quizzes link.

Teaching and Learning

Literacy and Reading Instruction

Information Literacy

Information literacy is the ability to locate information in various formats, evaluate its credibility, organize it, ethically use it to construct some form of writing or presentation, and communicate the findings. Because of advances in technology, information is more quickly and easily accessible than ever before; however, that does not mean all existing information sources are reliable. While it would be very difficult to have statistics on the amount of non-credible sources, it is well known that not all sources are valid or share accurate information.

In schools, the librarian holds a large portion of the responsibility for ensuring students can complete all these steps regarding information use. **Digital literacy,** the ability to functionally find information online; **media literacy**, the ability to understand, evaluate, and produce all types of media forms; and **academic literacy**, the ability to apply written content, are all crucial components of information literacy that should be taught in the library per the ALA Framework for Information Literacy for Higher Education. This framework document is revised cyclically by team members based on their own research.

Reading Literacy

Reading literacy is the ability to read, understand, and use written texts to construct meaning. Reading literacy is crucial to learning as it provides the basis of nearly all learning processes. Because of reading literacy's importance, extensive research has been completed to help educators understand the factors that influence it. A great amount of this research has shown that factors outside of the school's control greatly impact reading literacy, such as family income, parents' education, lifestyle, and other socioeconomic conditions. With that in mind, it is important to then consider the role the school plays in increasing reading literacy and, more specifically, what role librarians play. Across decades of research, it has been shown that schools with solid library programs tend to score better on standardized tests. This can be attributed to a variety of the benefits that libraries and librarians provide, such as an expanded access to resources that can spark student interests across grade and skill levels, direct instruction on literacy skills, professional development for teachers on locating proper educational resources, and an overall encouragement of reading.

Research-Based Activities Increasing Reading Comprehension

Because the primary purpose of the school library is to provide access to books and reading materials, it is logical it plays a role in **reading comprehension**, which is the ability to understand and interpret what is being read. One highly regarded way to increase reading comprehension in students is through read-alouds because not only do they allow for the modeling of reading strategies and thought processes, they allow students to practice with memory retention and vocabulary. School librarians often lead read-alouds and should use them as opportunities to model the aforementioned skills and implement and reinforce reading strategies taught in the classroom. Furthermore, librarians are at least partially responsible for creating a culture of reading, and with their knowledge of the collection, they are responsible for helping students find books that fit their needs and ability level. Additionally, librarians and teachers should have a collaborative relationship to ensure they provide the most support for students. They can work together to locate resources that fit content goals while also supporting students at their reading level.

Research-Based Reading Program Concepts

Research-based reading programs will vary in delivery method and content; however, they will all address fluency, vocabulary, phonemic awareness, phonics, and spelling. Regarding reading, **fluency** describes the reader's ability to read texts accurately with appropriate expression and speed. Reading **vocabulary** refers to the words one is able to recognize in print. **Phonemic awareness** is the understanding of sounds made by **phonemes,** the individual parts of a word that make a sound. Examples of phonemes include both individual letter sounds, such as the "s" sound in "sat," and sounds made by letter pairs, like "qu" in "quit" or "ch" in "chair." **Phonics** is closely related, as this is when phonemic awareness is applied to the decoding of words, meaning the relationship between sounds and letters is taught. **Spelling** fundamentals are a crucial part of reading programs as they teach the aforementioned phonics and phonemic awareness skills.

Diagnostic Process of Research-Based Reading Programs

Research-based reading programs, sometimes referred to as evidence-based reading programs, are meant to provide support in reading instruction. This support may be whole-group, small-group, or individualized instruction. All forms of instruction start the same, by having students take a diagnostic assessment to determine their strengths and weaknesses. This establishes the baseline data that will be used to determine the growth throughout the program. Using the data, the teacher can determine what kind of instruction is required and will deliver it using the prescribed content. Depending on the needs of the learner, instruction will cover one or more of the following: fluency, vocabulary, phonemic awareness, phonics, and/or spelling. Once that content is taught, students will complete another diagnostic assessment to show their growth and mastery. Students who show mastery will move on to the next determined step, while students who have not yet mastered the content will continue to receive the targeted instruction. The end goal of these programs is to have students reading on grade level.

Reading Workshops

Reading workshops are designed to provide direct instruction on the skills and strategies used by proficient readers. They consist of three components: a mini lesson, time to work on a related activity, and time to debrief. During the mini lesson, a specific reading strategy is taught, such as inferencing, predicting, or retelling. Following the mini lesson, students spend their time reading independently or working with the librarian or teacher in small groups to receive more guided instruction. Lastly, the group is called back together to review what was learned. Read-alouds during a class's time in the library can be easily modified to implement reading workshops as the read-alouds already provide direct instruction via modeling reading skills and strategies. Thus, librarians and teachers can easily coordinate to implement such workshops when classes are in the library.

Incentivizing Reading in the Library

Some reluctant readers may need incentives to read, while other students may just see incentives as opportunities to be rewarded for something they already do. Regardless, incentives and reading challenges are commonly seen in school libraries. Reading challenges motivate students with the promise of reward or recognition and through competition with other students. Tracking the progress students make in a visible manner also helps to maintain motivation. However, while incentives might work in some cases, the outcomes of reading challenges are not always as promising. Research has shown in many cases that the quality and length of the books that students read will decrease throughout a challenge as students work towards their goal. Furthermore, incentive programs also change the "why" behind reading. Students are no longer reading to learn new information or for leisure, they are reading to be rewarded. Overall, it is important for librarians to consider the positives and negatives of incentive programs before implementing them.

Principles of Reading

The five principles of reading are phonemic awareness, the ability to identify letter sounds in written words; phonics, the understanding of letter sounds in spoken words; fluency, the ability to read with expression and accuracy; vocabulary, the understanding of word meanings; and comprehension, the ability to understand what has been read. While teaching the skills related to these principles is not the direct responsibility of the librarian, there is an expectation that the librarian will support the curriculum. To do so, he or she must first be knowledgeable of these principles and use that knowledge to model the related skills during instruction and identify resources that provide support. An appropriate time for a librarian to model these skills is during read-aloud opportunities with classes. Also, the librarian should compile resources into kits for teachers to use in instruction; however, he or she may need to develop purchasing plans in order to gain these resources. The librarian is responsible for maintaining and housing these resources for schoolwide use.

Multiple Literacies

Multiple literacies refers to the ability to obtain information through multiple formats, including visual, textual, digital, and technological. This acknowledges that individuals gain knowledge through more than just written words and that instruction needs to occur for all types of literacy in order to develop successful students. Most library programs cover textual, digital, and technological literacies due to their nature, but they should consider the addition of visual literacy. The *American Association of School Librarians (AASL) Standards Framework for Learners* is a very detailed document outlining what students should be learning within the school library program. The Shared Foundations and Key Commitments cover what abilities students should gain through the school library program. This section of the framework can very easily be applied to all literacies, as it does not state the type of media to be used, only the skills needed to show proficiency. Many state guidelines are similar to those created by AASL and can be applied in the same ways. By using imagery to address visual literacy, books and other forms of texts to address textual literacy, online and e-resources to address digital literacies, and technology to address technological literacy, librarians can ensure students are being provided the instruction necessary to become fully literate in all contexts.

Teaching Methods Addressing Components of Multiple Literacies

Multiple literacies includes visual, textual, digital, and technological formats. To best address **visual literacy**, also viewed as extracting information from imagery, students need to be taught the skills necessary to associate images with meaning. This includes skills like inferencing, finding metaphors, and identifying the significance of selected imagery and the use of visual symbolism. **Textual literacy** is the ability to use text for understanding. This is most commonly achieved in classroom instruction but can be enhanced in the library by analyzing diverse texts and literature not used in the classroom. **Digital literacy** can be addressed by providing students with the skills they need to successfully use information found in digital formats, like websites and e-resources. Lastly, the need to address **technological literacy** has been growing with the digital age. Students need to be instructed on proper online etiquette, digital communication and collaboration, and how to use tech tools like word processors and presentation development software.

Assessing Technology Competency

As career fields continue to change with advancing technologies, it is vital that students' education reflects these changes. In order to best assess technology competency, educators can design assessments around the use of specific technology. An assessment can simply be having students create a presentation or product using a specific technology that was taught to them. For example, to assess students on their ability to use technology related to slideshows and videos, have students create slideshows or video presentations. Students must also be able to use some technologies, like calculators and other devices used to solve problems, proficiently in order to succeed in other areas of their education. As such, it is important that usage is assessed by ensuring students can perform the required steps to successfully access and use such technologies. This can be done through observation accompanied by a checklist. If technology competency cannot be assessed by having students demonstrate proficiency by effectively using the technology, one should consider assessing how comfortable and confident students are in using the technology independently.

Integrating Literature into the Instructional Program

While full of books, libraries are becoming more and more technology focused. While this is important for education and preparing students for the workforce, promoting and focusing on literature is still equally important. To do this, librarians can use **book talks** in their instruction; these are speeches or presentations about books meant to engage readers. This stimulates student interest in titles that may otherwise be overlooked and piques interest in independent reading. The librarian should also consider forming reading groups or clubs to promote and provide space for reading discussions. Collaboration with teachers is also a key component of integrating quality literature throughout the school in all subject areas. While the teacher is most knowledgeable about his or her own content, the librarian should know particular authors, illustrators, and titles to supplement the occurring instruction.

Facilitating Students' Development and Use of Content-Area Vocabulary

Libraries have a very specific set of content-area vocabulary. While these terms are used commonly in the library, they are not often heard elsewhere, so it cannot be expected that students will know them innately. As such, the librarian must provide direct instruction as appropriate on these terms. It is also beneficial to provide visual cues like posters throughout the library that represent these terms and the related actions. Once the terms have been taught, the librarian and students should use them to reference their actions and needs. It is also beneficial to inform teachers of this common language so they may use it as appropriate within the school to reinforce these concepts outside of the library.

Information Literacy Models and Teaching Information Literacy

Information Literacy

Information literacy is the ability to source, validate, and effectively use information. It encompasses materials and resources in all forms, such as books, articles, and digital media. Information literacy is made up of multiple steps, with the first being to define the task at hand. Once the task has been defined, a student should begin to locate sources and gather information from them. This may require him or her to combine information from several resources. With this information, he or she should be able to present his or her findings in an appropriate format such as a paper, multimedia presentation, or speech. The final step is to evaluate the outcome and determine if the task established in step one was completed. Because of their knowledge regarding research and literacy as a whole, librarians are most qualified to lead students in the information literacy process. Additionally, the library serves as an ideal workspace for this process to occur due to the obvious access to resources it provides. By providing this instruction, librarians are preparing globally competitive lifelong learners to succeed in the ever-changing workspace of the 21st century.

Origin of Information Literacy

Paul G. Zurkowski championed the importance of information literacy, and his 1974 report to the US National Commission on Libraries and Information Science was the first to use the term in writing. Directly following this report, discussion of the importance of information literacy began to grow in the library field. Several years later, the American Library Association (ALA) formed its Presidential Committee on Information Literacy, which released a statement in 1989 defining information literacy and addressing how important it would be in overcoming the challenges presented by the emergence of expanding and ever-evolving information and technology. The committee highlighted the need for information literacy across all populations and provided suggestions for how to implement the skills needed in library education. Since then, the ALA has continued to promote information literacy skills and refine the components that make up information literacy.

Eisenberg and Berkowitz

Mike Eisenberg and **Bob Berkowitz** are responsible for developing the Big6 research model. This model is meant for school-age learners and serves to support them through problem-solving and information seeking by providing a metacognitive scaffold. In order to understand the concept of metacognitive scaffolding, one must first understand the words separately. **Metacognition** is commonly referred to as "thinking about thinking," meaning having an awareness of the thought processes occurring within one's mind. In the education field, **scaffolding** refers to providing students with knowledge and lessons that build upon one another. Together, they refer to an external source providing support to a student's thinking to help him or her solve a problem. The research model created by Eisenberg and Berkowitz serves to provide this support by creating a defined process to follow. Using this model in the library has been shown to allow students to complete more complex problem-solving and inquiry activities as well as increase students' levels of engagement.

Keith Curry Lance

Keith Curry Lance is best known for cocreating the *Library Journal* Index of Public Library Service and for his work in library statistics. His most notable and highly referenced finding came from his research as principal investigator on the project "SLIDE: The School Librarian Investigation—Decline or Evolution." His team found a correlation between standardized test scores and the existence of school library programs. He found that students in schools that had a certified librarian present scored higher on standardized tests across all subjects than students who lacked the support of a librarian. This evidence of proficiency can be attributed to many factors related to the library, but the most notable are the promotion of reading, instruction on inquiry skills, and collaborative planning. This research supports the important role librarians play in instruction across the board.

David V. Loertscher

Over the last few decades, **David V. Loertscher** has successfully worked to prove that school librarians are an invaluable part of the student learning experience when they are performing as an educational partner. He found that the "support and supply role" for a librarian, in which the librarian provides a repository of books and other resources, is inadequate for student learning gains. His work helped to establish that the focus should shift instead to basic literacy, collaboration with teachers, learning through technology, and information literacy. This led to a massive shift in instruction within the library community to focus on these topics for the betterment of students as opposed to focusing on warehousing tasks. His research outlined the process of teaching information literacy and addressed how to apply it to special student groups, such as lower-level students, gifted students, multilingual learners, and several others. This has provided librarians both with the guidelines and a tool kit for effective information literacy instruction.

Carol Kuhlthau

Carol Kuhlthau is best known for developing the Information Search Process, a research model that focuses on a holistic, whole-student approach to inquiry. It outlines the feelings, thoughts, and actions a student is likely to be experiencing, having, and doing, respectively, based on where he or she is in the research process. Through this model, librarians and teachers alike are able to better support students in their learning by understanding their emotional status and thought processes in relation to where they are in their inquiry. Her work promotes an understanding that feelings of uncertainty and frustration are not only OK, but they are to be expected. This model helps students to reframe those emotions and work through them to create a product based on the students' findings. Additionally, it provides a framework for creating more meaningful library assignments as well as interventions to use in learning. Overall, Kuhlthau's work is considered to be some of the most empowering in the school library realm.

Ross J. Todd

Ross J. Todd was best known for his work in information literacy and inquiry-based learning. He was considered a world-renowned expert in adolescent information seeking due to his focus on understanding how children learn, find information, and construct new knowledge and how school libraries play a role in these processes. He was motivated by his understanding that the changes in technology would directly impact the 21st-century workforce, and librarians would play a critical role in preparing students for this change. His most notable research involved making information literacy the center of the library curriculum to test the impact it would have on student learning. The findings concluded that this style of instruction had positive impacts on learning outcomes and the overall views that students had of their own research journeys and abilities. An increased focus on information literacy made students better equipped to find and use information across all content areas to develop understandings they previously lacked.

History of Library Standards

In the 1920s, the first set of library standards was released by the ALA to outline the roles and responsibilities of the school library. Since then, many iterations of the standards have been published, including an updated set in 1945. Then, the American Association of School Librarians (AASL) was developed within the ALA to govern school library-related topics in 1951. The AASL released its newly revised standards in 1960 and has not stopped working on revisions to ensure success since. As technology and the way learners access resources both change, the roles and expectations set forth by the AASL also adapt. When school librarians stay abreast of these changes and make adequate efforts to adhere to these standards, they are ensuring students receive appropriate instruction to guide them in learning and inquiry for their lifetime.

Standards for the 21st-Century Learner

The AASL designed the *Standards for the 21st-Century Learner* as a framework to be used in collaborative instruction with classroom teachers. These standards focus on the learner and his or her abilities, and they are meant to ensure instruction is supporting the skills students need to be globally competitive learners. Unlike other frameworks, such as the *AASL Standards Framework for Learners*, these standards are broken down for different grade levels. However, there are four standards repeated throughout: inquire, think critically, and gain knowledge; draw conclusions, make informed decisions, apply knowledge to new situations, and create new knowledge; share knowledge and participate ethically and productively as members of our democratic society; and pursue personal and aesthetic growth. For each standard, there are four associated strands: skills, dispositions in action, responsibilities, and self-assessment strategies. For each strand, there are indicators, and beneath the indicators are either action examples or benchmarks that further dictate what must be taught in those grade levels to ensure students are meeting these standards.

21ST-CENTURY LITERACIES

As technology and the way resources are accessed has changed, so have related literacies. The following literacies are considered to be 21st-century literacies because they are vital for success in this ever-changing learning environment. **Digital literacy** highlights learners' ability to find and use information and resources in digital formats by using technology. This can be finding a book using a library management system, finding an article using a database, or finding any other form of media needed using any form of technology. This leads into **technological literacy**, which is the ability to use technology appropriately in communication, problem-solving, and accessing and using resources. Next is **textual literacy**, which is a student's ability to read and use texts and also write. It concerns all texts and not just those related only to technology-based formats. Similarly, **visual literacy**, the ability to use images for understanding, applies to all branches of information and is equally vital in digital resources. School librarians should align their instruction with these literacies to best prepare students to meet their educational goals. This can be done in collaboration with teachers or in personalized learning in the library.

STANDARDS FRAMEWORK FOR LEARNERS

The ***AASL Standards Framework for Learners*** is a set of standards meant to be used in conjunction with the *AASL Standards Framework for School Librarians* and the *AASL Standards Framework for School Libraries* to guide school librarians in developing curricula and programming to prepare students to be successful beyond the library. As such, the standards are meant for students in prekindergarten through 12th grade as well as anyone beyond that with the desire to broaden their own knowledge. They contain six standards, each one word, based on the Shared Foundations of the AASL: Inquire, Include, Collaborate, Curate, Explore, and Engage. These Shared Foundations are further explained by Key Commitments, which are one-sentence descriptions that explain the Shared Foundation's main objective: build, demonstrate, work, make, discover, and demonstrate, respectively. Each Shared Foundation is then explained within the context of each of the four Domains, which are Think, Create, Share, and Grow. Each Domain for each Shared Foundation contains a few listed Competencies, which are actions the learner should take to grow that Shared Foundation and Domain. When these frameworks are utilized in the library setting, students are provided with the best chance of being a successful learner for life.

STANDARDS FRAMEWORK FOR SCHOOL LIBRARIANS

To provide school librarians with a common directive in planning programming for both students and staff, the AASL created the ***AASL Standards Framework for School Librarians***. This framework is very similar to the one developed for learners as it features the same six Shared Foundations (Inquire, Include, Collaborate, Curate, Explore, and Engage), their Key Commitments (build, demonstrate, work, make, discover, and demonstrate), and the Domains (Think, Create, Share, and Grow). Where these two frameworks begin to diverge is in the Competencies within each Domain, as they are different for school librarians as compared to learners. These Competencies provide statements of what school librarians should strive to achieve and action steps to help them achieve it. The intention in creating this framework was to ensure library offerings are providing students across all grade levels with the skills they need to be successful in their own inquiries as well as to provide them with a culture of inclusivity and teamwork.

Standards Framework for School Libraries

Similar to the frameworks provided for learners and school librarians, the ***AASL Standard Framework for School Libraries*** serves to provide guidance in creating a learning environment in which students can work on personalized learning and have the opportunity to bridge learning gaps. The framework also provides best practices in library design in both a physical and instructional sense. It has the same Shared Foundations, Key Commitments, and Domains that the frameworks for learners and school librarians have. Its difference is in its Competencies, which for libraries are actually called Alignments. They still each provide actions for the libraries to accomplish within each Domain. One of the driving factors in creating the library framework was to ensure that the AASL maintains a high level of influence in decision-making related to libraries. The AASL acknowledges that school libraries must follow building-, district-, and state-level directives and decisions; however, the AASL should still maintain the highest level of influence on these directives and decisions with its research-based frameworks. In adhering with AASL standards, school libraries are able to best support students in their individual learning journeys.

International Society for Technology in Education's Standards

The **International Society for Technology in Education** (ISTE) first established **standards for technology**, the **ISTE Standards,** as they related to learning in 1998. Since then, it has continued to modify these standards to best fit the needs of learners as technology has continued to evolve. It has also released standards for educators, education leaders (i.e., administrators), coaches, and it has released the ISTE Computational Thinking Competencies. The student set outlines expectations for students to be empowered learners, digital citizens, knowledge constructors, innovative designers, computational thinkers, creative communicators, and global collaborators. Each standard features action statements to demonstrate how a student becomes those things. Regarding educators, the ISTE expects them to serve as learners, leaders, citizens, collaborators, designers, facilitators, and analysts. These are also followed by actionable steps to meet these standards. The general purpose of these standards is to provide an outline for preparing students to be successful learners and to thrive in technological fields by giving them the resources to adequately function and stay abreast of changes.

Impact of State and Local Standards on the School Library

There are state and district variations in the content being taught in schools. This is because the governing body that has jurisdiction over the school can decide what set of standards to follow. While individual states are free to select the standards they use, the most commonly adopted standard set in the US is **Common Core.** Like many standard sets, this features only language arts and math standards and requires states or districts to adopt or create a separate set of science and social studies standards. While these standards do not have a direct correlation to teaching expectations in the library, they do require a shift in functioning for the librarian so he or she can continue to collaborate with and support classroom teachers. The most notable impact these standards will have on the library is the increased need for narrative nonfiction. Additionally, school librarians can lead professional development for teachers based on the literacy standards as they are experts in this field.

State and National Guidelines for Information and Media Literacy Skills

Due to the rapidly changing nature of the development and access of information and media, it is vital that librarians play an active role in ensuring students have the skills required to navigate various forms of information and media to find what they need. These skills are defined at a national level through the AASL. Much of the AASL framework is dedicated to identifying the skills students need to successfully find, analyze, and use information across multiple formats.

Additionally, most states have their own set of library standards or guidelines reflecting what content must be covered to meet state requirements. Through adhering to both sets of guidelines, librarians can help to ensure student success in media literacy. Furthermore, digital resources play a vital role in learning and practicing these skills because the internet is the source through which most information is currently accessed. As such, it is important that students know not only what resources are reliable and how to navigate them, but also how to assess the credibility of resources on their own. Guiding students through the inquiry process to complete research is the most common way to help students develop these skills, as it allows them to pose questions and practice finding credible resources that they will use to draw conclusions.

Information Problem-Solving

Information problem-solving (IPS) is any instructional method that engages students in the solving of real-world, complex problems. These processes typically follow a model that requires students to identify a problem or task, find and use resources to gather information, use that information to create a product, and express their findings. These methods are meant to support students as well as educators by providing a predictable outline to follow.

Research completed by the ALA shows that students perform better and are more successful when librarians directly teach IPS. Because the school librarian is responsible for teaching inquiry skills like asking questions and finding relevant information, IPS is a natural extension. The library provides a workspace that is conducive to continued exploration and problem-solving and should be used as such.

Big6 Research Model

Created by Eisenberg and Berkowitz in 1990, the **Big6** research model is an information problem-solving model. It is meant to provide guidance in research, problem-solving, and metacognitive skills. The first step is **task definition.** It is at this point that a problem is established and the information needed to solve it is identified. During the **information seeking strategies** stage, step two, students need to identify all possible resources that can be used and determine which are best suited for the problem. **Location and access,** step three, and **use of information,** step four, go hand in hand. In step three, the student find where the possible resources are and locate where the relevant information is within those resources, while in step four, the students read the information and decide what is relevant for their problem. Step five, **synthesis,** is the point in which students take what they have learned and organize it into a presentable format. The final step, **evaluation,** asks students to evaluate the product they created as well as their own work within the process.

Information Search Process

Carol Kuhlthau proposed the **Information Search Process** (ISP) in 1991, which outlines the feelings, thoughts, and actions a student is likely to be experiencing, having, and doing, respectively, based on where he or she is in the research process. **Initiation,** step one, is usually filled with feelings of uncertainty as the student recognizes the need for new information. That uncertainty transforms to optimism as the student reaches stage two, **selection.** During selection, the student chooses a topic and process for how to proceed. Stage three, **exploration,** is highlighted by frustration and confusion as the student finds information and attempts to construct meaning out of it. Feelings become more positive once stage four, **formulation,** has been reached. As a focus begins to form out of the information gained, the student will begin to create a personal understanding and determine his or her focus. **Collection,** step five, is the opportunity for the student to find information needed to support or answer his or her focus. The student will feel confident and know the next steps in his or her query. In the final step, **presentation,** the student is able to use the information gained to demonstrate his or her learning and should feel either satisfied or dissatisfied based on results.

STRIPLING MODEL

Developed in 2003 by **Barbara Stripling,** the **Stripling Model** is a cyclical inquiry-based learning model to support students in the research process. It is different from other models due to its nonlinear nature. Because of this, there is no clear starting point within the model; however, students most commonly start in the **wonder** phase where they develop questions and make predictions and a hypothesis. From there, students may begin to **investigate** and find information to answer the questions they developed. Post-investigation, students may enter the **construct** stage where they will construct new understandings and draw conclusions. Once an understanding is constructed, students can **express** their findings by applying their newly acquired knowledge to a different context or by sharing what they have learned. **Reflection** provides the time to reflect on the experience and formulate new questions based on what was learned. Post-reflection, students may take time to **connect** their findings and reflections to themselves. It is again important to note that this model is a cycle. Students may enter at any point and may move in either direction throughout it to achieve their research goal. They do not have to follow the steps in the order they are written.

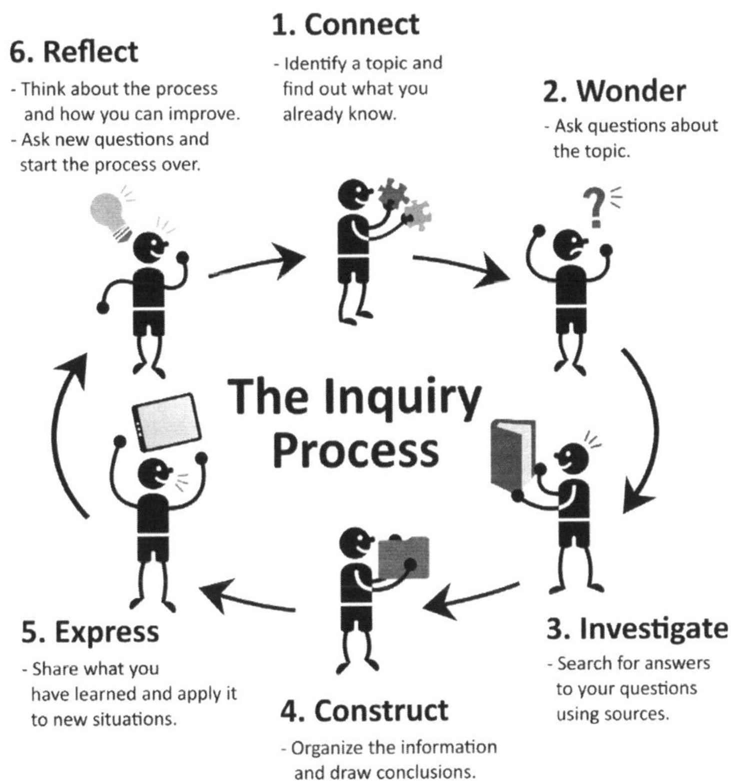

I-SEARCH

Ken Macrorie's intention in creating the **I-Search** (1988) process was to provide a new, alternative method to use when teaching research to students. It provides autonomy to the students by allowing them to select the topic they will be researching. His intention in doing this was to provide the opportunity to practice research skills without the negative connotation of forced topics that often lead to frustration. Unlike other research models, it establishes what the end product will be, which is a paper. To select a topic for their paper, students briefly freewrite about their own thoughts and then use that writing to select topics. Once a list of topics has been created, students narrow down their list and establish which topic will sustain their interest while also likely having multiple resources that can be used to address it. Students then compile related information from a variety of sources and begin to write their paper. According to the I-Search format, the paper should include an introduction, an explanation of the student's search process, the findings as they relate to the research topic, and a reflection of the overall process. In contrast to most styles of academic writing, the student is permitted to write in first person for all sections of the paper except for the research section.

Instructional Objectives and Lesson Planning

Cognitive Instructional Objectives

When planning instruction, one must first establish a measurable objective that students should be able to achieve. **Cognitive instructional objectives** address the intellectual side of learning activities and outline what students should be able to do by the end of a lesson or unit of study. These are the most common types of objectives in learning environments. They focus on a student's ability to remember, understand, apply, analyze, evaluate, or create based on the content within the lesson. The aforementioned list of verbs comes from the revised Bloom's Taxonomy and is hierarchical in the sense that students must master one level before moving to the next. For example, they must be able to remember before they can apply. Each step increases in complexity and is more abstract. It is vital to consider the current ability of students before establishing a cognitive objective to ensure they have mastered the lower abilities.

Review Video: Learning Objectives
Visit mometrix.com/academy and enter code: 528458

Review Video: Creating Effective Lesson Plans
Visit mometrix.com/academy and enter code: 100377

Affective Learning

While other styles of learning tend to focus on a student mastering a new skill or completing a task, **affective learning** targets and focuses on a learner's attitudes, feelings, emotions, motivations, perceptions, and values. This style of learning is most common in the early elementary years in which children are learning appropriate socialization and developing empathy for others. They may practice active listening with one another, role-play through scenarios, or model desired behaviors in social interactions. Affective learning may also be used to assist students in working through issues with peers or any other social-emotional needs. When addressing affective learning objectives, an educator may use words like accept, attend, cooperate, comply, or discuss. This verbiage reflects a focus on the student's emotional abilities as opposed to his or her technical abilities.

Psychomotor Objectives

Psychomotor objectives address physical movement as it relates to learning and establish physical actions students should be able to achieve as a result of instruction. Throughout the early years of their life, children progress from observing physical skills to mastering them. These skills include general and hand-eye coordination, speed, strength, and balance, as well as many others. They require instruction in order to become fully developed, whether through direct lessons or indirect modeling. The existing psychomotor skills of students in different age groups should be considered when designing lessons and establishing appropriateness for a class. Many studies have shown that an increased focus on psychomotor skills in education leads to overall higher cognitive functioning in students, thus emphasizing the need to focus on the whole child when teaching as opposed to only focusing on standard learning objectives.

Instructional Strategies

Instructional strategies are the methods through which an educator delivers a lesson. In order to meet the needs of all learners across a variety of settings, educators commonly use five types of instruction. In **direct instruction,** students are taught information in a structured, purposeful sequence. In the library, this may look like teaching routines and processes, or it could be instruction on locating information. **Indirect instruction** is more student-centered and has students perform a task based on their own learning. This could look like a reflective discussion after an independent reading activity. **Experiential learning** offers students the opportunity to learn through hands-on processes. STEAM (science, technology, engineering, arts, and math) and coding activities are good examples of this. Libraries are naturally great places for **independent learning** to occur as they house in-depth resources for all topics, providing students an opportunity to create their own learning experiences through reading. As such, students are able to answer their own self-guided inquires and independently solve problems. **Interactive learning** allows students the opportunity to respond verbally. This could be a group discussion following a read-aloud.

Learning Materials and Resources

Learning materials and resources are any items needed to successfully educate students. These materials and items will vary for each lesson and depend on each lesson's planned activities, manipulatives, and desired outcomes. Some simple examples commonly found throughout a school include pencils, crayons, and paper. In the library setting, books are the most commonly used resource at the center of a lesson. Databases are also frequently used in library instruction. Depending upon the curriculum being taught, resources for coding and programming, makerspaces, and robotics are also key learning materials. In many schools, the library houses resources that are shared among classrooms and teachers so that they can be properly cataloged for circulation and have a place to be stored when not in use.

Meeting the Needs of Diverse Learners

Schools tend to be diverse environments. This diversity can present in many ways but may include neurodiversity, racial diversity, cultural diversity, or diversity in ability. A librarian's goal is to ensure that the needs of all individuals are being met regardless of their background or academic and physical capabilities. Library programming and the lessons offered should be culturally sensitive and provide appropriate, adequate representation of all students. They should also feature instructional goals achievable by all the students for whom the instruction is intended, or the goals can be modified to accommodate differences in learning and abilities. Per the Individuals with Disabilities Education Act (IDEA), all accommodations mandated in a student's **Individualized Education Program** (IEP) apply in the library setting just as they would in the classroom. As such, the school librarian must be aware of and adhere to these. The same concept also applies to any accommodations listed in a student's 504 Plan per the Rehabilitation Act of 1973. Examples relevant to the library may include, but are certainly not limited to, increased font sizes for instructional documents, access to language dictionaries or translation devices, and shortened or otherwise modified assignments as specified in that child's plan.

Assessments

Assessments are a key part of any instruction as they provide an insight into student learning. The two most commonly used assessments in the school library are formative and summative. **Formative assessments** are informal, frequent assessments that take place throughout instruction. These may be conversations, check-ins with students, student self-assessments, or any other feedback collected during instruction that provides evidence of learning that is occurring. The data gained from formative assessments should be used to guide and make changes to instruction as a unit of learning is progressing. **Summative assessments** occur at the end of a unit of learning and serve to assess a student's overall learning. In a library setting, these are typically projects. Summative assessments also provide an insight on the effectiveness of instruction based on classwide assessment data, and the librarian can use this data to make changes to future instruction.

Bloom's Taxonomy of Educational Objectives

In **Bloom's *Taxonomy of Educational Objectives: The Classification of Educational Goals*,** Bloom created a hierarchical organization of the stages of learning, which is referred to as Bloom's Taxonomy. It was first introduced in 1956 but revised in 2001 to produce the version currently used in pedagogy. Bloom's Taxonomy is represented by a triangle with the base being the lowest level of understanding and the top being the highest. Students must achieve the lower level of learning before mastering the next. **Remembering** is at the base of the triangle and is the stage at which students should be able to recall facts from memory. Next, students reach the stage of **understanding**, in which they can explain what they have learned. This is followed by **applying**, the point at which students can take the information gained and use it in other contexts or to solve problems. **Analyzing** allows students to begin making connections between their learning and other contexts. In the **evaluation** stage, students can use their learning to make and justify decisions. The final step, **creating**, allows students to create something new or original from the knowledge they have gained.

Contributions of Benjamin Bloom

Benjamin Bloom was an educational psychologist who dedicated his career to gaining a better understanding of the way children learn. He is best known for Bloom's Taxonomy, which he developed with a team of other psychologists, of which he was the chairman. The taxonomy was originally published in 1956 and was created to provide a framework for how children learn. It demonstrated the hierarchical levels of knowledge development that must be achieved in order to gain mastery of content. This was later revised by Bloom's students and colleagues and republished in 2001 with some changes. This taxonomy is still used regularly in pedagogy and provides educators with an understanding of developmental stages, allowing them to develop appropriate plans for all learning stages. This can include using particular questioning strategies, deciding what style of assessment is appropriate, and what instructional methods should be used.

Inquiry-Based Learning

Inquiry-based learning is a type of active learning that occurs through high-level questioning, experiential learning, problem-solving, and making real world connections. Students begin with a question in mind, collect information related to the question, analyze the information, and then use it to draw conclusions. Many studies show that students find this style of learning to be more valuable than others because they are at the center of it. Since inquiry-based learning is so deeply rooted in asking questions and finding information, it aligns well with library objectives and can take place through library-based or classroom-based assignments in which the librarian has agreed to collaborate. School librarians are responsible for ensuring that students have the information literacy skills needed to locate, analyze, and use information, which are critical components of inquiry-based learning. Through ensuring students have those skills, librarians are providing them with the abilities required for meaningful learning experiences across many subjects.

Types of Inquiry-Based Learning

The four types of inquiry-based learning are structured, confirmation, guided, and open inquiry. These are listed in order of increasing student responsibility. **Structured inquiry** takes place in a whole-group setting. Students work together under the guidance of the teacher or another educator to establish a question, and then they work together under the same guidance with preselected resources to find the answer. In **confirmation inquiry**, students are provided with the question as well as a method or process to follow. In **guided inquiry**, a question or problem is still posed by the teacher, but then students are given a chance to complete their own research and then create a solution or product on their own to address that question or problem. **Open inquiry** allows for the most student independence. Students select their own topics, create their own questions, and are not provided with expected outcomes or any preselected reference materials or tools.

Assessment

Portfolios

When used as an assessment tool, **portfolios** are an organized collection of student work. They are meant to show student growth over a certain period of time, typically an entire school year. Portfolios contrast from many other forms of assessment as they feature a variety of works, some of which may be writing samples, student self-assessments, or any other type of formative assessment. In terms of the library, portfolios are most often used for students' professional development purposes. Librarians collect students' work samples related to students' professional goals and use the portfolios to demonstrate student growth related to those goals. The librarian may also use a portfolio to show his or her own learning and growth over the year for licensing purposes. Portfolios may be a physical collection of work housed in a binder (or similar organizer) or developed online in a digital format. Regardless, they will feature the same types of documentation.

Conferencing

Conferencing allows for students to talk with their educator about their own educational goals, strengths, and weaknesses as well as any related concerns. It provides a time for the educator to provide one-on-one, individualized feedback to a student, something much more beneficial to the student than receiving responses and criticisms from an educator while in a group. In the library, conferences are a critical way to gain insight into students' reading ability and interests. By spending time learning about individual students, a librarian is better able to find resources and materials to suit their needs and interests. It also allows the librarian to develop lessons to address any concerns with the students' abilities to locate and access information. While time-consuming, conferencing's personalized nature provides information about individuals that a librarian may not get through other forms of assessment.

Observation

Observation allows the educator to watch and assess students' learning, behaviors, and abilities in context as well as see the ways students interact with their environment. When using observation as an assessment tool, an educator should couple it with some type of written documentation in order to effectively collect and store data. This type of assessment varies from others in the fact it is used to collect qualitative and anecdotal data, not scores. This data is then used to guide planning decisions. In the library, it is important to observe students as they navigate the physical space and find information. This provides insight into the effectiveness of the library's layout and any instruction that was provided to teach students related skills, like library organization and routines.

Testing

Testing is one of the most common forms of assessment in schools. **Diagnostic testing** takes place prior to beginning a unit of instruction or at the start of the school year. The data from diagnostic testing is used to show what students already know, and it will influence what content should be covered in depth, what must be added, and sometimes what can be omitted. The data can be used again at the end of instruction to show how much students have grown from their pre-assessments.

Benchmark testing occurs at scheduled intervals throughout the year or unit of instruction. This shows how students are progressing and what content may need to be retaught. At the end of the year or unit of instruction, there is typically a summative test covering all related content. These are usually **norm-referenced** and thus are used to compare students to their peers within a grade level. They are often compared to diagnostic and benchmark tests to provide insight on student growth and achievement, which is then used to make decisions on altering lessons and curriculum.

Rubrics and Checklists

When given at the time of an assignment, a **rubric** provides students with explicit expectations for the assignment. The rubric is broken down into chunks of what will be assessed, and it provides detailed explanations for what scores will be given. A rubric could also be used to grade assignments. A teacher could return graded material to his or her students along with the rubric so the students could see the reasoning behind what grade they were given. These are most commonly used with projects, written essays, or other summative assignments to give students adequate guidance for their work. **Checklists** are similar in that they also provide guidance for work and list expectations; however, they do not provide the grading rationale given by rubrics. They can be used both by students, to check off what they have completed in their assignment as they work, and by educators when grading. In the context of the library, these may be used with any major project or assignment like inquiry-based learning projects, guided research assignments, or written reports.

Classroom Management

Space and Time Management

Proper space and time management are crucial in any learning space but especially in successful library programming. Libraries do provide storage for many books and resources, but they also serve as learning spaces; thus, classroom management must be taken into consideration when establishing the layout of shelves and storage solutions. For instance, librarians should be able to see students at all times. This is partially for safety, but also so that behaviors and actions can be monitored, corrected, or rewarded as appropriate. Keeping spaces in which students should be quiet and spaces in which students can collaborate separate and distinctly marked is also important and helps to manage student volume levels. From a classroom management perspective, time management involves creating and adhering to a routine. This establishes expectations and provides clear guidelines for what is to come so that students are able to fully participate in learning. By ensuring these aspects are in place, the librarian will develop a space that allows for successful programming.

Fixed and Flexible Scheduling

There are two common scheduling models in school libraries, fixed and flexible. **Fixed schedules** are commonly found in elementary schools and feature scheduled times for each class to visit the library on a weekly basis. The primary benefit of fixed scheduling is that it allows for consistent, planned instruction and ensures that every student is able to access the library regularly. The main drawbacks are limited library maintenance time and the librarian having limited autonomy over his or her own schedule. **Flexible schedules** are far less rigid than fixed schedules and involve scheduling library classes and lessons on an as-needed basis with classroom teachers. Classes coordinated between the librarian and teacher on a flexible schedule tend to be better aligned to support what students are learning in the classroom, since the library lessons have been specifically requested by the teacher. This style of schedule also allows for more free-flowing browsing throughout the day for students. The biggest drawbacks of flex scheduling are the facts that not all teachers will participate in collaboration and not all students will visit the library on their own time.

Review Video: Classroom Management - Rhythms of Teaching
Visit mometrix.com/academy and enter code: 809399

Positive Learning Environments

A positive learning environment is a safe space in which students feel they can fully participate in learning and receive the support needed to do their personal best. Students should feel comfortable and respected and have their basic needs met. Across many studies, it has been proven that students who learn in positive environments perform better academically, have better attendance, and are more motivated to succeed in school. Creating a sense of structure through routine is a simple way to create a positive learning environment in the library. When students know what is expected of them, they feel comfortable and confident in their ability to perform. Relationship building also creates positive learning environments. Students will know their librarian cares if he or she has conversations with them about their interests. Librarians can then use those conversations to more easily serve their students as patrons and provide them with materials that they are interested in. School libraries can also support students going through their own life experiences and traumas by providing access to written resources appropriate for their age that discuss their circumstances.

Expectations for Student Conduct

Expectations for student conduct are meant to keep students and staff safe and create a positive learning environment. It is vital that these expectations be clearly communicated throughout the year and practiced as needed. All expectations set should be reasonable based on students' age and ability levels. They should also be communicated using positive verbiage. For example, giving instructions to "walk in the library" is more effective than saying "no running" as it provides an example of what should be done. Some common student conduct expectations in the library include book-care rules, walking as opposed to other forms of movement, using appropriate volume, and returning books in a timely manner. Expectations that vary between libraries are routines for checking books in and out, the process for beginning library classes (if applicable), and the quantity of books that can be borrowed at one time. By communicating clear and reasonable expectations, librarians will make students aware of how they should behave, which will cut down on disruptions, distractions, and discipline issues.

Review Video: Promoting Appropriate Behavior
Visit mometrix.com/academy and enter code: 321015

Behavior Intervention Strategies

Behavior intervention strategies are any actions or plans set in place to improve student behavior. These may be specific to the student, like behavior charts or displayed routines, or used for the entire class or school, such as recognition programs, token economies, or universal signals for common needs such as quieting down. School librarians are part of an educational team responsible for the education and well-being of their students. As such, they are expected to use the appropriate behavior intervention strategies set forth within the school. For students with special considerations and strategies listed in their IEP or 504 plan, school librarians should use the behavior intervention strategies in place for students and document the results if applicable. School librarians may also choose to implement their own strategies within the library to help control student behaviors.

Review Video: Student Behavior Management Approaches
Visit mometrix.com/academy and enter code: 843846

Chapter Quiz

Ready to see how well you retained what you just read? Scan the QR code to go directly to the chapter quiz interface for this study guide. If you're using a computer, simply visit the online resources page at **mometrix.com/resources719/nbptslibmecya** and click the Chapter Quizzes link.

Knowledge of Library and Information Studies

Selection Policies

Guiding Documents for Library Selection Policies

As guiding documents for library selection policies, the **First Amendment** and the American Library Association's (ALA) **Library Bill of Rights** and **Freedom to Read Statement** outline some of the ethical and legal principles that govern free speech rights in the United States. Such principles include the freedom to view materials without fear of censorship or government interference and a guarantee that library materials serve all the members of a given population without discrimination. Library selection policies should be transparent about who makes decisions and which criteria are used to make those decisions, and they should emphasize that freedom of speech and intellectual freedom are prime mandates supported by the library. Selection policies generally explain that librarians should not allow their personal biases to influence policy and they should champion the mission of free speech and scholarship. Policies may also mention that materials are intended to meet a wide range of personal beliefs and interests, which includes materials that may be deemed objectionable by certain parties.

The ALA's **Code of Ethics** and position statements, including those on the topics of diversity, confidentiality, and the school library's role in education, serve as guiding documents for school selection policies. The code outlines the professional decorum expected of librarians and includes the following mandates: serve all peoples with dignity; respect and protect freedom of speech and intellectual property; and protect and promote the values of intellectual freedom and privacy. Selection policies should include language on how the collection supports academic inquiry and the process of discovering and verifying new information. In the many position statements put forth by the ALA, inclusion and inquiry are two values that are highly emphasized, and they are regarded as primary values that the school library must embody. Selection policies take these two values into account by ensuring that libraries can provide materials in numerous formats, languages, subjects, and accessibility options so that a wide variety of needs can be met.

Review Video: Ethical and Professional Standards
Visit mometrix.com/academy and enter code: 391843

Determining Which Materials Are Selected or Deselected for Collection

Library materials are selected for collection or deselected according to a variety of criteria. Generally, the **CREW** method is used, which stands for **C**ontinuous **R**eview, **E**valuation, and **W**eeding. To decide whether certain materials are eligible for weeding, the **MUSTIE** evaluation is used, which refers to materials that are **M**isleading, **U**gly, **S**uperseded, **T**rivial, **I**rrelevant, or obtained **E**lsewhere. Thus, materials that reflect the opposite values would be good qualities for selection, including those materials that are factual, in good condition, current, have scientific or literary merit, are relevant to the community, and are not easily obtained from another source. Other criteria that librarians take into consideration during the selection process include price, availability, positive reviews or feedback from trusted sources, community interest, curriculum support, and program support. All materials in a given collection must serve a purpose, whether that is educational or recreational. All materials that do not serve a purpose should be discarded.

Regular evaluation is necessary to determine whether items in the collection are serving such a purpose.

Writing, Implementing, Reviewing, and Revising Selection Policies

Librarians are generally responsible for all aspects of a library's selection process, including writing, implementation, review, and revision. Library staff like paraprofessionals or volunteers may also be involved in the selection or deselection processes at the implementation level or at the writing and review levels by providing suggestions and feedback. This may take the form of suggesting particular resources, such as types of resources that are missing, or taking part in regular weeding procedures. The selection policy should clearly state who is responsible for the selection and deselection of materials and how the materials are selected and deselected. Selection policies should be regularly evaluated by librarians in order to determine whether curricular and recreational needs are being met. This can often be done through circulation statistics and curriculum mapping. If a particular aspect of a selection policy is actively interfering with the effective administration of the library's collection, it should be reviewed and adjusted to align with the needs of the library.

Print Collection Organization Methods

Popular Organization Methods for a Library's Print Collection

When choosing a method of organization for a library's print materials, there are a few standard options used by the majority of libraries (school or otherwise) worldwide. Perhaps the most well-known system is the **Dewey Decimal Classification**, which organizes books into large buckets based on subject. While Dewey can be used for fiction, most public and school libraries have adopted a method of sorting fiction alphabetically by author's last name and sorting nonfiction using Dewey or another classification system. Some school and public libraries use **BISAC Subject Headings** to organize their nonfiction collection, which sorts materials by broad subject alphabetically rather than by grouping them into just 10 large classes (like Dewey) that may not necessarily suggest the relative physical location in the library. Some schools prefer BISAC or a more freeform organization method due to the smaller size of their collections, where it might be more important to have a "world literature" section rather than several subsections for countries that might contain few or no materials. Some school libraries and most academic libraries use the **Library of Congress Classification (LCC)** for both fiction and nonfiction, which groups materials into 21 classes, giving far more flexibility for large collections like those housed in universities.

Selecting and Maintaining Resources

Curriculum Mapping

The process of **curriculum mapping** involves the use of a diagram to outline all the educational objectives and lessons being taught throughout the school for a given year (now or in the future). By comparing actual lessons to standards and objectives required by state and federal laws, teachers can be sure that their curricula are actively meeting the needs of their students. In the same manner, curriculum mapping can be used by librarians in conjunction with classroom teachers to ensure that the library collection supports the curricular needs of students. A visual diagram of content standards and associated lessons and projects will give librarians a reasonable approximation of the types of materials that are necessary for students to be successful in learning subject content. By aligning selection policies with content curriculum maps, libraries can reduce budget waste and ensure purchased materials will accurately reflect classroom educational needs.

School Community and Material Selection

Since library collections are designed to support the specific needs of the populations that they serve, there will naturally be variance in the types of materials required by one library when compared to another. One way this manifests itself is the languages in which materials are offered. A library population that contains a large Hispanic community should collect materials in Spanish as well as materials that might be of particular interest to Spanish speakers. On a broader level, student tastes may influence the number and kinds of materials that are collected. For example, a particular school may have a strong love for romance and nonfiction books, while science fiction and fantasy languish (according to their circulation statistics). Such a library may want to devote more of its budget to the types of materials that circulate heavily (romance and nonfiction), while sticking only to the highest-profile books in less-popular genres (science fiction and fantasy). Being observant and responsive to the needs of a particular community is key to ensuring that the collection is most effective.

Library Collections Support of School Curricula

Library collections support school curricula and the needs of diverse learners in a variety of ways. When libraries consider curricular and diverse population needs during the selection process, budgets can be utilized effectively to provide materials necessary for these purposes. Curricular objectives in the classroom are supported by materials that are actively used during lessons, such as databases, subject nonfiction materials, and fiction related to lesson subjects. A library's reference materials also broadly support the mission of all school curricula. It is important to select and maintain appropriate materials to support the needs of diverse learners, such as assistive devices like magnifiers and reader software or materials in languages other than English. The library's collection can also provide students with access to outside resources like reading lists, webpages, and bibliographies that support the needs of specific groups like students interested in subjects not taught in school or students who need extra help with a particular classroom subject due to a disability.

Popular Platforms for Selection and Collection Development

As a means of beginning and maintaining a particular collection for a library age group or genre, **EBSCO**'s **NoveList** service provides **Core Collections**, which are lists containing well-reviewed and well-regarded materials to support librarians and their collections. By comparing these collections to a library's current or proposed collection, gaps or overlaps can be identified and new materials can be lined up for purchase. These Core Collections are a great way for a new librarian to start a collection filled with materials that have been selected for quality and relevance. Other popular selection formats are **bookfinder.com** and **Follett Titlewave**. These resources give excellent information on books in particular interest areas or age groups and give great bibliographic, Lexile, award, and review information for library materials. Titlewave in particular is a great resource for the librarian in search of materials to support a specific educational objective or to align with a current-interest topic.

Using Statistical Information to Evaluate Resources

Statistical information is a key tool at the librarian's disposal when evaluating the overall quality of the library's collection. It is possible to evaluate the collection by calculating the overall age (by copyright date), the number of items, and the cost (in dollars spent) of each category in the collection. Collections like nonfiction and reference materials need to be kept current to ensure they are accurate and useful, so the average age of materials is particularly useful here. Further, circulation statistics and the physical space allocated for each category of the collection can give a lot of insight into how the library is organized and which categories are circulating or not. Aligning budgets with circulation statistics is a key way to ensure that money is being spent to support appropriate collections and not being heavily dedicated to collections that are not of interest to the students.

Planning, Designing, and Evaluating Media Products

Different types of media products are used to meet a variety of needs and can include instructional videos and tutorials, pathfinders, lesson kits, or any other type of media usable by patrons. It is often the responsibility of the school librarian to create or compile these resources, and it is often by request of administration or when the librarian sees a wide need for these products. The first step in planning a media product is to establish a goal based on a need. Once this goal has been established, the librarian can begin to design a product to meet it. He or she should consider what type of media will best address the concern, such as a video, multimedia presentation, or written document. These media products can then be shared with the intended audience, typically staff or a student group. Once the audience has had time to use the shared media, it is important for the librarian to check in and gather feedback. By doing so, the librarian will know if the media is addressing the established goals, and that feedback can be used to improve the media and create additional high-quality media products to meet future concerns.

Media

Media is any type of material or instructional tool an educator might use within a lesson. This can include simple supplies like paper, pencils, or crayons, but also includes videos, multimedia presentations, and any other resource used to deliver educational content. The proper use of aligned media in instruction enhances the educational content's quality. In order to best meet instructional goals by using media, the educator must first consider the desired learning outcome based on the standards or unit of study he or she is addressing. The educator may then select or create media that aligns with said learning outcome. Because there are various types of media resources available, it is important to ensure they are being used ethically and legally (regarding any copyright issues). Adhering to fair use policies is the best way to ensure this when using media that was not created by oneself or when using reference materials to create new media.

Maintaining Library Catalogs and Bibliographic Integrity

Library catalogs provide in-depth information about what a library collection has to offer. As such, keeping a catalog up to date is a key librarian responsibility. The best way to catalog a resource will vary based on the type of resource and content within it; however, entries most often include the title, author, illustrator (if applicable), publication date, and location of the book (for physical text resources). Digital resources are cataloged similarly but typically also include access information. Non-text and specialty resources, like manipulatives and curriculum kits, are typically cataloged with a name, description, and location within the library. The Library of Congress (LOC) and the ALA have established best practices for cataloging any related bibliographic information and should be referred to for any specialty cataloging. By adhering to the guidelines established by the LOC and ALA, librarians are able to maintain bibliographic integrity, which leads to streamlined, effective catalogs with appropriate bibliographic information.

Conducting a School Library Media Collection Inventory

Regular collection inventory in the school library has several benefits. Inventory helps maintain the accuracy of a school library's catalog by ensuring books are not only actually in the library but are in the correct places based on their bibliographic information. Another benefit is the role it plays in weeding. Inventory allows time for librarians to be hands on with all the books to establish which, if any, should be removed based on their physical integrity. Finally, inventorying a collection allows for loss analysis, providing detailed information on what books are missing and how much they are worth. While the detailed process will vary based on the catalog system used, the general process for inventory is typically the same. Using the cataloging system and a handheld scanner, the librarian scans each book in a section one at a time. Once that section has been completely scanned, the system compiles a list of books not scanned that should be in the library and are not out on loan. The information generated provides the information needed to correct any inaccuracies in the library catalog.

Using Standard Review Tools to Guide Selection Decisions

Standard review tools allow the school librarian to maintain a quality collection without the necessity of personally reading every single resource purchased. These tools provide reviews on quality, age-suitability, and other information relevant to the selection process. Some of the most popular tools include ***Booklist*** and ***Kirkus Reviews*** (all ages), ***School Library Journal*** (school ages), and ***The Horn Book*** (children and young adults). By regularly referring to these resources during the selection process, librarians can get a good idea of some of the current popular reads for specific interest and age groups, and they can read reviews of the materials to ensure they are suitable to meet the needs of their intended audience. Other review resources exist for readers in specific genres, including those that support the genres of science fiction, short story, and poetry.

Using Bibliographic Sources to Guide Selection Decisions

Bibliographic sources help librarians to make selection decisions by providing in-depth information about the various characteristics that make up a resource, including content, physical dimensions (if applicable), cost, availability for purchase, and much more. The careful and purposeful use of these tools will result in a collection that is robust in offering materials in a wide range of formats, interest areas, and reading levels. Some potential sources for bibliographic information include **ProQuest**'s **Books in Print** database, the **Library of Congress Catalog**, and various other periodical publications. Bibliographic sources are used by librarians alongside other selection tools like review platforms, selection and development platforms, and vendor catalogs to develop a full view of potential materials for the collection.

Pros and Cons of Using Vendor Catalogs

Vendor catalogs, like those belonging to popular vendors **Follett**, **Mackin, Amazon,** and **OverDrive**, will provide librarians with a curated, one-stop shop experience for various collections. For the sake of simplicity and convenience, many schools partner with a single vendor to supply their library resource needs. One of the major benefits of such a relationship is the customer service opportunities. Engaging in a relationship with a vendor provides a certain level of hands-on support for librarians in the selection process. Another point in favor of utilizing vendors for selection is that it reduces the number of irrelevant resource options, which might otherwise overwhelm an inexperienced librarian. On the other hand, a more experienced librarian may wish for a larger number of resources, which might not be available with a particular, single vendor. Vendor catalogs also have a financial interest that bibliographic or professional publications may not have, influencing the number and kinds of materials offered.

School Library's Professional Collection

A school library's **professional collection** is designed to serve the ongoing professional education needs of the library and teaching staff. Such collections will typically include materials concerning the education and motivation of students and materials that train educators on new techniques and ideas in their subject fields. Professional journals, conference abstracts, and other subject publications will make up the bulk of these resources. Due to the speed at which educational disciplines evolve and the importance of providing the absolute best experience for children, it is critical that a professional collection is regularly updated and reviewed by librarians and subject specialists. A core group of librarians and subject specialists should meet regularly to discuss gaps, potential selections, and outdated items in the collection.

Importance of Keeping a Professional Collection Up to Date

More than any other collection in the school library, the professional collection demands currency in order to operate effectively. This is due to its purpose as a tool to keep educators current with developments in their fields, especially those that directly relate to education and motivation of students. If educators rely on materials in the professional collection that espouse old, disproven methods to educate students, the students may suffer irreparable harm. Therefore, it is critical to keep professional collections current with the latest peer-reviewed articles and publications in subjects that support curricula and the professional development of faculty. Professional collections require the most current information, followed by digital databases, print nonfiction, and, finally, print fiction.

Selecting Various Non-Literature Items

In addition to evaluating print and digital literature resources, librarians must also evaluate and purchase a variety of other materials such as **library management systems** (LMS) to organize the day-to-day operations of the library, audiovisual and computer equipment, and various online subscription services like creativity software or internet privacy services. Each of these non-literature items requires collaboration with school technology professionals so that the professionals can give insight into the pros and cons of various options and provide support in implementing and maintaining them. Like any other library material selected, non-literature items should support the needs of the library and the school's educational objectives while remaining as cost-effective as possible. Purchasing computer hardware and software is a particularly expensive endeavor, and both will need to be maintained and repurchased with regularity in order to ensure their practical use for students.

Role of a Jobber

A **jobber** is a wholesaler who purchases materials from manufacturers or publishers and sells them directly to libraries. Jobbers reduce some of the complexity in purchasing materials by handling many of the earlier steps in sourcing and purchasing materials in bulk. Many jobbers will offer school libraries book processing services, which mean the materials reach the library immediately ready to be shelved with barcodes, stickers, and any other physical processing requirements already included. Some jobbers like Follett and Mackin offer catalog integration in addition to physical processing, which further reduces the need for library staff to enter newly received materials into catalogs. The convenience of using a jobber is its primary advantage, while increased costs are the primary disadvantage. Weighing a jobber's services and materials offered against its costs, especially in comparison with other jobbers, is a great way to select the one that will best support a library's selection needs.

Vendors for Materials

Pros and Cons of Purchasing Materials Directly from a Publisher

One of the major benefits to purchasing directly from a publisher is the potential for bulk purchase or frequent-order discounts. Since publishers may sell their products to businesses like wholesalers and retailers, cutting these intermediaries out can result in cost savings for libraries. Libraries may also see the benefit of publishers directly advertising their new products to them, saving some time and effort on the part of the librarian in locating materials. On the other hand, such advertisements can be one of the major downsides to publisher acquisition. Publishers, like other businesses, have a monetary interest at the heart of their business, so they may try to advertise and sell products that the library might not ordinarily want. Publishers are also limited in the kinds of materials they sell since they will generally only carry items that they help produce or provide editing services for. Other acquisitions sources like wholesalers and retailers may have access to a wider variety of products.

Types of Materials Purchased from a Publisher vs. Another Source

One of the most common material types to be purchased directly from publishers is reference materials, particularly those that need to be updated frequently and thus purchased regularly. Print reference materials like encyclopedias, dictionaries, and bibliographies are likely to be kept continuously in print, and these are typically collected by the library from the same publisher for convenience. It can be useful to keep a standing order for the latest reference materials if the library has the budget for it or to have an understanding that when it is time to update the print reference section, the regular publisher will be the library's first consideration. There may also be a benefit to purchasing computer software from a publisher. Specialized computer software that is either used by the back end of the library (e.g., integrated library system, accounting software) or by the patron-facing computers (e.g., photo editing, 3D modeling) may require specialized support, which publishers are able to provide. Being able to troubleshoot software problems and receive help with installation and maintenance is a major benefit to purchasing directly from the software's publisher.

Pros and Cons of Purchasing Materials from a Wholesaler

Library wholesalers (**jobbers**) are businesses that purchase materials directly from many publishers and then offer a one-stop shop experience for libraries. Common library wholesalers include **Follett**, **Mackin**, and **OverDrive**. The major benefit of purchasing materials from a wholesaler is the simplicity and ease of access to a much wider range of materials than can be provided by an individual publisher. Wholesalers can also provide their customers with cost savings by buying materials from publishers in bulk at a discount and passing along a portion of the discount to their customers. Another advantage of using wholesalers in library acquisitions is the potential for catalog integration and materials processing services. Many of the largest wholesalers offer specialized integration with a library's catalog and will process materials before sending them on to libraries, saving a lot of time and effort for library staff. The primary disadvantage of a wholesaler relationship is the lack of access to all materials a library might be interested in acquiring. Since many libraries will maintain a relationship with a single wholesaler, there will naturally be desired materials that wholesaler does not carry, and that would necessitate another acquisition source.

Subscription Services

Libraries are relying more than ever on subscription services that they use either internally or offer to patrons as part of their collections. Some of the common kinds of services libraries might subscribe to include various databases, e-book and audiobook platforms, web hosting services, software licenses, print and digital periodicals, and video platforms. Publishers may be the preferred vendor for software licenses since they can provide user support. For most digital offerings like databases, e-books, audiobooks, and videos, a wholesaler partner specializing in digital collections will likely be the best vendor. Other subscription services like web hosting are likely to be purchased from individual vendors, such as those who develop or publish the resource in question, as this might be the only possible place to purchase the subscription.

Choosing a Subscription Service

With the abundance of desirable subscription-based offerings, it is important that librarians carefully select the right number and kind of subscription services that maximize resource availability while minimizing costs. One thing to keep in mind while making purchasing decisions about subscriptions is the ongoing nature of their costs. Compared to other one-time material purchases, subscriptions will bill at a regular interval and must be budgeted accordingly. Subscriptions are also, due to their ongoing nature, subject to change in ways that one-time purchases are generally not. Thus, it is important to ascertain whether and how subscription resources might change, how they are updated, and who is available to support end users should they need it. Subscriptions that provide access to digital resource platforms that offer e-books, audiobooks, or videos should be evaluated for the number and quality of offerings and how well those offerings support school curricula. These digital collections must also be evaluated for overlaps with the print collection, which may serve as enhancements or redundancies depending on the habits of users.

Selecting a Vendor

When selecting a vendor for a particular materials acquisition, it is important to consider a variety of factors that will determine the best source for a given purchase. Most vendor selections will start from the location of a desired material, and the most suitable vendor will be selected after this point. In the case of a wholesaler that provides most of a library's materials, the vendor may be selected first, and then materials will be selected from that vendor's catalog. Vendors for a given item should be compared to each other and evaluated according to cost of the material, cost of other materials that might interest the collection, support services offered, customer reviews, and shipping and handling practices, among other factors. Libraries should start with a desired material and then eliminate vendors that don't offer the material. Based on the vendors who offer the material, the appropriate vendor should be chosen based on major price considerations.

Materials Purchased Through Various Types of Library Vendors

Libraries acquire a wide variety of materials for their collections, as well as furniture, cleaning supplies, office supplies, programming supplies, computer hardware and software, and more. While there is a large budgetary emphasis on the acquisition of literature, since this is the primary offering of libraries and occurs with great regularity, other types of purchases are important in ensuring an effective library operation. Cleaning and office supplies may be purchased through wholesalers that specialize in these products, while furniture and materials to support programs may come from the same wholesaler or another one depending on the organization. Office supply stores can handle each of those needs and may reduce some of the complexity in purchasing these materials. Specialty library suppliers can offer library furniture and supplies like bookends, displays, accessibility aids, and materials-processing supplies. Computer hardware and software may be purchased from publishers or specialty computer supply companies, depending on the needs of the library.

Government Agency Assistance

Government agencies assist school libraries with the purchase of certain kinds of materials as a means of supporting the education of students. The **Federal Communications Commission's (FCC) E-Rate** program provides schools and libraries with needs-based discounts on telecommunications and information services in the form of reimbursements. This may help subsidize the cost of internet services, materials that help students work from home like tablets and laptops, accessibility supplies, or Wi-Fi equipment like hotspots. These types of equipment and services may be prohibitively expensive for libraries but are still critical for the educational needs of students, making the E-Rate program an important form of government assistance for school libraries. Another form of governmental assistance is the **Library of Congress (LOC) Surplus Books Program,** which provides free books to support libraries in need.

Resource Acquisition Processes

Bidding Process When Choosing Between Suppliers

A bidding process for acquiring resources requires a librarian to make decisions between various vendors in a formalized manner by comparing their bids for a particular good or service. Such a bidding process will begin with the determination of the good or service that is to be purchased, followed by a **request for proposal** (RFP). An RFP is a formal announcement that a resource is being sought by the library, and potential vendors are welcome to submit private proposals for providing that resource. After a set date, generally contained in the RFP, all received proposals are considered by the librarian (and potentially other interested parties) and evaluated for suitability of price, timeline, vendor capability, and other factors. Once the best bid is determined, the librarian will contact the vendor, accept the proposal, and make plans to purchase the goods or services requested.

Purpose of a Bidding Process

Bidding processes are a good practice for many organizations and purchase types and may be mandated by law or organizational policies for certain institutions that are funded publicly. The purpose of such a process is to create transparency in purchasing procedures, reduce the potential for favoritism or other unscrupulous purchasing practices, and ensure purchases are made for the least possible price. This last point is particularly salient for local and federal government-funded organizations like school libraries, as funding bodies (or the public) want to ensure that funds are being spent in the best possible manner. Without a bidding process, it is possible that goods and services might be purchased without proper consideration and end up costing more than necessary. It is also possible for fraud or generally unethical behavior to occur when making purchases without a bidding process. A person or organization with private interests may purchase materials from a vendor that is not the cheapest or otherwise not the best suited for the purchase, which costs libraries money and diminishes the overall quality of offerings. Bidding out important purchases drastically reduces the possibility of fraud.

Encumbered Funds

Encumbered funds are those that are earmarked for a specific purpose, generally one that occurs regularly or that will occur in the future. These funds will not be spent except on the designated purchase and are thus said to be encumbered because they cannot be freely spent on other purchases. Subscription services generally create encumbered funds since they are regularly occurring expenditures that the library can plan for on an annual basis. A large event that is being planned for later on in the year may necessitate an encumbrance of funds as a means of ensuring that money will remain available to fund the event. Monetary donations to the library may also come with encumbrance clauses that specify the kinds of materials or services that can be purchased with the donation. For example, a science educator may donate to the library on the condition that the money only be used to support and enhance the science curriculum in the school.

Best Practices to Use with Encumbered Funds

Encumbered funds should be clearly tracked both before and after disbursement in order to make sure that funds are correctly saved and spent. It is important to reserve a certain part of the library's budget for unforeseen purchases or those that might occur on short notice, such as a replacement of a crucial reference work or the repair of the library's catalog computer. Over-encumbrance of the library's funds will make it less flexible in responding to short-term opportunities and may limit the kinds of purchases that it can make, particularly those that are one-time payments as opposed to regularly occurring. Spreading out encumbered funds over various line-item budgets may promote flexibility by retaining "free" funds, which can be spent in each of the budget categories the library maintains. It is also important to regularly evaluate the kinds of funds that are being encumbered, both to ensure the amounts set aside line up with their intended purchases and to determine whether the purchases continue to be necessary or desirable.

Kinds of Budgets Used

Generally, library budgets will fall into a couple major categories: line-item budgets and program budgets. While the **lump-sum** budget may be used by extraordinarily small or poorly managed organizations, it is advisable to organize funding into categories in order to properly allocate, spend, track, and evaluate spending. **Line-item budgets** allocate funds according to specific items being purchased, such as books, supplies, staff salaries, etc. Funding by line item allows libraries to accurately track how much is being allocated and spent on specific items. **Program budgets** allocate funds based on specific objectives or programs, such as circulation, staffing, or physical space requirements. Program budgeting helps give libraries a sense of the cost of each program's objectives, and each program will have separate budgets that align with the actual costs of administering it. Some programs may duplicate individual expenditures such as books since they will be required by both circulation and staffing (in the form of professional collections). Most library budgets will contain a mixture of program and line-item budgets depending on the mindset of the librarian and the kinds of purchases being made.

Creating Line-Item Library Budgets

Line-item library budgets are commonly used to ensure that funds are allocated and available to appropriately support each kind of purchase the library makes. Generally, line-item budgets are created by determining how much money needs to be spent at minimum on a particular resource as well as how much money would be spent on that resource in an ideal situation. One way to begin budgeting each line item is to determine how much was spent on that resource in prior years or by looking at organizations that have a similar size and financial situation. Since libraries will always be interested in purchasing new books, for instance, a line-item budget for materials acquisition is likely to be desirable and should be regularly evaluated to ensure that the amount allocated is not too much or too little to meet the needs of the collection. When used in conjunction with program budgets, line-item budgets can give insight into the actual cost of various parts of the library's operation and how those costs factor into the operation of a particular library program like circulation or information literacy education.

Using of Purchase Orders

A **purchase order** (**PO**) is the formalized request for a purchase sent by a buyer to a seller that specifies the number and kind of goods or services requested as well as the terms of the sale, including the fulfillment timeline, liability transfers, and price. POs are compared to packing slips upon receipt of goods to ensure that ordered goods were received in the agreed-upon condition. After the completion of a bidding process, librarians will generally send formal POs to vendors to request desired goods or services. Depending on the organization, a PO may be accepted as the formal documentation of a purchase and will be retained for reporting and budgetary purposes. POs can assist with tracking funds that have not yet been spent but that are allocated for a purchase that will occur in the short or long term. They are also used as legal documents that show a written contract between the buyer and seller, and they can help resolve disputes that may occur during the purchase process.

Process of Creating a PO

Librarians will be the primary actor in the creation of a PO and in any follow-through on the purchase process involving it. Depending on the organizational structure of the school, the librarian may initiate the PO process and then pass the PO along to school financial specialists for execution or follow-up. Coordinating with school legal experts and financial specialists will also ensure that PO terms are agreeable. This will help protect the library and school from potential financial or legal trouble in the future. School financial specialists may have standardized PO templates that can be customized by the librarian, reducing the need for creation of POs from scratch and saving valuable time and energy. Depending on the library's relationship with a wholesaler, there may be support available on the vendor side for the creation and initiation of a PO as well.

Cataloging Methods

Cataloging in Publication

Cataloging in Publication (CIP) is a bibliographic record created by the Library of Congress (LOC) before a work is published. It is generally found on one of the first few pages of a print book and is helpful for cataloging and processing purposes. It exists as a partial record containing some key information that is used when preparing for the physical or digital arrival of a work and that allows for some basic cataloging to be done ahead of time. CIP records are generally abbreviated versions of the final records that would be contained in MARC (Machine-Readable Cataloging) records after publication. Generally, CIP records contain information about the work's title, author, publication date and location, description, subject headings, and various identification numbers like the Library of Congress Control Number (LCCN) and the International Standard Book Number (ISBN).

Sears List of Subject Headings

The **Sears List of Subject Headings** is an abbreviated list of the complete **Library of Congress Subject Headings** and is thus an organized, standardized list of headings and subheadings that can be used by organizations for cataloging purposes. For instance, a library's nonfiction selection may be categorized based on a classification system like the Dewey Decimal Classification or the **Library of Congress Classification (LCC)**, with subcategories drawn from Sears. The Sears Subject Headings allow for a library to categorize its materials without separating works on similar subjects into smaller, more distinct categories, such as sports and athletics. The Sears Subject Headings are best suited for use by smaller libraries that will not have a need for the vast number of detailed subheadings offered by the full LOC system.

Resource Description and Access

The system of **Resource Description and Access (RDA)** is a descriptive cataloging standard that outlines a set of rules used in creating cataloging records. These rules are generally used to construct bibliographic records for catalogs, including MARC records. RDA is commonly used in libraries, museums, and other catalog-heavy industries as a standard language to create cataloging records, and its greatest strength is its widespread use. As long as records are constructed according to RDA guidelines, they can be freely shared by organizations with little or no modification needed. RDA is the successor to the previously popular ***Anglo-American Cataloguing Rules, Second Edition* (*AACR2*)**. Compared to *AACR2*, RDA's primary strength lies in its international nature. *AACR2* was, by design, oriented for and by a specific audience and retrofitted for use by other international organizations. RDA was designed to be more robust for use in other languages and by international cultures and organizations.

Replacement of *AACR2* by RDA

AACR2 was an outdated set of descriptive cataloging standards used by many organizations to outline the writing of bibliographic records. In 2010, RDA was adopted as the successor to *AACR2* in order to reflect a changing world with new needs and requirements. In comparison to *AACR2*, RDA was designed to be more intuitive for use in digital environments and provide more rigorous descriptions for digital-only content. Another change from *AACR2* to RDA was the removal of the "Anglo-American" title, which no longer reflected a system that was translated into two dozen languages and used in more than 40 countries worldwide.

Dewey Decimal Classification

The **Dewey Decimal Classification** is a system used by libraries to organize various parts of their collections in a logical, organized manner. Like other organization systems, Dewey's strengths lie in its ability to provide categories for all items in a collection to make cataloging and physically locating each item easier. Dewey is divided into 10 primary classes, which are as follows: 000 (computer science, information, general works), 100 (philosophy, psychology), 200 (religion), 300 (social sciences), 400 (language), 500 (science), 600 (technology), 700 (arts, recreation), 800 (literature), and 900 (history, geography). Within each primary class there are a variety of subclasses that can further classify related items and locate their proximity. Smaller libraries like school libraries are well suited for Dewey since it provides logical groupings for materials without providing too many categories that might not have many items included. Most libraries that use Dewey will use it strictly for nonfiction, choosing to organize fiction alphabetically by author's last name rather than including it in the 800 literature class.

MARC Records

MARC Records

As a bibliographic record type, **MARC** (Machine-Readable Cataloging) records were designed to contain all the bibliographic information about a work and explain how that information should be read and understood. MARC records can be read by computers and are thus made searchable and form the basis for the online cataloging used in libraries today. MARC records are formatted in a long string of data types called **access points** that include a variety of code characters called indicators and tags that tell the computer a new field is to be read and the type of data within the field. Without these indicators and tags, the computer would not be able to interpret the data within a given field or read the language that we may use to interpret MARC records in day-to-day conversation. Ultimately, MARC records serve as a standardized method of recording bibliographic information that can be transmitted and interpreted by computers.

Library of Congress Control Number

The three-digit tag used for the **Library of Congress Control Number (LCCN)** in MARC is **010**. The LCCN is a unique control number assigned by the LOC to each MARC record, and it is used to locate an individual record in national databases. A MARC entry for the LCCN (e.g., "$a 85152473") does not utilize either indicator, and it may include subfields like National Union Catalog of Manuscript Collections (NUCMC) control number (e.g., "$b ms89003179"), or a canceled/invalid LCCN ("$z"). A sample MARC field could look like [010 ## $a 85152473 $b ms89003179].

International Standard Book Number

The three-digit tag used for the **International Standard Book Number (ISBN)** in MARC is **020**. The ISBN is a unique product number used by publishers and retailers as a shorthand for a specific title and format. A MARC entry for the ISBN (e.g., "$a 9781984802781") generally contains no defined indicators (##) and may include subfields like terms of availability (e.g., "$c $11.99") or qualifying information (e.g., "$q acid-free paper"). A sample MARC field could look like [020 ## $a 9781984802781].

Author Main Entry

The three-digit tag used for the **author main entry** in MARC is **100**. This field uses three common first indicators (0 for first name, 1 for surname, and 3 for family name), no second indicator, and may include subfields like name (e.g., "$a Smith, John"), title (e.g., "$c esq."), or dates associated with the name used to distinguish similar names (e.g., "$d 1900-1960"), as well as many others. A sample MARC field could look like [100 1# $a Smith, John, $c esq., $d 1900-1960]. Note that 100 entries end with a period and subfields are separated by commas.

Title Information Entry

The three-digit tag used for the **title information entry** in MARC is **245**. This field uses the first indicator to note whether an access point should be added for the title. A 0 indicates that an entry should not be added (used when there is no 1XX author field), and a 1 indicates that an entry should be added (used when there is a 1XX author field). The second indicator is used to indicate whether any characters should be skipped when filing the entry alphabetically (0-9 digits skipped). For example, an indicator of 12 would suggest that an entry should be added for title and that two characters should be skipped when filing the title entry. This is often used in the case of a title beginning with "a" or "the," which would be skipped when alphabetizing. Some common subfields include title (e.g., "$a Splat! 2:"), subtitle (e.g., "$b a tale of two splats"), and statement of responsibility (e.g., "$c Splatburn, Milton"). A sample MARC field could look like [245 10 $a Splat! 2:, $b a tale of two splats, $c Splatburn, Milton]. Note that 245 entries end with a period and subfields are separated by commas.

Edition and Imprint

The three-digit tag used in MARC for **edition** is **250** and the tag for **imprint** (publication) is **260.** Edition has no indicators and commonly uses only a subfield for edition statement (e.g., "$a 3rd ed."); though, there are a few others used. Imprint has a first indicator of undefined, 2 (used when publisher has changed), or 3 (latest publisher) for publication sequence and no second indicator. The most commonly used subfields include publication location (e.g., "$a New York, NY"), publisher name (e.g., "$b Random House"), and publication date (e.g., "$c 1994"). A sample MARC record including both edition and imprint information could look like [250 ## $a 3rd ed. 260 3# $a New York, NY $b Random House $c 1994].

Physical Description

The three-digit tag used for the **physical description** in MARC is **300**. Physical description does not use either indicator and has many common subfields. Some of these include extent, which generally includes number of pages, volumes, or playing time (e.g., "$a 303 pages"), other physical details like color or illustrations (e.g., "$b color"), and dimensions (e.g., "$c 30cm"). A sample MARC field could look like [300 ## $a 303 pages $b color $c 30cm]. Knowledge of the physical description of an item helps librarians ensure that the materials will fit on their shelves.

ANNOTATION

The three-digit tag used for **annotation** in MARC is **520.** This field is used for a variety of notes about the work and is categorized by the first indicator including summary (undefined), subject (0), review (1), scope (2), and abstract (3), among others. The second indicator is not used. The most commonly used subfield is the note itself (e.g., "$a A really great book."), though others may be used. A sample MARC field might look like [520 ## $a A really great book.].

TOPICAL SUBJECT HEADING

The three-digit tag used for **topical subject heading** in MARC is **650.** This field adds a subject heading to the record, allowing for reference based on subject or topic. This field uses the first indicator to note the level of the subject as not specified (undefined), primary (1), or secondary (2). The second indicator notes which system, if any, was used to construct the subject heading, with 0 (Library of Congress), 1 (LC for children's literature), and 4 (not specified) commonly used. Common subfields include subject or geographic name (e.g., "$a spelunking"), chronological subdivision (e.g., "$y 1900-1999"), and geological subdivision (e.g., "$z North America"). A sample MARC field might look like [650 10 $a spelunking $y 1900-1999 $z North America].

SHELF ORGANIZATION

A library's shelves should be organized according to a purposeful, systematic method of organization based on the classification system used for the collection. Materials should be organized in an attractive manner and be easily accessible for patrons of all abilities. In order to meet ADA compliance standards, shelves should be 32 inches apart, and shelves should max out at 48 inches tall (or come with signs offering assistance reaching upward). Depending on the classification system being used, shelves should be organized logically into neat sections, perhaps by fiction, nonfiction, and other media, and alphabetized according to the classification system's call numbers. A library which uses a classification system other than Dewey or LCC may sort fiction by genre or some other organization scheme. Materials should be shelved regularly and stored between loan and shelving in a logical way that maximizes the ease of reshelving, such as by physical library location, genre, and alphabetically.

Loan, Reserve, and Renewal Procedures

PROPERLY IDENTIFYING THE BORROWER OF PRINT LIBRARY MATERIALS

Thousands of dollars are spent each year on library materials. These materials are meant to be shared with the entire school community. When items are borrowed but not returned, it creates a financial burden on the school to replace the resources, a professional dilemma for the librarian who must satisfy a request with an alternate resource, and if no replacement item is available, a disappointed student. While it is impossible to ensure that every item ever borrowed will be returned, a **library media specialist** (LMS) can increase the probability by properly identifying each borrower. Library automation software will keep track of who borrows what, but the librarian must demonstrate diligence by checking out every item and verifying a borrower's identity through valid school identification or, if applicable, simple recognition.

UTILIZING THE LOAN FUNCTION OF A LIBRARY AUTOMATION SYSTEM

Circulation starts with loaning materials. Depending on the type of user information uploaded into the system, an LMS can **loan items to individual students** or **to entire classes by teacher or**

homeroom. In the case of the latter, the teacher is then considered to be the borrower and is responsible for the timely return of all borrowed material. Student borrowers can be searched in the system by first or last name, student identification number, or by grade. Many systems also allow for resources to be loaned to the library itself with an **in-library loan** feature. This is particularly helpful when the librarian wants to temporarily remove print items from the collection to repair them or to keep track of books that are removed from the shelf for a display or a class research cart.

Fair Loaning Policy for Sharing Resources

When multiple students are assigned the same project, an availability issue may arise. An LMS who has been in place for several years knows which resources are necessary to have on hand to avoid this problem. But an LMS who is not as familiar with the curriculum or one who has a small budget might not be able to meet the immediate research needs of large groups. In this case, creating a class resource cart is a good idea. This can be done by using the in-library loan feature of the automation system to check out all books on a certain topic. The books are placed on a cart for students to research in the media center only. Loan limits for e-books can ensure all students have an opportunity to access digital material, and if e-book subscriptions are in place, the librarian can recommend those unlimited resources to students. Creating this policy will make students and faculty feel confident that print and electronic resources will always be accessible when needed.

Setting Flexible Loan Periods

Students borrow materials for different reasons. Setting different loan periods for different item types takes into consideration the needs of the borrower. A student doing research will probably not need a resource for more than two weeks, as he or she is bound by an assignment due date. Requiring nonfiction items to be returned within two weeks also ensures the resources will be available for others whose assignments might have overlapping topics. Often, students who borrow audiovisual materials or fiction will use them in their free time, which, depending on personal circumstances, might not amount to much. A longer loan period of three weeks is practical and will probably result in fewer renewals. The circulation feature in a library automation system allows the administrator to manipulate due dates for different item types.

Circulation

Circulation in a library refers to the flow of library resources between members of a particular user set. Different user sets might include a school, a town, or a business. Circulation allows for the smooth transfer of materials between users, and circulation policies ensure the materials are shared fairly within the set community. Proper record keeping is crucial to tracking the items circulating at any given time. There are two types of circulation systems that facilitate record keeping in different ways. An **automated** circulation system is electronic, involves a software subscription, and stores information digitally. A **manual** circulation system can be managed different ways, but it usually involves a librarian assigning physical cards to each print and audiovisual item detailing book and borrower information and due dates. Manual systems have become less common as automated systems that offer more valuable circulation statistical analysis tools have become more affordable.

Reserve and Renew

A **reserve** is a hold placed on an item to save it for a particular borrower. This is a useful service for borrowers who need an item that is currently circulating to ensure they will, upon return of the item, be next to check it out. An LMS can place a reserve for a student, or the student can reserve the item remotely through an online catalog that offers the reserve option. A borrower can, through the online catalog, also place a reserve remotely to hold an available item for a short time. When a reserve is placed on an item, a notation is made on the record preventing it from being borrowed or renewed. To **renew** an item is to extend the loan period of a borrowed item for a specified time. The LMS sets the renewal policy and can conduct the renewal at the borrower's request. Some automated systems offer a function allowing the borrower to renew his or her own item.

Restriction Policies Regarding Reserving, Borrowing, and Renewing Books

The LMS strives to support the research and recreational reading needs of the students, but to serve the school community properly, it is necessary to set limits to ensure resources are shared fairly. These rules can also apply to libraries with single-user e-book collections. A time-sensitive hold or reserve policy gives the borrower a chance to save a title, but not indefinitely. A librarian may limit the number of books per subject or author that a patron can borrow or allow only a certain number of renewals before a book must be returned. Presenting borrowing guidelines in a clear and transparent manner will promote the importance of the consideration of others.

Ensuring Physical Materials Are Returned

Students might not return borrowed items on time for a variety of reasons. Regardless, to protect the assets of the library, policies must be in place to address this problem. Progressive attention should include:

- An overdue reminder notice
- An offer to renew if the item has not been placed on reserve
- A second overdue reminder notice
- A hold on further transactions
- A late fine
- A statement of cost to replace the item
- A withholding of student records until all fees have been paid.

Return policies should be posted near the circulation desk or other areas where students who are borrowing will be able to see them.

Types of Print and Non-Print Resources

Responding to Student Information Needs

For a librarian to properly respond to a student's information needs, the student must first be able to identify what he or she needs. This begins with teaching students about what different library resources can do for them. For example, a particular portion of the nonfiction section may fulfill their need for information on a school assignment, while a portion of the fiction section addresses their own needs for entertainment. The next step is to teach students how to access and engage with library resources. This requires instruction in using the library's catalog management system and available online and digital resources as well as teaching students general library skills related to the way in which the library is organized. This will give students the skills required to independently fulfill their needs. The manner in which the library is organized and labeled should also lend itself to easy access for students. Sections of the library and what they contain should be clearly identified with easy-to-read signs. A librarian may find it beneficial to provide direct instruction to students on navigating the library based on the organization used in each section, such as the Dewey Decimal Classification, alphabetization, or genrefication.

Ensuring Print Books Remain Relevant Sources of Information

Nonfiction books are the most popular print resource. The information available in nonfiction books includes all subjects within call numbers 000 to 999. They can be hardcover or less expensive softcover. Most library media centers (LMCs) still house print books and update the print collection every year. Print books need to be examined periodically to maintain currency, relevance, and condition. When the information in a book becomes outdated, the book should be removed from the shelf and replaced by one with more current information. The LMC collection should reflect the school's curriculum, so as the curriculum changes, it may be necessary to add or remove books from the collection. Because books are handled, they sometimes need to be repaired or replaced. Properly maintaining the overall state of the print book collection will encourage students to make more use of this investment.

E-Books

E-books are electronic books that can be accessed on any device with an internet connection. They can be a digital version of a print book or they may be published only in their electronic format. E-books in the LMC have grown in popularity because of the practical and financial advantages they offer. A student doing research is physically capable of carrying only a certain number of print books, but with only one device, a student can access hundreds of e-books. Because programmers can continually update information in e-books, they can usually be considered a relevant resource. They are also budget-friendly because the publishing costs are lower than those for print books. Often, increases in the cost of paper, ink, and production are reflected in the price of print books. When the library media specialist (LMS) chooses to purchase electronically produced books rather than print books, the lower costs may allow the library to order more books overall. Cataloging new e-books is also quicker and easier than processing new print books, which also saves the LMS time.

Academic Journals, Periodicals, and Serials

Many libraries offer print resources other than books, such as journals, periodicals, and serials. **Academic journals** are subject-targeted publications with articles written by experts in the field. They are usually science- or humanities-based and contain research drawn from case studies and experiments. **Periodicals** are publications printed at regular intervals, and they are usually subscription-based, such as magazines. Periodicals can be research-based or offered for general interest. **Serials** are resources that are dated or assigned volume numbers to hold their place in a series. Some examples include newspapers, newsletters, yearbooks, and records such as meeting minutes. These types of resources are rarely cataloged in an LMC but are, instead, listed in guides. Since some are not easily replaced, they are often housed behind the circulation desk so that loans can be monitored and they can be treated as reference materials that may not leave the library.

Audiovisual Resources

Audiovisual resources such as videocassettes, CDs, and DVDs are cataloged and housed as resources in the LMC the way print materials are. When a student is searching for information by topic, an audiovisual item may be part of the search results. Movies, songs, documentaries, pictures, and audiobooks are all resources that can be found in these audiovisual formats. These are valuable as they offer knowledge on a topic in a different context. With these resources, students can extract information from what they see or hear. In automated systems, the borrower can often determine the item type by an icon displayed near the title. Thus, if a title is available in formats other than print, the borrower can choose his or her preferred format.

Databases

A database is a collection of information that is stored in electronic files and that can be accessed by computers or other devices with an internet connection. When an LMS refers to a database, he or she means a research database containing information specifically collected and offered for research. The information is usually in the form of articles written by professionals and organized by topic. Some databases specialize in certain topics, and others cover a wide variety of subjects.

Students find databases particularly helpful with research because they offer search tools that produce more targeted results. Research databases usually require a subscription and are password protected. The subscriptions can be costly, but they are considered an essential resource for research. As an administrator, the LMS can track the usage statistics to justify the cost.

VISUAL REFERENCES

Atlases and maps are visuals that help with research by using scale to put locations in perspective. Print maps can be physical, single-page resources or a collection bound in books. Print atlases contain multiple region-specific maps and charts. Print atlases and maps should be continually reexamined for accuracy due to the nature of constantly changing boundaries.

Posters and photographs are often included as reference material for the historical detail they provide. Most posters and photographs used for research are images of the originals that are found in books or on websites. Original posters and photographs with historical value are usually part of a special collection housed in museums.

REFERENCE MATERIALS USED FOR RESEARCH

Reference materials in the LMC can be print or electronic. They are considered nonfiction resources and include encyclopedias, almanacs, dictionaries, and thesauruses. **Encyclopedias** contain fact-based entries on subjects of general knowledge or specific subjects. Print versions come in sets and offer the information alphabetically in many volumes. Electronic encyclopedias offer the same breadth of knowledge but, because they can be conveniently updated, have more current information. **Almanacs** are collections of general or subject-based facts and statistics used for researching history and science and can serve as the basis for future predictions. They are often organized by year. Sports and record-keeping almanacs are popular general nonfiction resources. Dictionaries and thesauruses are guides for English and foreign language usage. **Dictionaries** are a comprehensive list of definitions and pronunciations. **Thesauruses** offer alternative vocabulary choices such as synonyms and antonyms.

Print reference materials are cataloged but do not usually circulate, meaning they cannot be removed from the library. Most libraries have a designated area, floor, or room for print reference materials, and offer tables and seating for easier use. Electronic reference materials are usually accessed through the library's database collection.

Community Resources

Partnering with Community Resources

Community resources are people, materials, supplies, funds, or other assets existing in a community that are or can be made available for use to the public. Common examples include public libraries, museums, retail stores, health service offices, outreach programs, and community colleges. Resources with physical spaces and academic goals, such as libraries and museums, are often used for collaborative programming to reach a common goal and increase patronage at that location. Retail stores and businesses are commonly able to make monetary and material donations to school libraries with which they are partnered. They can also assist in fundraising by hosting events on behalf of the library. Partnerships with offices, outreach programs, and community colleges provide a wealth of guest speakers and access to materials that can provide students with insights on topics of health, educational planning, and future careers. Additionally, these organizations may own physical resources of value to lend to school libraries, such as tools and technology. These are just some examples, and a librarian is not limited to these. He or she should use the needs of the library's patrons to select and implement the community resources that will be the most valuable.

Advocacy

Advocacy is the act of promoting or showing support for a cause. In a school library setting, this can include reaching out to decision-making bodies, speaking at events such as school committee or school board meetings, or educating others on the needs of the library. In these instances, advocating is most often for receiving funds and resources. Community partnerships can help fulfill these needs. Philanthropic organizations and businesses in communities often offer grants and donations to causes that benefit schools and education. A librarian should be able to express the needs of the school library and explain the benefits of receiving funds in order to obtain these financial supports.

Positive Impact of Using Community Resources

Community resources can refer to people or materials, among other things. Regarding people, community members are often willing to volunteer their time, which means the library may have experts on various topics come at no cost to the library and teach students new and helpful information. Additionally, lending from organizations within the community is a key way to obtain resources for a short amount of time without having to spend additional money. A primary example would be borrowing technology resources, like computer hardware and robotics, from local colleges and universities; however, this can also include any niche tools necessary for certain hands-on learning experiences, such as gardening tools, musical equipment, experiment kits, or recreational equipment. Borrowing allows students the benefit of gaining experience while keeping costs minimal for the library.

Author Visits

Author visits are beneficial for all school members. For students, these visits create a memorable, positive event associated with reading. They also help motivate and empower students to be creative and dedicated in their own writing and activities. Students are also likely to be more motivated to read and write following the event, which will lead to an increase in library visits, material circulation, and writing resource usage. Data representing these increases can then be cited in the justification of acquiring additional resources to maintain the library's collection. For librarians and teachers, these visits serve as reference points that they can call back to during instruction. Additionally, many authors create and share curriculum materials aligned with their work that can be used in the library or classroom.

Guest Speakers

Hosting guest speakers in the library exposes students to life in their communities outside of school, and such events can be tailored to meet the specific goals of a school, library, or class assignment. Inviting individuals with specific educational experiences and success in their field provides students with the opportunity to engage with an expert. This can increase student interest, engagement, and motivation in the topics that the speaker covers. For the librarian, hosting helps establish relationships with guest speakers, and these relationships can lead to future events with the speakers or to developing contacts with other professionals for future events.

Storytellers

As the name suggests, **storytellers** verbally retell stories for audiences. These stories can be dramatic retellings of classic tales, their own fictional works, or stories from their personal experiences. Storytelling differs from a read-aloud, as the host is not reading from a book but reciting the story from memory. Because the storyteller is not reading, he or she is able to maintain eye contact and engagement with the audience, which usually leads to an increase in audience interest and provides the opportunity for students to work on listening skills while simultaneously hearing new vocabulary and phrases in context. As students listen, they tap into their critical thinking skills to predict what will happen next, follow the plot, and analyze characters. The lack of images in storytelling requires listeners to use their imaginations and develop mental imagery based on what they are hearing. Overall, hosting storytellers provides students with opportunities to continue developing both academic and social skills.

Legal and Ethical Issues

Confidentiality of Records

Students' rights to confidentiality are protected under the Library Bill of Rights as well as the constitutions of many states. The American Association of School Librarians (AASL) asserts that children and youth have the same rights to privacy as adults. As such, any records stored in the library should only be used for helping to maintain the collection, such as using circulation data to help make purchasing decisions or weed the collection, and should not be used or shared in any other capacity.

To maintain the right to privacy, it is best practice to interfere as little as possible with a student's search for information. Information sought out or borrowed by patrons is covered under the aforementioned rights to privacy. If any law enforcement agency requests records to assist in an investigation, it must go through the appropriate legal channel to request them. Overall, any information linking individuals to their use of resources is to be kept confidential unless the librarian is legally required to disclose it.

Copyright and Fair Use

Copyright law is a federally governed statute designed to protect an individual's intellectual property from unethical use. **Intellectual property** is any original work or creation and can include, but is not limited to, any form of writing, artwork and designs, musical compositions, and computer programs. Copyright controls the usage of these materials and ensures creators are compensated for the use of their works. **Fair use** allows for small portions of copyrighted materials to be quoted or otherwise used for academic or reporting purposes without the need to compensate the creator. For example, a small portion of a book, such as a passage or chapter, may be reproduced for a lesson; however, it is against copyright law to copy the book in its entirety.

School librarians share a responsibility with teachers for ensuring students are appropriately using information in a manner that does not constitute copyright infringement. As the experts in the building, the librarians must not only teach students copyright and fair use, but they must also lead professional development opportunities for teachers.

Plagiarism

Plagiarism is defined as the act of using another person's work or ideas and claiming them as one's own. Plagiarizing work is often a violation of academic, ethical, or honor codes and can lead to disciplinary action that can extend up to expulsion from academic institutions. As such, it is vital that students learn how to appropriately, ethically, and legally incorporate the works of other individuals to enhance their own. This is where responsibility falls upon the school librarian.

To avoid plagiarism, students must first understand what does and does not constitute it. While copying the work of someone else and claiming it as one's own is plagiarism, it's still possible to reference someone's works ethically. In order to do so, proper citation practices should be taught. Librarian-created guides to citation can be made and distributed for student use. By teaching the concept of plagiarism and how to appropriately cite used work, librarians can help prevent, combat, and correct plagiarism within a school.

Acceptable Use Policies

Acceptable use policies outline the best practices and expectations of users. In most school library situations, these policies concern technology with internet access and internet access itself. Appropriate use of library equipment and internet services entails visiting only lawful sites and refraining from sharing inappropriate materials, altering or installing any software, violating copyright and fair use agreements, logging in using someone else's credentials, and/or monopolizing equipment. Librarians can tailor these policies as they see fit for the populations they serve.

In the school library, these policies should be explained and distributed on hard copies to students so that they (and sometimes their guardians) can sign them in agreement. When these policies are violated, they often lead to the immediate revocation of privileges.

Internet Filters

Internet filters use software to block access to specific websites and searches that display certain types of content. These filters are most often purchased by a school district and implemented on all district-owned devices. Depending on the software used, teachers and staff may be able to override filters by logging in with their assigned credentials, while other software may require overrides be initiated at a higher level. Search filters are meant to serve as a form of protection and adherence with acceptable use, not a form of censorship. They block minor students from accessing information deemed inappropriate; however, filters are not always reliable and may under- or over-filter search results and access to sites. As such, it is important to teach students how to find information that is safe and reliable without needing to rely on these filters.

Bibliographic Citation

Teaching Citation Skills

School librarians have a responsibility to work with both students and staff to ensure proper citation methods are taught so that students can maintain academic integrity. Failure to properly cite used works can result in plagiarism. Librarians may choose to teach citation skills directly, create guides for staff and student use, or do a combination of the two. While the style of citation used in writing varies based on the assignment and the content of the class, it is vital that students learn how to locate, list, and format the information required for citations. This includes proper titles, author(s), publication information such as publisher name, publication year and/or publication location, and access information. The information must also be italicized, bolded, and/or capitalized as required by the citation style being used.

Bibliographic Citation

Bibliographic citation serves to provide information about the author, titles and type, and publication information for any resources used in a paper. If a digital resource can be accessed through a URL, the URL should be listed in the citation. Using citations to provide credit to the author(s) or creator(s) for quoted, paraphrased, and otherwise used work prevents plagiarism and maintains students' academic integrity. Additionally, citations provide information for the reader, be it the person grading the assignment or a peer, to find the used resources so that he or she can view the original if needed.

Styles of Citation

The most commonly used citations in academic writing are American Psychological Association (APA) style, Modern Language Association (MLA) style, and Chicago style. The style of citation used on a writing assignment is most often established by the class and subject matter being covered. APA style is most commonly used in writing covering behavioral and social sciences; MLA style is used in the humanities; and Chicago style, published by the University of Chicago Press, is primarily used when writing about history. It may also be used for the humanities but is used less often than MLA in those circumstances. The use of these styles can also vary by teacher, school, or other preference. Each style has its own set of rules for capitalization, punctuation, and formatting, as well as rules for where and how citations are written.

In-Text Citations

In-text citations are citations that are placed directly within a writing and can be formatted as parenthetical, numerical, or note citations, depending upon the citation style required. **Parenthetical citations** directly follow a quote or information used in writing. What information is inside the parentheses is determined by the citation style. The author's last name, publication year and/or page number where the information used can be found is usually included. **Numerical citations** use a subscript font to number cited information. These citations must be used in numerical order throughout the writing and match the used resource on the reference page at the end of the writing. **Note citations** include footnotes and endnotes. For the former, a numerical citation is used next to the writing containing a reference. Reference information is written in the footer of the paper, hence the name *footnote*. Endnote citations are similar to numerical citations; however, the references are listed at the end of a section or chapter as opposed to at the end of the entire work.

What Information to Cite or Not Cite

Proper citations are the best way to protect against plagiarism and provide credit to the creators of works used in one's writing. Any resource from which information was obtained for the writing assignment at hand should be cited. Aside from the widely known need to cite direct quotes and unmodified information, citations also include data used to draw conclusions and make statements, verbally given information taken from interviews, or any lesser-known facts.

The list of writing that does not need to be cited is much shorter. Facts that are widely known and any original ideas or information written from first-person experiences do not need citations.

Awards in Literature

American Library Association (ALA) Awards Given to Children's Books

The **John Newbery Medal** is awarded yearly to the author of the most distinguished contribution to children's literature published in the United States that year. Eligibility for the award is decided by a committee judging only the text of a book. The committee may consider the theme, plot, characters (and their development), and setting in their judging. Recent winners include *When You Trap a Tiger* by Tae Keller and *New Kid* by Jerry Craft.

Similar to the Newbery Medal, the **Theodor Seuss Geisel Award** is also awarded for distinguished contributions to children's literature as determined by a committee; however, this award is given to both the author and illustrator. Recent winners include *See the Cat: Three Stories about a Dog* written by David LaRochelle and illustrated by Mike Wohnoutka and *Stop! Bot!* written and illustrated by James Yang. **The Robert F. Sibert Informational Book Medal** is awarded annually to the most distinguished informational children's book of the previous year as voted on by a committee, and it is also given to the author and illustrator. Recent winners include *Honeybee: The Busy Life of Apis Mellifera* written by Candace Fleming and illustrated by Eric Rohmann and *Fry Bread: A Native American Family Story* written by Kevin Noble Maillard and illustrated by Juana Martinez-Neal. All aforementioned awards also recognize runners-up and award them honors.

The **Caldecott Medal** is the most well-known book award given yearly to acknowledge distinguished illustrations in American picture books. It is named after Randolph Caldecott, an English illustrator who worked in the mid-to-late 19th century. It is given based on illustrator technique, how well the images represent the story, the style used, and overall presentation. Runners-up are also chosen and awarded honors. Recent winners include *We Are Water Protectors* illustrated by Michaela Goade and *The Undefeated* illustrated by Kadir Nelson.

The **Odyssey Award for Excellence in Audiobook Production** is annually awarded to the producer of the most distinguished audiobook for children and/or young adults. There may be one or two Odyssey winners each year. Honor books are also selected. The committee that awards it has representatives from both the Young Adult Library Services Association (YALSA) and the Association for Library Service to Children (ALSC). This award is given to audiobooks available in English and in the United States. In contrast to many other book awards, the Odyssey Award is not given based on the content of the book; rather, it is solely judged on the audio production. In addition to narration, sound quality, musical choice, and sound effects are also taken into consideration. Recent winners include *Kent State* produced by Paul R. Gagne and written by Deborah Wiles and *Hey, Kiddo: How I Lost My Mother, Found My Father, and Dealt with Family Addiction* produced by Scholastic Audiobooks and written by Jarrett J. Krosoczka.

The **Pura Belpré Award** is named after the first Latina librarian at the New York Public Library. Pura Belpré was also an author and storyteller. A committee within the American Library Association (ALA) awards one medal winner for each of the following categories: children's narrative, youth illustrator, and young adult narrative. Each category also usually acknowledges at least one to three honor books. The awards are given to Latino writers and illustrators whose work has been published in the US or Puerto Rico and positively portrays and celebrates Latino culture from any Spanish-speaking region. Recent winners include *Efrén Divided* by Ernesto Cisneros, *¡Vamos! Let's Go Eat* by Raúl the Third (Raúl Gonzalez), and *Furia* by Yamile Saied Méndez.

The **Children's Literature Legacy Award** is awarded to authors and illustrators whose works have shown long-lasting contributions to children's literature. It was formerly known as the **Laura Ingalls Wilder Medal** but was renamed in 2018. The award is now given annually; however, in the past, the time between awards ranged from two to five years. The committee assembled by the ALA may consider either the author's entire body of work or portions that relate to children's literature. Recent winners include Mildred D. Taylor, Kevin Henkes, and Walter Dean Myers.

Unlike other book awards, the **Mildred L. Batchelder Award** is given to American publishers of children's books, not to authors or illustrators. It is awarded annually for the publication of a translated children's book. To be considered for the award, the book must have originated outside of the US, originally written in a language other than English. A committee under the ALA reviews translated books and looks at multiple aspects, including accurate and high-quality translation, overall design, and illustrations in some cases. This award is given annually, with honors usually given to about one to four other titles. Recent winners include Yonder: Restless Books for Young Readers for the publication of *Temple Alley Summer* and Enchanted Lion Books for *Telephone Tales.*

Young Adult Library Services Association

The **Young Adult Library Services Association (YALSA)** is a division of the ALA that selects high-quality books for ages 12 to 18. It awards books and authors based on a variety of criteria. The **Alex Awards** honor 10 adult books each year that appeal to teen readers. The **Morris Award** is given each year to an author who has been published for the first time and produced writing for teens. The **Printz Award** is given to the overall best teen book published each year, regardless of any former publications. YALSA representatives are also part of the committee responsible for awarding the Odyssey Award for Excellence in Audiobook Production. The Odyssey Award for a children's book is given by a different branch within the ALA. As the name suggests, the **Nonfiction Award** is given yearly to the best nonfiction writing for teens. The **Margaret A. Edwards Award** is awarded yearly to an author for his or her works and long-lasting contributions to teen literature and efforts to help adolescents feel seen.

Pulitzer Prize

Named after newspaper magnate Joseph Pulitzer, the **Pulitzer Prize** was created in 1917 and is awarded to distinguished works of journalism, music, and literature. It is often revered as one of the most prestigious honors in writing. Currently, there are 23 categories awarded per year. As it relates to the school library and older readers, there are awards for fiction, drama, history, biography, memoir, poetry, and general nonfiction. Columbia University assembles a board of judges who vote on submitted works. There are no set criteria for what is considered distinguished writing, and the nominating juries are to decide what exactly "distinguished" means in relation to the category they are judging. Until recently, only US citizens were eligible for book, drama, and music awards, unless a work was a history book, in which case authors of any nationality were considered for writing about the US. Starting with the 2025 awards, the eligibility requirements have changed, and now only US citizens, permanent US residents, and longtime US residents will be eligible for book, drama, and music awards. These new requirements also apply to the history category. Awards may be given posthumously. As with other awards, the Pulitzer highlights the quality of work and helps to guide students in their book selection for both academic and leisurely reading.

Prominent Figures in Literature and in Library Media Science

Notable Library Leaders

The following are notable library leaders and their contributions to the library community:

- **Melvil Dewey**: Dewey's development of the Dewey Decimal system, which was first published in 1876, keeps many libraries organized to this day. Dewey also contributed to the development of the ALA and is acknowledged as the father of modern librarianship.
- **Mary Kingsbury**: Kingsbury was the first professionally trained school librarian in America. She worked at Erasmus Hall High School of Brooklyn beginning in 1900 and began to pave the way for professional school librarians.
- **S.R. Ranganathan**: Ranganathan was an Indian librarian and mathematician and is considered the father of library science. He is credited with creating the colon classification system as well as the five laws of library science.
- **John Cotton Dana**: In the late 1800s, Dana saw the need for changes to libraries to make them more accessible to the general public. He developed a more conducive stack management system that allowed for easy browsing, extended library hours, made it easier for community members to get library cards, and developed children's rooms, which are found in most public libraries.

Prominent Children's Book Author-Illustrators

The following are prominent children's book author-illustrators whose works center around easy reader and picture books:

- **Eric Carle:** Carle won nearly 100 awards across the US, Europe, and Asia, including the Children's Literature Legacy Award and several other ALA awards. His most prominent works are *The Very Hungry Caterpillar*; *Brown Bear, Brown Bear, What Do You See?*; and *The Grouchy Ladybug.*
- **Theodor Geisel/Dr. Seuss:** Geisel's most notable books are *The Cat in the Hat*, *The Lorax*, *How the Grinch Stole Christmas!*, and *Oh, the Places You'll Go!* His many awards include three Caldecott Honors, a Pulitzer Prize, and a Children's Literature Legacy Award. Additionally, the ALA awards the Theodor Seuss Geisel Award yearly to the author and illustrator of a distinguished children's book.
- **Tomie dePaola:** dePaola produced more than 260 books in his lifetime, including *Strega Nona*—his most notable work—*Tomie dePaola's Mother Goose,* and *Now One Foot, Now the Other.* He won the Children's Literature Legacy Award as well as both Newbery and Caldecott Honors.
- **Arnold Lobel:** Responsible for the *Frog and Toad* series as well as *Mouse Soup*, Lobel produced more than 40 books in his lifetime. He won many awards, including both a Caldecott Medal and a Newbery Honor.

Classic Literature for Young Adult Readers

The following authors are responsible for creating classic literature for young adult readers:

- **Lois Lowry:** Lowry has received numerous national and state-level awards and twice has been a finalist for the international Hans Christian Andersen Award. Her bestsellers *The Giver* and *Number the Stars* both received Newbery Medals, a rare feat for authors.
- **Harper Lee:** Lee only published two books in her lifetime; however, her first novel, *To Kill a Mockingbird,* was an instant success and won a Pulitzer Prize a year after it was published. She was also awarded the Presidential Medal of Freedom for her contributions to literature.

- **John Steinbeck:** Author of the Pulitzer Prize-winning *The Grapes of Wrath*, Steinbeck was awarded the Presidential Medal of Freedom as well as a Nobel Prize for his contributions to literature.
- **Gary Paulsen:** Best known for *Hatchet* and the books that followed in that series, Paulsen received three Newbery Honors. He was also awarded the Margaret A. Edwards Award for his lifetime contributions to young adult literature.
- **Christopher Paul Curtis:** Author of the Coretta Scott King Award-winning novels *Bud, Not Buddy* and *Elijah of Buxton*, Curtis has received one Newbery Medal and two Honors as well as many smaller state-level awards.
- **S.E. Hinton:** Author of *The Outsiders*, she received the inaugural Margaret A. Edwards Award and has won many lesser-known awards as well.

Classic Chapter Books and Middle Grade Fiction Works

The following authors are responsible for creating classic chapter books and middle grade fiction works:

- **Kate DiCamillo:** DiCamillo's novels include *Because of Winn-Dixie*, *The Tale of Despereaux*, and *Flora & Ulysses: The Illuminated Adventures*. She is one of only six authors to have won the Newbery Medal twice. Other awards she has received include the Geisel Award and Mark Twain Award.
- **Beverly Cleary:** Cleary published over 40 books in her lifetime. This includes her series about Ramona Quimby, which starts with *Beezus and Ramona*, and Ralph S. Mouse, which starts with *The Mouse and the Motorcycle*, as well as several stand-alone novels such as *Fifteen* and *Muggie Maggie* and autobiographical works. She has won over 40 awards, most notably the Newbery Medal and the Children's Literature Legacy Award.
- **Judy Blume:** Most popular for *Are You There God? It's Me, Margaret*, Blume has written over 25 books. Of the over 90 awards she has received, the Margaret A. Edwards Award for lasting and significant contributions to young adult literature is the most notable.
- **C.S. Lewis:** Having written more than 30 books, Lewis is most well-known for his series *The Chronicles of Narnia*, which has sold over 100 million copies.

Well-Known Illustrators

Illustrators are responsible for enhancing books through imagery, a crucial component of children's books. As such, they are acknowledged similarly to authors with several different awards, the most prestigious being the Caldecott Medal.

- **Jerry Pinkney:** Best known for his watercolor illustrations and having illustrated over 100 books, Pinkney was one of the most well-known children's book illustrators. He won several awards, including a Caldecott Medal for *The Lion & the Mouse*, five Caldecott Honors, the Orbis Pictus Award, and five Coretta Scott King Awards. He was also nominated for the highly regarded international Hans Christian Andersen Award.
- **Marcia Brown:** Though she was also an author, Brown was most acknowledged for her illustrations. She won three Caldecott Medals, six Caldecott Honors, and the Children's Literature Legacy Award. Her most recognizable works include *Stone Soup*, *Once a Mouse*, and *Shadow*.
- **Ezra Jack Keats:** Best known for his Caldecott Medal-winning book *The Snowy Day*, Keats was both an author and illustrator; however, his illustrating was more highly awarded than his writing. In total, he illustrated over 85 books. His work was so influential that schools, playgrounds, and even a skating rink are named after him.

Graphic Novelists

There are three big awards specifically for comic books and graphic novels, the Eisner Awards, the Harvey Awards, and the Ignatz Awards. Each of these is awarded for various categories. Graphic novels can be eligible for other book awards, depending upon the criteria.

- **Art Spiegelman:** Spiegelman is the cartoonist responsible for the only Pulitzer Prize-winning graphic novel, *Maus.* He has also won multiple Eisner Awards for his work.
- **Raina Telgemeier:** Best known for her award-winning autobiographical graphic novel *Smile,* Telgemeier has also written the Eisner-winning graphic novels *Sisters*, *Ghosts*, and *Guts*.
- **Dav Pilkey:** While Pilkey has not yet won any major awards related to his work in graphic novels, his series *Dog Man* as well as the spin-off *Cat Kid Comic Club* are atop the list of bestsellers. They have been translated into several languages and bridge the gap between picture books and novels.
- **Jerry Craft:** Craft is the creator behind the first graphic novel to win a Newbery Medal, *New Kid*. The novel also won the Coretta Scott King Award and the Kirkus Prize. He has several other graphic novels that have won smaller awards and sit atop multiple best seller lists.

Award-Winning Middle Grade and Young Adult Work

The following authors are currently creating award-winning middle grade and young adult work:

- **John Green:** Green has won the Printz Award and Printz Honor for his books *Looking for Alaska* and *An Abundance of Katherines*, respectively. His eight novels have won many additional awards, including *The Fault in Our Stars*, which is one of the best-selling books of all time.
- **Markus Zusak:** Zusak has received Printz Honors for his best-selling books *The Book Thief* and *I Am the Messenger.* He also received the Margaret A. Edwards Award for his lasting contributions to young adult literature.
- **Nancy Farmer:** Farmer has written several young adult novels but her most famous is *The House of the Scorpion*, which received both Newbery and Printz Honors and the National Book Award for Young People's Literature.
- **David Levithan:** Levithan has created several novel series, stand-alone novels, short stories, and comics. For his efforts, he has been awarded the Margaret A. Edwards Award as well as many other awards for his work in representing marginalized groups of teens, specifically LGBT youth. Several of his novels have been adapted into films, including *Nick and Norah's Infinite Playlist.*

Characteristics of Types of Literature

Characteristics of Fiction

Fiction is usually characterized by five elements: plot, setting, characters, narrative perspective, and theme. The **plot** refers to the intermingled sequence of events of the story that grows into a climactic event before falling into a resolution. **Setting** refers to both the physical setting of the book as well as the time during which the story takes place. Within a fictional work, **characters** develop across the plot, and the story is sometimes told from the point of view of one character, many characters, or a narrator—this is the **narrative perspective**. Lastly, fiction works feature a **theme**, or an underlying meaning, highlighted by the events within the story.

Review Video: Myths, Fables, Legends, and Fairy Tales
Visit mometrix.com/academy and enter code: 347199

Characteristics of Short Stories

Short stories are typically written in prose and are far shorter than novels. Their length can vary, but they are usually between 500 and 10,000 words and able to be read fully in one sitting. As a rule, short stories are fiction, but they may contain real life inspiration. Additionally, they can fall into other various fiction genres, such as horror, romance, or comedy. These stories can be further divided into three categories: lyrical, flash fiction, and vignette. **Lyrical** short stories are written to seem musical and rhythmic and contain vivid imagery and metaphors. **Flash fiction** includes short stories containing full plots. These stories can fit a proper beginning, middle, and end into a short text but may not contain the typical character development noted in longer fiction writing. **Vignette** short stories describe in rich detail a small part of a much larger story and usually incorporate a lot of imagery.

Characteristics of Biographies

A **biography** is the story of an individual's life that is written by someone else. While most biographies are nonfiction, they are intended to read like fiction works with a beginning, middle, and end. Most often, they are about well-known public figures and contain information about the struggles they overcame, their outstanding accomplishments, and the significant events of their lives. The included dialogues and the retelling of certain incidents and events may not be completely accurate due to the time elapsed since the events occurred and their private nature; however, biographies are still marked as nonfiction due to their historical accuracy and the research used to retell events. In the school library, biographies can come in many forms for all age groups, ranging from picture books to full-length books.

Elements of Poetry

While poems consist of many elements, the most common are line breaks, rhythm, and specific literary devices such as simile, metaphor, alliteration, repetition, and personification. **Line breaks** separate the end of one line and the beginning of the next line in a poem by creating a physical space between them. These are deliberately placed and create the appearance of the poem, whether it is a long poem with short lines or a short poem with long lines. These line breaks also impact the **rhythm** of a poem, or the flow of stressed syllables. Other literary devices can be used to convey the author's feelings or ideas as appropriate.

The three common types of poetry are lyric poetry, narrative poetry, and dramatic poetry. As the name suggests, **lyric poetry** is often songlike. It is usually written in first person with the intention of expressing emotion. **Narrative poetry** tells a story with a plot. It is written in verse and has a clear beginning, middle, and end. These poems typically contain a rhythmic theme, but it is not required. **Dramatic poetry** portrays a story or situation. As a rule, it contains a rhythm or rhyme. These are typically meant to be read as a monologue or acted out.

Literary Dramas

A **drama** is a written story presenting a conflict that is usually meant to be acted out in the format of a play. Dramas can be written in prose or verse, and the events portrayed can be fiction or nonfiction. They are written in **acts** or **scenes** (i.e., a portion of the writing containing its own beginning, middle, and end) and contain **stage directions** (i.e., instructions pertaining to the actions of the actors in the play) as well as descriptions of the setting. They also feature directions for lighting and related prompts such as **blackouts** (i.e., turning off all stage lighting) and curtain closing. Popular examples of literary dramas used in schools include *Romeo and Juliet* by William Shakespeare and *Oedipus Rex* by Sophocles.

Folk Literature

Folk literature, also sometimes referred to as folklore or oral tradition, defines a variety of story types communicated orally and not in written form. These can include narratives, songs, and poems. Some of the most popular genres within folk literature include myths, fables, tall tales, legends, and fairy tales. Before the abilities to read and write were widespread, stories were passed along solely by word of mouth, and so every culture developed its own folk literature that was representative of its own experiences. As civilizations developed, these oral retellings were replaced by written literature; however, folk literature still exists in many communities and within family units. Some examples of common folk literature include "Chicken Little," "Stone Soup," "The Little Red Hen," and "The Gingerbread Man."

Graphic Novels

Graphic novels are narratives conveyed to readers in the format of a traditional comic book. They contain a plot, characters, settings, and all the other elements of a fiction novel aside from being written in prose. Many of the elements of a story, such as the setting, characters' appearances, and characters' actions, are conveyed through the imagery used. In recent years, the popularity of graphic novels in the young reader community has grown. Many significant works of literature have been turned into graphic novels to help younger or lower-level readers more easily digest them. Examples include *The Hobbit, A Wrinkle in Time, Anne Frank's Diary, To Kill a Mockingbird, The Giver,* and *Les Misérables.* In addition to these adaptations, original works have been created including single titles as well as series. A few popular titles include *Maus* by Art Spiegelman, *El Deafo* by Cece Bell, and *Roller Girl* by Victoria Jamieson. Current popular graphic novel series include *Dog Man* and *Cat Kid Comic Club* by Dav Pilkey and *Amulet* by Kazu Kibuishi.

Informational Texts

Informational texts, also referred to as expository texts, are a subgenre of nonfiction. They serve to educate or inform the reader about matters that are typically scientific or social. Unlike other nonfiction works, they do not contain characters or recreated dialogue. Some examples include how-to guides, field guides, newspapers, textbooks, brochures, and encyclopedias. Informational texts also include those same examples in their online and digital formats. Text features such as bold or italicized terms and phrases, glossaries, images with labels, graphs, tables, and charts may be used where needed to clarify or convey additional information.

Chapter Quiz

Ready to see how well you retained what you just read? Scan the QR code to go directly to the chapter quiz interface for this study guide. If you're using a computer, simply visit the online resources page at **mometrix.com/resources719/nbptslibmecya** and click the Chapter Quizzes link.

Leadership

Library Media Science Organizations

American Library Association (ALA)

The mission of the American Library Association (ALA) is to provide guidance and resources related to libraries and librarians, offer professional development resources, and develop and share guidelines for best practices in the library. It acts to protect library users' First Amendment rights and their information-seeking processes. The ALA also acts as an advocate for libraries at all levels, primarily through letters written to governing bodies as well as testimonies and official comments. It holds large annual conferences to provide librarians with opportunities to share their research and for professional development. In relation to school libraries, the ALA developed the American Association of School Librarians (AASL). Through this division, it provides frameworks for education in the library that are meant to help students acquire the skills needed to be successful in the 21st century. The ALA also uses its platform to promote the research-based fact that schools with fully funded and professionally staffed libraries perform better overall in standardized testing.

American Association of School Librarians (AASL)

The AASL was developed by the ALA to focus specifically on school libraries. The primary goals of the AASL are to provide guidance and professional development opportunities for librarians, advocate for school libraries, and help ensure students are receiving the library education they need to be globally competitive. Through obtaining an AASL membership, librarians can become part of a global network that uses regular communication to provide one another with insight and assistance in their field. Additionally, they can access AASL-created professional development courses to help them hone their skills in many different facets of the library. Aside from the overall advocacy work of its parent organization, the AASL has published tool kits to help librarians advocate for their library. It has also published several frameworks since its creation, the most recent being the *National School Library Standards for Learners, School Librarians, and School Libraries*. In doing so, it provides guidelines and expectations for learners, librarians, and libraries to help develop successful library programming and provide the education needed for students to be successful information seekers.

Young Adult Library Services Association (YALSA)

The Young Adult Library Services Association (YALSA) is a branch of the ALA that was developed with the intention of ensuring libraries are adequately and appropriately staffed and stocked to accommodate teen readers. Its primary goal is to ensure all teens have equal access to quality literature and needed information regardless of any existing barriers. In order to do so, it provides continued professional development opportunities that focus on involving teens in the library and providing resources to meet their needs. YALSA is responsible for awarding the Alex Awards, Edwards Award, Morris Award, Nonfiction Award, Odyssey Award, Printz Award, and Pura Belpré Award. Its Teen Book Finder Database is a tool that allows users to quickly identify these high-quality and award-winning titles for teen readers. This is helpful in guiding librarians in collection development as well as in guiding teens in book selection. YALSA memberships provide librarians with access to more professional development opportunities, grants, and networking opportunities. Its professional development opportunities are also accessible through the symposiums and conferences it hosts throughout the year.

Association for Educational Communications and Technology (AECT)

The Association for Educational Communications and Technology (AECT) is a professional community centered around the use of educational technology. While it is not library specific like many other related organizations, its work and emphasis on technology in education aligns directly with the role of the school librarian in preparing students to be lifelong learners. Through its international forum, it can update and share information as it changes and evolves with the rapid growth of technology. AECT's goal as it relates to the school library is to develop and promote best practices related to education technology. To do so, it has published several books and briefings and continues to publish two bimonthly journals that highlight the importance and appropriate usage of technology. In partnership with the AASL, it developed the Learning and Teaching Principles of School Library Media Programs, which solidified the role school libraries play in technology education and vice versa.

International Society for Technology in Education (ISTE)

The International Society for Technology in Education (ISTE) focuses on the use of technology to enhance education at all grade levels. ISTE focuses on many aspects of educational technology, including digital citizenship, STEAM (science, technology, engineering, arts, and math), artificial intelligence, computational thinking, and online learning. It offers online courses and certifications for all educators to assist them in developing curricula and lessons that meet their educational goals for students and integrating appropriate and safe technology use. It hosts annual summits as well as in-person and virtual learning symposiums for educators and also offers related books, blogs, podcasts, and journals for more independent professional development. Its work directly relates to that of a librarian in the 21st century, whose role as the educator responsible for teaching the proper and effective use of educational technology has been established by many studies and frameworks.

Association for Library Service to Children (ALSC)

The Association for Library Service to Children (ALSC) is a branch of the ALA that focuses on library services for children. It is the largest organization in the world with this focus. Its work provides professional development opportunities for librarians, book lists for use in collection development, and information on best practices for children's library programming. Through this, it offers librarians guidance on developing and maintaining successful children's programs. An ALSC membership also offers librarians access to a network of professionals as well as opportunities to serve on committees, task forces, and discussion groups. Additionally, it offers live meeting and lecture opportunities for professional development related to children's librarianship. The ALSC is responsible for deciding the winner of several book awards, including the Newbery and Caldecott Medals and Geisel Award. It also provides scholarships and grants to members.

State and Local Library Organizations

While there are several national and international organizations to provide guidance and information on best practices for librarians, other similar organizations exist at the state and local level. The most important for school librarians are the bodies that determine licensing criteria. They establish the level of education, standardized testing, and experience required to become a licensed school librarian. These decisions are typically made at the state level. Many of these organizations also provide librarians with grant opportunities for their library. Similar to larger organizations, state and local groups provide networking and professional development opportunities. Because the roles and responsibilities of local and state organizations vary, it is the responsibility of the librarian to remain informed of such organizations' actions in order to remain in compliance with any mandates and best practices that they establish.

National Guidelines

The AASL is the leader of national guidelines for librarians in schools. Through its publications, it shares research-backed common beliefs and standards for students, librarians, and libraries. The **Common Beliefs** needed for a successful school library program are established by the AASL and outline what is required of a school librarian to run an effective library that produces well-rounded and successful learners. These beliefs directly impact the role of a media specialist by establishing high expectations that can be achieved only by adhering to the standards framework, also developed by the AASL. The AASL's ***National School Library Standards for Learners, School Librarians, and School Libraries*** establish Shared Foundations for learners, librarians, and libraries, and those foundations are Inquire, Include, Collaborate, Curate, Explore, and Engage. This framework directly impacts school librarians by not only establishing nationwide expectations they themselves must meet, but also by creating standards that must be met by the students and the library in order for librarians to be considered effective in their roles.

Professional Development

Continued Professional Development

It is vital that school librarians stay abreast of changes to ensure they are best serving their patrons. Regular participation in professional development is one way to do so. Technology has continued to evolve over the last few decades, and in order to ensure students are ready for life and work, librarians must be capable of providing their students with up-to-date knowledge and skills. To best do this, librarians must put in the necessary work themselves by attending workshops and courses to learn more about technology. Continued professional development opportunities will also benefit collection development. Not only will they provide librarians with information on award-winning literature and tips for overall collection maintenance, they will also help librarians stay on top of trends and use them to increase reader interest. From a more technical standpoint, continuing education units are required for most librarians to maintain their licenses, and professional development courses offer these credits.

Professional Learning Communities (PLCs)

Professional learning communities (PLCs) are groups of professionals in the same or similar fields or roles that gather to work collaboratively on a variety of topics. In schools, these are typically composed of teachers within the same grade bands, elective course teachers, or support staff. Within a district, there should ideally be a PLC composed of only school librarians. When meeting in these PLCs, librarians work to establish common practices within the district, collaborate on programming, and share stories of success to provide assistance to their peers. They also typically take on large tasks for the benefit of the whole group, such as establishing library-related processes for the district (e.g., the request process for books to be banned). Where these PLCs do not exist or there are not enough personnel to create them, librarians may turn to networking spaces to help develop study groups with a similar purpose. Study groups will examine and discuss current events as they relate to the school library, develop best practices, and discuss implementation of policies. By doing this, these groups are ensuring librarians have the support and professional guidance they need to be successful.

Library Conferences and Workshops

Attending library conferences and workshops is a key way for librarians to stay abreast of changes in their field as well as acquire continuing education units. The ALA and its branches host several conferences throughout the year, including the ALA Annual Conference and Exhibition, YALSA's Young Adult Services Symposium, and the AASL National Conference. These events provide workshops, small group seminars, and speeches from top professionals in the field to provide learning opportunities to librarians. State library organizations also put on conferences that host speakers and learning opportunities for librarians and other educators who focus on literature and technology education. By attending events, librarians are able to gain the ever-changing knowledge they need while becoming a part of a professional network. As virtual learning continues to grow in popularity, these events are becoming more accessible for all to participate in, even if they cannot participate in person.

Mentors

Like with most positions in the education field, library study programs usually require someone to have hands-on experience from an internship or in-service program prior to receiving a degree or license. Candidates for these degrees and licenses work under the supervision of an experienced librarian serving as their mentor. One of the primary functions of a mentor is to ensure candidates are completing the necessary experience hours and tasks outlined in their programs; however, another primary function is serving as a source of knowledge and providing guidance and feedback based on his or her own experience. Mentors are also able to provide more targeted support based on what type of library they work in, such as an elementary or high school library. Because no textbook can cover all of the scenarios one may experience in the library or provide all of the tips and tricks to every library system, learning from mentors is one way to ensure new librarians are fully prepared for their future roles. Mentors also provide support during what can be a challenging experience as their mentees learn and work.

Resources Indicating Trends in Teaching and Learning

Education is constantly changing and shifting, and while staying abreast of these changes can be difficult, there are a variety of resources that librarians can use to stay up to date. For library education specifically, the AASL and the ALA keep pace with the trends and disseminate information to librarians in regular communications and publications. For general education trends, the National Education Association (NEA) offers up-to-date information. Regularly attending professional development opportunities offered from one's place of work or previous educational institutions, along with taking courses offered from a variety of qualified sources, allows educators to stay up to date with new resources, changes in curriculum, and other trending education topics. To ensure educators are adhering to changes in their own state, it is important they remain up to date with communications and publications from their state and county's department of education.

Professional Collaboration within the School and Community

Collaboration Within a School

School librarians are expected to provide students with adequate guidance and education to be successful in and beyond school. Initiating and facilitating this collaboration will look different based on the scheduling the school utilizes. Students participating in fixed scheduling will come to the library for instruction on a regular basis, so the need to initiate collaboration is minimized; however, students on a flexible schedule may need to be invited in. As such, the librarian needs to make his or her presence and what he or she has to offer known to students by completing some form of outreach. Once students are in the library and prepared to collaborate, they can begin to work in partnership with the librarian to meet their educational goals. Librarians also need to make sure that staff are aware of how the librarian can support them. This can be initiated by email or some other schoolwide bulletin offering the opportunity of collaboration. The librarian and teacher will work together to plan and facilitate learning opportunities.

Planning and Implementing Staff Development

Staff development is typically planned and delivered as needed based on what ideas or items are new to the staff. Some examples include new software and hardware, learning programs, curricula, and anything being implemented schoolwide. In many cases, the school librarian is brought on to lead professional development related to the aforementioned software and hardware. Planning successful lessons for staff is much like planning for students in that the librarian must first establish the desired outcome, such as the ability to design instruction or create a product using the new technology. Once that has been established, the activities used to meet those outcomes can be planned. Activities for staff should be engaging and appropriate for adult learners while fulfilling the needed learning targets. Following a staff development session, it is vital to ask participants for feedback. Allowing staff to share their opinions and using that input to guide future sessions will aid the librarian in offering meaningful development opportunities for staff.

Teaching and Assisting Staff New and Emerging Technologies

The school librarian is often tasked with leading professional development and instructing staff members on the application of new technologies like software, hardware, and digital access to resources. The technology referred to here may be tools that can address the needs of entire classes or may be more specialized for individual student needs, like assistive technologies. In order to create instruction for full and proper use of the technology, the librarian should determine a goal for the lesson or instruction being provided. The librarian should then establish what methods should be used to reach staff. While meeting in person is usually best, it is occasionally necessary to use asynchronous teaching methods. Additionally, a form of direct instruction is not always necessary. In some situations, sharing information containing tutorials, instructional tools, and other helpful details regarding the technology being discussed is sufficient for staff. Once the method of lesson delivery has been established, the librarian may then find, develop, and compile the necessary media and resources to address the topic being covered.

Collaboration Within the Community

Community partnerships play a big role in the school library. They offer opportunities for receiving funds and hosting speakers, events, and unique experiences for students. To successfully collaborate, librarians must first initiate contact by reaching out to individuals within the community or representatives of the organizations they wish to collaborate with. The librarian should be prepared to communicate how the goals of the library align with the goals or beliefs of the organization or individual they are contacting. If contact is successful and the organization or individual wishes to collaborate, the librarian should then create a plan. This plan should detail what is going to take place, who is responsible for what portions of the plan, and the overall desired outcomes. The librarian is responsible for continuing to nurture and grow these community partnerships for the benefit of the library.

Selecting, Using, Evaluating, and Producing Media

A librarian should be prepared to assist staff in locating, creating, and using media so the staff can then use that media on their own in the future. While librarians often pull and compile media resources directly for educators, it is a valuable skill for teachers to be able to do so independently. As such, librarians should offer professional learning opportunities to staff in which they cover the resources available for use, such as the library catalog and any resources to which the school is subscribed. In the event that there is no existing media resource that satisfies the need of the teacher, the librarian may offer assistance in creating the media or offer lessons to cover the tools used in media production. These tools may include word processing software, presentation software, video creation software, and any other resource used to produce a tool that can be used in education. The librarian may also choose to create pathfinders with reference materials about using these resources as opposed to holding professional learning opportunities.

Chapter Quiz

Ready to see how well you retained what you just read? Scan the QR code to go directly to the chapter quiz interface for this study guide. If you're using a computer, simply visit the online resources page at **mometrix.com/resources719/nbptslibmecya** and click the Chapter Quizzes link.

Administration

Library Decision-Making

Key Stakeholders Affected by Library Decisions

Some of the key stakeholders affected by library decisions include librarians, library support staff, students, administrators, parents, teaching faculty, and information technology (IT) professionals. **Librarians** are affected by every decision made regarding the library since their mission includes the effective administration of all its aspects. **Library support staff** are interested in nearly all the same things that librarians are, but they are less directly involved with certain operational aspects like budgeting and vision. **Students** are invested in the overall experience of visiting the library, which includes having access to a wide selection of books, a knowledgeable staff who can assist them, fun and educational programs, and research or technology assistance tools. **Administrators** want to ensure that the library operates effectively (e.g., meeting goals, aligning with the school mission) and efficiently (e.g., within budget). **Parents** are likely to be concerned about the educational experience of their children and may wish to ensure that their children are being protected from materials they deem inappropriate. **Teaching faculty** and **IT professionals** want the library to support the instructional needs of the school, which includes providing research, technology, and teaching assistance to students and faculty.

Benefits Associated with a Diverse Library Decision-Making Board

A diverse library decision-making board that includes members of the various stakeholder groups will enjoy many benefits, such as improved school buy-in, inclusive and effective decisions, and a wide variety of perspectives, which promote new or different ideas. Including the various groups affected by library decisions on the board allows each group the opportunity to explain their unique viewpoint on a given issue, which will help the board avoid potential problems before they occur. For instance, a library board that does not include IT professionals might make a decision that relies on technology resources the school does not have the knowledge base to operate. Including each of the library stakeholders in decision-making also has the benefit of increasing overall enthusiasm for library programs and has the potential to increase funding from parents and administrators who feel they are part of promoting an effective library that is taking their particular needs into consideration.

Challenges Associated with Shared Decision-Making

Shared library decision-making can be challenging at times since the decisions are made by a group of different people with different needs and wants. The power dynamics of the various groups involved can exacerbate these challenges. These groups include students (low power); parents, faculty, and librarians (medium power); and school administrators (high power), all of whom view their involvement as important. Ultimately, it is up to school librarians and administrators to determine the needs of the library and make final decisions, but it is important to ensure that each stakeholder group feels heard and understands how decisions will benefit them. If this is not possible, it is desirable that all stakeholder groups understand the necessity of a decision that does not directly benefit them. Giving each group equal time and respect during group discussions goes a long way in promoting a civil and respectful library board meeting.

Library Philosophies and Mission Statements

School Library Philosophy

A school library **philosophy** is a statement or statements that describe the library's **purpose**, the library's **values**, and how the library **supports** those values in practice. An effective written philosophy is one of the guiding principles of a school library that can help with decision-making and both short- and long-range planning. Common library values include ethical research, respect for others and their works, community, curiosity, and lifelong learning. By considering the school library's stated values, the administration can make decisions and plans that support those values and evaluate decisions and plans based on how well they support the library's philosophy and its values.

School Library Philosophies vs. Mission Statements

While a school library's philosophy states the various values that are emphasized in library offerings, a library's **mission statement** (or statements) is more practical in nature and describes the various goals of the library and the methods used to achieve those goals. While both are key components of library decision-making and planning processes, philosophies and mission statements serve related but different purposes. The philosophy serves the library by describing key interests and ideas it hopes to promote, while the mission statement gives concrete goals tied to library values that can be directly measured. An example of a mission statement is as follows: "It is the mission of the school library to provide equal access to materials to all students regardless of background."

Parts of a Library Mission Statement

A library mission statement typically consists of a **goal**, **methods** for achieving that goal, and **reasoning** for why that particular goal is needed. An effective mission statement does not need to specifically include all three of these parts, but each is important in crafting a useful guiding statement for library decision-making. Without a goal, a library mission statement does not exist. A goal gives the mission statement something to achieve and lets stakeholders know something that the school library intends to accomplish through its short- and long-term operations. The methods for achieving a goal give stakeholders information about how the goal will be accomplished and can generally be measured to track progress. The reasoning for a particular goal can reassure both library staff and other stakeholder groups that the goal is worth accomplishing, and it can explain why the library is invested in achieving this desired result.

Goals and Objectives for Library Programs

Selection of Library Programs

Library programs are the various structured resources, events, and services that the library provides to patrons. Programs are selected for a variety of reasons, including to support a particular school mission, promote literacy and education, encourage a particular stakeholder group to invest in the library in some way, or highlight a particular library offering. Library programs are ultimately selected by librarians and staff, but both broad and specific programs should be supported by various stakeholder groups throughout the program's lifetime. Programs should be tailored to the audiences at which they are targeted (e.g., seventh-grade boys, fifth graders learning about research methods, high school students interested in young adult romance novels) and should be aligned with library and school philosophies, values, and missions. By considering the target demographic for a particular program during the planning process, librarians and staff can tailor the program to that group by ensuring the program is actually of interest to them and meets their needs and wants. Effective library programs directly support the educational and social objectives of the library and school and cross-promote various library services.

Direct Impact of Goals and Objectives

Library programs are driven by goals and objectives from start to finish. An effective library program has a purpose, measurable goals, and a plan to achieve those goals. An example program might have the purpose of attracting more young male readers to the library; have a goal of increasing male student patronage by 10 percent over the next year; and have a plan to achieve this by surveying young males for the kinds of programs they want from the library, creating programs aligned with those survey results, and promoting those programs. The planning, execution, and evaluation processes of library programs must always keep in mind the program's goals to ensure the programs are effective and efficient. Without goals, library programs are unlikely to succeed at promoting the larger mission of the library and school and will not effectively contribute to the educational, social, and entertainment goals of the school and library.

Evaluation of Library Programs

Library programs are evaluated according to how well they achieve their stated goals, align with and support the various philosophies and missions of the library and school, and support the educational objectives of classroom teachers. Programs should be evaluated by the various stakeholder groups impacted, which will be unique to a given program. For example, a program targeted at sixth-grade history students should be evaluated by library staff, history teachers, sixth-grade history students, and perhaps other groups (depending on the specifics of the program). Methods for evaluating program success will vary but may include surveying stakeholders, comparing initial measurements (e.g., prior program participation, pretest scores, attitude surveys) to post-program assessments (e.g., current program participation, posttest scores, attitude surveys), and assessing program results to determine whether the program is in alignment with school and library missions.

Library Planning

Short- vs. Long-Range Library Planning

Short-range library planning is concerned with library operations and programs that will occur within the next 6 to 12 months, and it is generally based on previous long-range planning efforts that have been split into manageable pieces that can be accomplished over various short terms. **Long-range** planning, then, is concerned with planning broader operations and programming efforts that will occur over the next three to five years, with some occurring over 10 years, depending on the organization and the plans being developed. While both types of planning are concerned with similar library operations and programs, the immediacy of short-term planning requires more thorough and detailed planning and will include things like the next semester's programs, classroom projects, purchasing, and material selection and deselection. Long-range planning expands these same ideas out further to ensure that the library is achieving its goals in the long run, which includes proper budgeting procedures, alignment of library resources with school missions and educational needs, overall program offerings and objectives, and future areas of school growth and development.

Importance of Long-Range Planning

Long-range planning is designed to ensure that the school library is prepared for programs, procedures, and policies that may take effect further than one year in the future. For instance, a large-scale library renovation may be planned to begin in five years' time, which would prompt the library to ensure that the next five years are spent preparing for such a large-scale disruption. By having plans in place, a library can break up large problems into manageable pieces and handle them in the short term. Long-range planning also gives the library some insight into how well it has achieved its goals by allowing it to compare long-range plans to the actual events that later occurred in the short term. Essentially, long-range plans allow school libraries to better organize, plan, and promote library resources and services by tackling larger tasks over a longer period.

Deciding Short- and Long-Range Plans

The length of a plan is proportional to the scale of the project being tackled. A program that is offered every year, for instance, likely has a large amount of the work required to plan it already completed from the previous year, so it can be slightly modified at the start of each year for implementation in the middle of the year (short range). A larger program, perhaps one with the goal of increasing student reading levels by 10 percent across the board, is likely to take a much longer time to complete (long range). By deciding the procedures and milestones much further in advance, the librarians have time to prepare and regularly reevaluate the plan. Once plans have been decided, it is important to write them down in terms that can be measured so they can be evaluated during and after implementation to show how well they've achieved their stated goal. For example, if student reading levels have only increased by 9 percent after five years, it may be time to reevaluate the methods used, the length of time allotted to achieve the goal, or the goal itself.

Needs Assessment Process

Needs Assessment

A **needs assessment** is the process of determining whether a particular library program or offering is meeting its intended purpose. In practice, this means evaluating a given program or offering (e.g., nonfiction reference materials), determining how it should be functioning (e.g., current and quality materials that support the curriculum), and comparing that to how it is actually functioning (e.g., quality materials that support the curriculum but are many years out of date). The **needs gap** between current and desired states is where the library should focus its efforts in correcting the issue. In the case of programs, the needs may include time, volunteers, money, or supplies required to meet the program's intended purpose, such as a book fair that has the goal of providing a quality event that matches students with great books.

Types of Scenarios Prompting a Needs Assessment

Needs assessments should be conducted regularly for each of the various offerings of the school library, including programs and resources. Some resources that might need regular needs assessments include various library collections (e.g., visually impaired materials, magazine subscriptions, online databases), the library's physical space (e.g., seating, computer access, ADA compliance), or technology (e.g., computer performance, audio/visual equipment, photo editing software). Some programs that benefit from needs assessments include book clubs, career fairs, or makerspace tutorials. In each case, the current offerings' effectiveness in achieving stated goals should be compared to the desired offerings' effectiveness.

Importance of the Needs Assessment Process

Library needs assessments are critical to ensure the proper utilization of library resources such as time, money, and space. Without properly assessing the needs gap between the current and desired states of a program or resource, efforts may be wasted on a program that is already performing up to standard or even overperforming. For example, the nonfiction books on Greek mythology may be showing lower-than-expected circulation numbers, causing a librarian to believe that perhaps the titles should be deselected. If, however, the titles are necessary for an annual history project, then student needs are being met and deselecting the titles would be counterproductive and waste time and money. The reverse is also possible, where a given resource is not recognized as underperforming even though it continues to not meet the needs of the group it is intended to serve. By conducting regular needs assessments, librarians can spot both performing and underperforming resources and align staff time and money to the appropriate efforts.

Financial Objectives and Budget Management

Short-Term vs. Long-Term Financial Objectives

Short-term financial objectives are those with expenses that, along with the associated items used or obtained, will be paid for within one fiscal year or within another relatively brief financial period. Generally, the majority of regular library purchases will be short-term and will be made each semester or year. **Long-term** financial objectives are those with expenses that will be paid for over multiple fiscal years or other, broad financial periods. These are generally larger purchases or multiple purchases associated with a single large project that may exceed the typical budgeted amount for a given fiscal period; thus, they require money to be spread out over multiple years in order to remain within budget. Typically, library budgets include a mix of short- and long-term objectives that relate to the various budget priorities that come and go during the normal course of library business.

Examples of Projects, Programs, and Resources

An example of a short-term library objective might be the semesterly or annual purchase of new print books for the fiction and nonfiction collections. Each of these two collections has different needs and requirements for the purchasing timeline, but both will have regular purchases making up a large portion of the annual budget. Some other potential short-term objectives might be to update a particular section of the library with new furniture or replace a particular computer bank with updated hardware. A long-term objective may include reducing the amount of money spent on print books and instead increasing the funding for digital materials. A project of this size would likely require multiple years of planning and money to fully realize itself, so this would constitute a long-term objective. Another long-term objective might be overhauling the library's makerspace capabilities, including the purchase and maintenance of new equipment, staff training, and the development of programs to utilize the new equipment.

Prioritizing Budgets

Library budgets are prioritized according to current short- and long-term library objectives, taking into account overall school and library missions as well as librarian and administrative priorities. A key strategy that many librarians utilize to effectively prioritize their limited funding is making **prioritized lists** of potential purchases. When librarians are speaking with various library stakeholders, new potential purchases will either be implicitly or explicitly suggested, and it is critical that these suggestions are written down in order to consider their merits for future purchasing cycles. As each item is added to the list, it should be accompanied by an estimated cost and intended use. When items are purchased, they should be added to another list (or budgeting software) that details the date, cost, and use of each expense so the information can be referred to during future budget planning processes. Prioritized lists also allow for a more visual representation of potential uses for the budget and give librarians a quick method of locating an appropriate potential purchase when short-window budget windfalls occur (usually near the end of the fiscal year).

Influence of the Missions of the Library and School

Library budget priorities are heavily influenced by the overall missions of the school and library. Ultimately, this comes down to allocating funds that will actively promote the values and priorities of both, so the purpose of budgeting is to ensure that these priorities are properly funded. For instance, if the number one mission of a particular school library involves the active participation of people from all walks of life in the learning process, the library budget should reflect this mission by highly prioritizing materials and programs that promote and enhance a multicultural perspective. By actively considering why a particular line item is a priority, library budgets can be not only more efficient (i.e., spending money where it is useful), but also more easily understood by various library stakeholders.

Arguments Justifying Budgetary Needs

Librarians may need to justify overall budgetary allocations as well as specific line-item purchases. A major mission of most school libraries is to serve the educational needs of the school by providing resources, programs, and training opportunities that align with and enhance those educational needs. By assuring administrators and other monetary decision-makers that library purchases and staffing directly support school educational goals, library budgets can be justified and potentially increased. A popular argument for justifying current or increased library budgets is one of student success. Some studies show that students tend to perform better academically when school libraries have larger collections and are better staffed. Another possible justification for library budgets is an explanation of what the negative outcomes for students would be without the expenditure. For example, a school that highly emphasizes science, technology, engineering, and mathematics (STEM) may strongly benefit from a well-funded makerspace that includes 3D printing hardware, design software, staff training, and furniture that promotes collaboration. By explaining how the lack of such a program could negatively impact students' learning experiences in these fields, a librarian could justify such an expensive project.

Challenges Encountered During the Process of Budgeting

One of the potential challenges librarians may face during the budget process is a lack of the funding needed to accomplish all desired goals and fund all desired purchases. As school budgets get tighter, library budgets can sometimes be seen as an easy place to make some cuts. Librarians should find ways to promote the great importance of library programs and the many benefits libraries provide to student education. They should also educate administrators on the various resources available at libraries in order to defend their budgets and justify future investments. A prioritized list of desired purchases should be consulted to determine where funds must be spent to support school curricula and which purchases can wait. Another potential challenge librarians may face during budgeting is a lack of information about resource purchases. For example, how can a librarian determine whether one database is better than another (and in what way) in order to justify a significantly larger price tag? By relying on professional library networks like the American Library Association (ALA) or the American Association of School Librarians (AASL), librarians can gain information and advice from trusted sources on how to properly evaluate various resource packages like databases or online catalog providers.

Best Practices to Tracking Past and Future Spending

In concert with school financial experts, the librarian is responsible for maintaining an accurate record of past and future expenses. A properly maintained budget will include upcoming expenses, and a librarian should actively and immediately record when those expenses have been purchased. Careful and regular accounting is crucial to maintaining an accurate budget record, so it is advisable to periodically (e.g., daily, weekly, perhaps monthly) record expenditures and be aware of the amount of funds remaining for a given period or expense category (e.g., print books, promotional materials, training, etc.). By keeping long- and short-term expenditures together, librarians might be able to spread long-term expenditures out over multiple fiscal periods to avoid getting into a situation where funds no longer remain to cover an unexpected cost. Proper utilization of trained library staff paraprofessionals can greatly assist in the process of tracking library expenditures.

Evaluating a Budget Plan

The primary purpose of evaluating budget plans is to ensure that the budgeted costs for resources and programs are adequate enough to provide the desired level of service. If a librarian completes a **needs assessment** regarding the various line items of the budget and the combined library offerings, it is possible for to determine the effectiveness of a particular budget. If it is clear that a particular resource or program is not providing the desired level of service at the currently budgeted cost, it may be discovered that it is not being adequately funded. Similarly, a particular program may be overfunded, with money going to waste while funding a program that is already performing up to expectations. Another way to evaluate a budget involves comparing past expenditures to current and future (planned) expenditures across the same line items and related categories (e.g., print books or teen programs). Utilizing a consistent format for budgets every year makes comparison much easier and allows librarians to see how certain programs or resources have performed over time compared to how much has been spent on them annually.

Contributors to a Library Budget

Library budgeting, like other library decision-making processes, should be a collaborative process that includes representatives from each of the various library stakeholder groups. The various collaborators whose input should be considered when putting together library budgets include librarians, library support staff, school technology professionals, financial professionals, faculty, principals, and students. Each of these stakeholder groups will have different opinions and emphases when it comes to where and how money should be spent, so it is important to weigh the pros and cons of each group's input when making final decisions. Librarians are likely to be one of the most important decision-makers in this process since they hold the responsibility of operating the library and should be the most knowledgeable about its overall vision, needs, and offerings. On the financial side, school financial professionals and principals are also very important since they hold the keys to proper disbursement and management of library funds. Input from library support staff, technology professionals, faculty, and students will also be valuable since they have intimate knowledge of the day-to-day workings of the library, know its technological needs and capabilities, and are the most regular users of the library.

Alternative Methods of Funding

Today's librarians are facing a crisis of dwindling funding at all school levels. This is largely due to the increasing costs of operating public schools, including the costs associated with meeting standardized testing achievement standards. In many cases, libraries are seen as entities that can operate with reduced funding or staffing because, at a glance, they do not appear to directly support testing goals in the way that classroom teachers do. Therefore, it is critical for school librarians to seek alternative sources of funding to continue providing adequate levels of service to the school populations they support. One such alternative funding source is the direct donation of materials, time, or money from school parents or other unaffiliated community members. Another alternative funding source might be state or federal funding through grants. Grants can help provide funding for books, programs, and staff, and grant writing is an invaluable skill for the public librarian of today.

Managing Staff and Volunteers

Roles vs. Duties of Librarians, Library Paraprofessionals, and Volunteers

Librarians, at the top of the library hierarchy, perform most of the higher functions in the library, including budgeting, supervising library employees, short- and long-term planning, and selecting and deselecting materials. **Library paraprofessionals**, then, support the librarian and the mission of the library by completing tasks like circulation, budgeting assistance, and more face-to-face student interactions. Librarians and library paraprofessionals also perform many similar duties, including day-to-day operating functions such as circulation, materials advisory, and technology support. **Volunteers** also have some duties in common with paraprofessionals, such as lower-level functions like shelving, organizing, cleaning, and program assistance. Volunteers, however, aren't typically involved with any sort of library decision-making, and they tend to only assist with necessary tasks that don't require much knowledge of library operations.

Benefits and Limitations of Working with Volunteers

The primary benefit of working with volunteers is budgetary. Since volunteers are unpaid, they are an invaluable resource, especially for underfunded libraries. Volunteers are often enthusiastic and desire to give their time and effort to improving the library and assisting with day-to-day tasks like shelving or helping with various projects. Volunteers are also likely to be some of a library's biggest supporters out in the community, advertising library programs or any resource or funding needs for free. Properly training volunteers to be library champions is essential to ensure an involved and enthusiastic community. Volunteers, unfortunately, are limited in the amount of time they can work and the kinds of work they can do. Since they are not paid, it is unreasonable to expect volunteers to do work at the level performed by paraprofessionals or librarians, so they don't work with students' personal information, assist with circulation, or help with library budgets and planning. They are, therefore, best suited for work that does not require much decision-making but is still necessary for library operations, like shelving or doing various other repetitive tasks, freeing up paid library staff to utilize their time on other projects.

Keeping Library Staff Current with Development Opportunities

All library staff, including librarians themselves, should keep up to date with current practices in effective library operation. It is an important responsibility of librarians to mentor and train staff (particularly paraprofessionals) to give them the skills necessary to function effectively in the school library. A well-trained library staff can be more attentive to stakeholder needs and better respond to situations that require high-level decision-making to find creative solutions. A staff that is not trained regularly may continue using ideas and methods that have been shown to be ineffective or less effective than new methods or ways of thinking. Regular training sessions, both formal and informal, are critical to ensure that staff members have the best tools at their disposal. Formal training sessions include lectures and hands-on training on specific topics and should occur at regular intervals. One effective method of providing a broad range of training topics involves bringing in experts in various aspects of library operations, like school technology or financial professionals. Informal training sessions are more likely to take the form of active mentorship or links to professional articles and videos, and these should occur on a daily or weekly basis.

Considerations for Choosing Which Trainings to Administer

Depending on state or school guidelines, library support staff may be required to meet certain education, training, or certification standards. These standards should largely inform the training schedule for staff, ensuring they are performing up to expected standards in a variety of skill areas. Another method of selecting training topics is through observation or direct discussion with staff. Particular policies, procedures, or subjects may need more in-depth training sessions or ongoing support, such as library ethics, intellectual freedom, and legal considerations for library staff. Staff may also request specific training that directly supports their current positions or broadly relates to the field of library science and supports their career aspirations and professional growth. It is vital that trainings be selected and tailored to address specific needs for maintaining an appropriately trained staff.

Methods of Communication to Use with Library Staff

Communication with library staff is performed through a few channels, and those channels vary depending on the purpose of the communication. For more formal communication, structured channels like regular or ad hoc meetings are preferred. These types of meetings might see librarians discussing upcoming events, new library processes, advertising campaigns, or changes to existing operational procedures. For more informal or less impactful announcements, email, group communication platforms like Slack or Teams, or one-on-one communication may be appropriate. Some kinds of information shared in these informal channels might include ideas for programs, day-to-day operations communication, and team-building exercises. It is important to use the appropriate channel because the method of communication can convey the relative importance of the information being shared. Information shared in an improper channel may not be given the importance it deserves. For example, using a text message to communicate that there is a new schoolwide goal that will heavily influence the library may not be the best method to convey the intended importance of such news.

Keeping Library Staff and Volunteers Active and Engaged

Communication between librarians and staff should be an ongoing dialogue, with both sides speaking and listening to each other. Through existing library communication channels, staff can be informed and kept engaged by giving their thoughts and input to ongoing and future decision-making processes. As key decision-making stakeholders, library staff have valuable input to give and need a regular place to give feedback to librarians. When library staff feel heard, they are more likely to buy into the library and perform to the best of their capabilities. Regularly requesting this type of feedback from staff, as well as creating a culture that rewards two-way communication, is critical to achieving this mission. Setting aside time in regular meetings and promoting a culture of open communication in a digital group communication platform are both great low-effort and high-reward ways to increase communication and promote an enthusiastic staff.

Staff Evaluations

As with any organization that employs paid staff members to complete tasks, it is critical to ensure that library staff are properly evaluated on a regular basis. By checking in with staff and comparing their actual performance to expected performance, librarians can identify areas of strength and weakness and can know what future training to emphasize. If staff are not regularly evaluated, problems can go unseen for longer than necessary, and library operations will suffer as a result. Some particularly important areas for library staff (primarily paraprofessionals) include circulation functions, materials advisory, shelving procedures, financial assistance, and technology support. Ensuring that staff are properly performing up to expectations in each of these areas is necessary to ensure they are meeting the objectives of library operations. Another key benefit of staff evaluation is the opportunity for formal one-on-one communication between librarians and paraprofessionals, which may offer insights into a staff member's interest areas for future personal or professional growth. Staff who feel supported and heard are more likely to feel motivated to perform effectively in the library.

Formal vs. Informal Evaluation Methods

An informal evaluation of library staff takes place every time librarians interact with library staff or view their work. This may take the form of mentally noting how well a particular task is being completed or observing a particular quality in a patron interaction, such as a warm greeting or good listening skills. Informal evaluations may also include praise, comments, or suggestions to staff about a particular skill or interaction that was observed. More formal evaluation takes the form of one-on-one conversations, which are generally scheduled, and may include written comments as well. Formal evaluations generally utilize data-driven performance markers that can compare current and expected levels of performance to past performance. Formal evaluations are generally kept for record-keeping purposes, to measure employee performance progress, and as a means of supporting staff in future improvement areas.

Key Policies and Procedures

Circulation Policy

A **circulation policy** is necessary as a means of codifying how the various resources in the school library are allowed to be used by patrons. Generally, this means written rules on loan periods, renewal policies, checkout limits, fines and fees, and library-use items. A library's circulation policy is the one that all other policies hinge on, since without the loan of materials, a library's primary purpose cannot be achieved. A comprehensive circulation policy can ensure materials are either loaned to or used in-library by the largest possible number of students without unduly depriving other students. Such a policy can also assist with the retention of materials since loan periods and fines are well advertised to borrowers.

Borrowing vs. Circulation Processes

Under the umbrella of a library's broader circulation policy lies an implied **borrowing** procedure, which is the act of lending out a particular library resource for a student to take home. Most libraries will allow the majority of their print and electronic materials to be borrowed, but they may have other resources that they only allow to circulate in-library without a borrowing option. Examples of such materials for which in-house circulation may be more appropriate include rare or valuable materials, large and cumbersome history or reference volumes, or materials that are difficult to account for quickly (e.g., board games, puzzles). Borrowing, on the other hand, is likely more appropriate for the vast majority of print materials, e-books, and other materials that students might need for an extended amount of time outside the library.

Determining and Implementing Borrowing Procedures

A library's circulation policy, which includes the terms of the borrowing agreements for the various kinds of resources in the library's collection, is the backbone of the library's mission to provide materials to patrons. Each type of library resource needs to have a specific borrowing procedure associated with it so that it is clear how long it may be borrowed, by whom, and with how many renewals (if any). The majority of a library's borrowing collection will generally stick to a single loan period, which may vary from a few days to weeks depending on the library. Some specialty materials like hotspots or computer equipment necessary for a particular course may be loaned for a whole semester or year, while more in-demand or valuable items may only have loan periods of a single day. It is important to determine how long a patron might reasonably need to borrow an item when determining the standard borrowing procedures. A renewal system, whereby materials can be kept longer than their original loan periods, is a way for libraries to extend the length of their loan periods on a case-by-case basis as necessary.

Interlibrary Loans

An **interlibrary loan** (commonly referred to as **ILL**) is the process whereby one library loans its materials out to another library so that a patron may check out a resource that is not available at his or her home library. Some libraries belong to a consortium of libraries, which facilitates easy interlibrary loans between members and allows members to pool resources together and share materials. As with circulation policies, ILL policies are intended to ensure a library's collection can serve the maximum possible number of patrons without any undue hardship to others. In-demand or cumbersome items may be better saved for home patrons. Another thing to consider when writing ILL policy is cost. It may be costly to loan out materials through the mail, and if home patrons are not then utilizing ILL services with partnered libraries, the cost may not return a benefit for the home library. Comparing a library's collection to that of the web of ILL-friendly libraries can give some insight into the benefits of participating in such a partnership.

Considerations When Writing Selection Policies

A library's **selection policy** outlines the kinds of materials purchased by the library, who is in charge of purchasing items, which processes are used, and the purchasing schedule. Broadly, such a policy explains how materials are chosen (i.e., selected) or removed from the collection (i.e., deselected). As a central part of their mission, school libraries must support the academic achievements of the students in their schools, namely through direct instructional support and through making reference, leisure, and technology resources available for borrowing. Thus, school library collections need to contain materials that support school curricula. Another important consideration when writing school library selection policies is the age range of the typical patrons. An elementary school's selection policy will look different than a high school's policy. It is also important for school libraries to consider how parents may be involved in evaluating the materials a library collects, and selection policies should reflect how libraries manage parental influence in this area.

Acceptable Use Policy

To ensure that students are making good use of technology and internet resources, it is important to consider an **acceptable use policy**. Such a policy generally includes an agreement signed by parties who wish to use computers or other internet-enabled devices owned by the school that outlines what those parties will or will not use the devices or the internet for. Its purpose is to protect students from illegal or inappropriate materials online, promote good internet security habits, shift legal liability for internet misconduct away from schools, and ensure productivity when using school technology resources. The agreement itself and regular reminders of good online behavior are the major methods used to enforce acceptable use policies. Other enforcement methods include punishments or verbal admonishments for infractions, maintaining a schoolwide culture of good internet behavior, and the loss of privileges for major or repeated infractions. A more preventative approach to enforcing an acceptable use policy involves the use of internet filtering software, which prevents students from even accidentally breaking the policy agreement.

Legal and Ethical Considerations Addressed by an Acceptable Use Policy

One of the major purposes of an acceptable use policy is to protect schools and libraries from legal and ethical concerns that might cause harm to students or others. Many acceptable use policies explicitly prohibit the access of materials that are illegal in nature, and many others limit materials that are deemed to be ethically or morally inappropriate for access by students. Without such policies in place and agreed to by users, a legal burden could be placed on a library if one of its users accesses the internet for nefarious purposes or comes to some harm on the internet. By referring to a written policy, libraries can advertise to internal or external organizations that they are actively taking steps to protect users of their resources and are committed to the safe use of the internet and technology resources.

Reconsideration Policy

The term **reconsideration** is used for the process by which a given item in the collection is considered for removal, specifically through the formal challenge process initiated by a patron or staff member. Materials are challenged for a variety of reasons, some of which include being deemed as irrelevant, obscene, untrue, or inappropriate for a particular age group. A library's reconsideration policy will outline the steps that a reconsideration event takes from start to finish. This policy will detail the types of materials a library does or does not collect, on what grounds, and how a patron might go about formally requesting the removal of an item. Many such policies elaborate that the library upholds the First Amendment of the US Constitution, which protects free speech, or the American Library Association's (ALA) Library Bill of Rights, which mandates that libraries "challenge censorship." During the challenge process, it is important to remain transparent in deciding whether to remove challenged material, and referring to the formal reconsideration policy can help provide this transparency.

Materials Donation Policy

A **materials donation policy** is one that outlines the kinds of materials that can be accepted for donation by the library and for what purpose. Generally, these are in place to create an official transfer of ownership from the person donating to the library, and most specify that once donated, materials are free to be collected, sold, or discarded for any purpose deemed appropriate by the library or librarian. Two reasons for this policy are to ensure those donating understand what might happen with their donations and to prevent someone who has second thoughts about his or her donation from having any recourse in asking for the materials back. Some libraries do not accept donations at all or will accept donations purely as a recycling service, either of which would be stated in a materials donation policy. Many libraries also use donation receipts alongside their official policies as a way to formalize a given donation and retain records for legal purposes.

Partners Involved in the Process of Writing a Conduct Policy

A library's **conduct policy** is a form of **acceptable use agreement** that states the actions patrons should take or should specifically refrain from while in the library in order to promote a welcoming environment for all. To that end, it is important when writing a conduct policy to consider the opinions and perspectives of individuals of various backgrounds to ensure such a policy is comprehensive. Some of the key partners who should be involved in writing a conduct policy include librarians, school legal counsel, administration, students, staff, faculty, and behavior interventionists. This group of partners will provide guidance on the sorts of behaviors that should be expected of patrons as well as those behaviors which will not be tolerated.

Legal and Ethical Issues Related to Policies and Procedures

Partners Involved in Making Legal and Ethical Decisions

Library decisions involving matters that concern ethical or legal decisions typically need to be vetted by a variety of decision-making partners to ensure that libraries are operating in a proper manner. Some of the most important key approvers in this process are a school's principal, legal counsel, and superintendent. The school's legal counsel is going to be the foremost expert and day-to-day approver for a library's legal and ethical matters, so building a strong working relationship with the counsel is desirable. Some decisions may even require approval from a school board, city council, or state government. All library policies and actions must remain within guidelines set by federal, state, and school governing bodies in order to remain compliant with the law at various levels. For public schools that receive funding from government sources, it is especially critical that regulations be followed so as to not jeopardize funding opportunities.

Due Process

The phrase **due process** refers to a Fifth Amendment-supported idea of a person's right to a thorough and fair process in handling matters that might deprive him or her of a particular right. In a library setting, this means handling sensitive library matters to the letter of the official policies. These official policies are made more transparent and fair to help protect a library from being seen as infringing upon the rights of its patrons. Some of the specific policies that most concern due process include reconsideration, selection, hiring, and circulation. For example, it is very important to follow reconsideration policies to the letter in order to ensure that patrons feel that their (sometimes very personal) concerns are being heard and addressed in a fair and timely manner. It would go against the notion of due process to dismiss a reconsideration challenge out of hand without properly considering the facts and evaluating the circumstances of a particular challenge.

Reasons Materials May Be Challenged

It is a regular occurrence for materials to be challenged at any library level, but school libraries see a greater number of challenges due to the direct involvement of a patron group that is exclusively composed of minors. Challenges are brought against materials for a variety of reasons: being deemed as inappropriate for sexual, religious, political, or cultural reasons; being seen as unnecessary or outdated; or being seen as inappropriate for a particular age group. The first and last of these three make up the bulk of challenges in school libraries, and many challenges are aimed at books that contain sex, drugs, violence, racial issues, or strong language, or books that depict groups that some have deemed subversive, like political out-groups, people who don't fit into the gender binary, or people who are not straight. Regarding a reconsideration challenge, the First Amendment is generally going to protect the rights of students to have access to materials regardless of their content (barring hate speech or materials that are pornographic, among other exceptions). Courts have repeatedly upheld the right of libraries to collect materials without concern for censorship and outside influence.

Legal Rights to Students Regarding Privacy and Confidentiality Matters

Students are afforded a number of rights that protect their privacy and make their library records confidential, and most of these rights are based on the ALA's Library Bill of Rights. Primary among these is the right to browse whichever materials they desire without any interference from library staff or other interested parties. Students' browsing history is also protected and should not be shared with parties other than the student. School libraries, in accordance with federal law, have a limitation or exception to this privacy in the form of the Family Educational Rights and Privacy Act (FERPA). FERPA states that parents may have access to their underage child's educational records until their child comes of age, and this can limit some of the true privacy students may have. FERPA also includes provisions for educational staff to access records that are directly related to students' education, further limiting the privacy of students in certain circumstances. Schools have an ethical obligation to ensure that the access to student information is not treated frivolously and only accessed in situations in which private information is considered necessary and impactful for informing educational decision-making processes.

Library Policies Protecting Students' Privacy and Confidential Information

In order to protect the privacy of students, library policies should be written in such a way as to make it as difficult as possible to accidentally violate student privacy rights. Circulation policies should include language and procedures that do not violate student privacy, such as private secure checkout processes, library hold processes that do not reveal students' requested materials, and staff trained not to disclose students' browsing habits where other students may hear. Another part of a library's circulation policy may involve the collection of various types of student data. Reducing the amount and kinds of student data collected can reduce the likelihood of the accidental disclosure of student information. Technology policies can also help protect students' privacy by obscuring search history, not advertising students' interests or currently checked out materials, and providing secure, private channels for students to discover materials without requiring any outside assistance. Students should also be informed of their rights and given the assurance that library staff are committed to the mission to protect their privacy.

Intellectual Freedom

A student's **intellectual freedom** is his or her ability to explore ideas and topics of interest without interference from other parties. Along with protecting students' privacy, the chief mission of the school library is to protect and encourage students to express their intellectual freedom to seek knowledge. One of the ways a school library's policy can protect intellectual freedom is through the selection and deselection processes. By selecting a wide range of materials, libraries can ensure students have true access to all information they may seek without accidentally (or purposefully) excluding information on a given subject. Library training policies should also include language on assisting students with the search for information and giving students the tools they need to actually search for information in the first place. Library missions and objectives should clearly state their support for the value of intellectual freedom, and they will be further supported by federal laws and library interest groups like the ALA and the American Association of School Librarians (AASL).

Partners Protecting Students' Intellectual Freedom

There are a number of key partners involved in protecting students' intellectual freedom in the school library. These include librarians, library staff, faculty, administrators, technology staff, and the school legal counsel. Librarians and library staff have the dual mandate of encouraging students to explore their interests without fear and protecting their freedom through rigorous policy and advocacy. Faculty should encourage students to explore their curiosities as well, with the additional responsibility of ensuring that instruction does not stifle creativity or restrict freedom to explore topics that are suitable for a particular assignment. School administrators are responsible for ensuring that school policy supports library policy in encouraging and protecting intellectual freedom. This general school policy directly relates to the school technology policy, which should protect students from outside actors while not restricting their ability to express their intellectual freedoms. Finally, the school legal counsel directly supports administrators and library staff in writing appropriate and effective policies and defending those policies in times of challenge.

Ethical Equal Access Policies

Ethical and equal access to the school library and its offerings means a commitment to welcoming all potential students to access the library with as little inconvenience as possible. For many students who belong to various minority groups, like speakers of other languages and those with various disabilities, this means a concerted effort toward inclusion through a wide selection of materials that meet the needs of a diverse audience. Physical library considerations such as shelf height, aisle size, and inclusive accessibility features for people with visual and hearing impairments are also important pieces of an effective equal access mindset. All students, regardless of their unique characteristics, have an equal right to use the library, and it is critical that libraries protect this right through policy and advocacy. There may also be state or federal guidelines that can help libraries begin to assess their operation procedures to see whether they align with providing equal access to all students.

Privacy and Confidentiality in the ALA's Library Bill of Rights and COPPA

Students' rights to privacy and confidentiality in the library are protected under the ALA's Library Bill of Rights. This information should be used to establish clear privacy policies in the library. Any records pertaining to a student in the library, such as circulation history and password information, are to remain private; however, there are times when there are exceptions. When there are concerns for the safety of a particular student or the safety of others, it may be necessary to share information with others, such as administration or law enforcement. It is up to the librarian to be familiar with the laws in his or her state and ensure the library is adhering to them. Additionally, it is important for school staff not to use programs that interfere with student privacy by collecting data, per the Children's Online Privacy Protection Act (COPPA). Students should be well informed by their librarian of their privacy rights, what they can do as students, and what will be done by staff to protect them.

Ethical Course of Action for Copyright or Plagiarism Issues

The best way to address issues related to copyright and plagiarism is to prevent them from happening by providing necessary instruction on citation and usage; however, there are times when students are equipped to ethically use information yet fail to do so. Most schools have an honor code that strictly prohibits plagiarism, and they have guidelines in place for when infractions related to unethical use of information occur. Where these do not exist, the librarian should campaign for their development. Typically, the issue is first addressed by the educator who identifies the misuse of information, and usually the offending student receives an incomplete or zero on the assignment. On some occasions, likely when the misuse was unintentional, students are permitted to complete the assignment again. Following infractions, it is important to remediate students on the steps of ethical use to prevent it from recurring.

Collaborating with Other Libraries

Collaborative Relationships Between Libraries

A library can improve its collection in a cost-effective manner by maintaining relationships with other libraries. Libraries commonly enter **consortiums** within their school districts or states to develop mutually beneficial relationships with other libraries. Each library is an individual consortium member. A consortium's primary benefit is the increased access to resources for patrons, both students and teachers. While the types of resources available will vary based on each library's purchased materials and subscription services, they will often include access to print and digital resources, a variety of databases, homework help sites for students, gamified and virtual learning tools, professional development resources, and other subscription-based education resources. Financially, this lowers the cost of goods and services by dividing it between consortium members. By purchasing within a consortium, access to resources is increased while cost per member is decreased. Additionally, interlibrary loans typically occur between organizations within a consortium. This increases patron access by allowing patrons to borrow resources owned by other libraries with no increase in cost to the patron's library.

Initiating and Building a Relationship with a Public Library

Before a school library begins to develop a relationship with any outside entity, school administration should be made aware and give its approval. Once this occurs, the school librarian should establish a primary contact at the public library. Most often, this is the children's librarian or youth services librarian. The school librarian should contact him or her with introductory information and an invitation to meet. The initial meetings should include discussions on what services both libraries have to offer as well as information on what the school library needs and is expected to do. At this point, the school librarian and public librarian may collaborate to develop goals and plan mutually beneficial programming to reach those goals. At the completion of the programs, it is important for the librarians to meet again and use data to determine the effectiveness of the collaboration and develop plans to continue their partnership.

Programming Between Two Libraries

When planning any program or event, begin with the end in mind. The end goal should fulfill a common need for both libraries in the relationship. Ensure that the goal is measurable so that it may be evaluated after the programming ends. Once both stakeholders have collectively established what participants should know or be able to do when the programming is completed, they can then use that to determine the steps required to get there. These events and partnerships are typically student-based, but they can also revolve around teachers or parents when needed. During planning, maintain regular communication regarding the programming's progression and the needs of both parties. Ensure the workload is appropriately divided and progress will adhere to the agreed-upon timeline. This phase is most important in determining future collaboration, as future decisions are often based on satisfaction in the planning process. As mentioned previously, the established goal should be measurable. Data collected after the event should be used to evaluate the effectiveness of the programming in meeting the goal. With that data, improvements to programming can be made to benefit all involved parties.

Partnership Events with Public Libraries

Partnership events are held as a collaboration between stakeholders. In this context, the stakeholders are the school and public libraries. By collaborating and using their own professional experiences, the librarians can plan events that reach the goals of their own institution while splitting the costs and responsibilities.

The most popular partnership events are **summer learning programs**. These are developed to prevent learning losses in students over their extended break from school by incentivizing reading through the public library. The public library benefits in increased patronage while the school library benefits by having students who have maintained their reading skill levels and the interest in reading they gained during that school year. Other potential events include programming around book weeks (e.g., children's book week, teen reads week, etc.), author or illustrator appearances, college fairs, technology skills courses, and even course offerings for parents of students.

Negative Effects of Library Partnerships

When working and planning programs together, it is not uncommon for one party to feel they are doing the bulk of the required work, or at least more than their fair share. To prevent this, all involved parties should participate in the development of a cohesive plan outlining each member's responsibilities and deadlines. In large collaborative groups, such as a cohort of all librarians in a district, it is important to have established norms and roles. This avoids any confusion of appropriate behaviors and responsibilities. These should be established early in the relationship and referenced regularly.

Interlibrary Loan Process

Interlibrary Loan

Interlibrary loan is the process in which a library borrows a resource from or lends a resource to a library with which it has a relationship. It allows patrons to access and borrow both physical and digital resources owned by libraries other than the one where they are members. By temporarily obtaining a resource on patron request, a library is not spending any additional money on niche resources that may only be used irregularly, but it is still filling the needs of the patron. This is one of the simplest and most budget-effective ways to fulfill patron needs. Because no two libraries have identical collections, partnering with another library will increase the quantity and quality of available resources without increasing costs.

Process of Borrowing

Interlibrary loan processes are split between two components, borrowing and lending. The process of **borrowing** allows patrons to access resources not available through their own library. An interlibrary loan is initiated by a patron search on the library management and circulation system to digitally search collections. This is either completed by the patron him- or herself or on his or her behalf by library staff. How results are received will vary based on the library management software used; however, there should be options to search the collections of all libraries with which a partnership exists. Once the desired titles or resources are located, selected, and the user information required for loaning is entered (usually through a username and password) the requested resource will be processed for loan.

If the requested materials are physical, they will be delivered via the agreed-upon method. For most school systems, resources are delivered via a courier completing interoffice mail, but mailing services may also be used. Digital resources are immediately available to access virtually or as a download for e-readers where applicable.

Process of Lending

Interlibrary loan processes are split between two components, borrowing and lending. The process of **lending** resources requires a librarian to locate and prepare resources for shipment. First, the library management and circulation system alerts library staff to completed interlibrary loan requests, and then these materials are located and pulled from the shelves. These resources should be visually assessed and their quality before checkout should be noted. They are then checked out to the individual patron or under the name of the library where the patron is a member. Materials are shipped in an agreed-upon method, typically some type of courier; however, loans may also be completed via mailing services. It is best practice to locate and send materials within 24 to 48 working hours of the request being received.

Dispersing and Returning Materials

When physical resources on loan are received, their condition should be assessed and any damage should be noted. In some instances, the resources will already be checked out to the individual patron. In other cases, the resource is checked out to the library itself. In this case, a temporary catalog entry will need to be created for the resource within the library management and circulation system. Once that is completed, the resource can be circulated to the patron who requested it. Books on interlibrary loan typically have a shorter loan period and are either not eligible to be renewed or have limited renewals; thus, the policies surrounding this should be stressed to the patron so that he or she is able to adhere to them and not incur fines.

Regarding digital resources, they are automatically recalled, and access is ended by the lending system once the return date is reached. The patron may choose to return them earlier if they are no longer needed.

Limitations of Interlibrary Loans

While interlibrary loans increase access for patrons, there are some drawbacks to this resource-sharing system. The resources being borrowed belong to a different library, and that library's policies may vary from one's own library. For some resources, there may be a smaller limit on renewals or no option to renew at all, which may require that the resource be potentially returned before the patron has finished using it. There is also potential for the resource to be recalled by the owning library. If a patron of the owning library requests the resource, it may be immediately recalled and the borrowing patron in possession of the book may be required to surrender it. If these or any other policies are not adhered to, the patron and library may be subject to fines. When it is time for the book to be returned, it should once again be assessed for any damages. If a temporary record was created, the book should be checked back in and the record deleted. If no record was created, it is ready to be returned to the owning library. In both cases, it should be processed and returned in the agreed-upon manner.

Alignment of the Library Media Program with the School Curriculum

Aligning Library Programs with School Curriculum

In order for school libraries to have the greatest impact on student learning, the content delivered must align with the school's curriculum. While the standards and curriculum used to meet them will vary between school districts, the most commonly used standards in the US are Common Core. The AASL has developed a crosswalk that aligns Common Core reading standards with its *National School Library Standards for Learners, School Librarians, and School Libraries* in order to best assist in aligning library instruction with a school's curriculum. For sets of standards for which crosswalk documents do not exist, it is vital for the librarian to find commonalities between the standards used by the school and the standards set forth by the AASL. Beyond direct instruction, the librarian is responsible for developing a collection that supports the chosen curriculum. This could mean purchasing additional titles in certain genres such as narrative nonfiction to support Common Core goals, or removing any outdated or biased resources.

Supporting School Curriculum with Library's Collection

A library often serves as a warehouse of physical and digital resources available to the whole school. The librarian is responsible for developing a collection policy designed to support and supplement the curricular goals of the school. Purchasing supplemental texts on standard topics above and below the prescribed grade level is one way to do this. It provides struggling readers with the resources to learn more about the topic at their level while also providing gifted readers with a related challenge. These supplemental texts can also be used to extend learning because they will go beyond what was covered in the classroom. Additionally, librarians often provide students with technology and databases that can help them access additional learning assistance tools, like homework help tools or online tutoring services, or help them perform deep dives into topics covered. Supporting the curriculum may also include weeding invalid or outdated books and replacing them with more relevant titles and maintaining access to research databases.

Librarian's Role in Curriculum Selection and Support

Per its guidelines, the AASL expects that school librarians join committees that make decisions regarding curriculum. This can be at the district, school, or department level. It is a fitting task for librarians as they are expected to collaborate with teachers to meet curricular goals. By serving on a curriculum committee, librarians can use their specialized skills to collaborate with teachers and other decision-makers to enhance the quality of instruction and the learning objectives within the school. It will also allow for the needs and concerns of the library to be represented. This will help to ensure librarians are able to support the selected curriculum through library programming.

Keeping Abreast of Changes in Library Curriculum

An ever-adapting and changing society requires school and library curriculum to adjust so that students can be best prepared to enter the working world. Although changes to school and library curriculum are influenced by changes to state or national standards, they are ultimately established by decision-makers within the district and communicated at the district level. To stay abreast of changes to library curriculum, the librarian must remain up to date on the actions and publications of library-related national and state decision-making bodies such as the AASL and the Florida Department of Education, respectively. This can be done by joining the AASL and interacting with its regular publications and by familiarizing oneself with the standards and expectations established by a state's department of education. Regularly participating in professional development opportunities and discourse with other librarians is another way to stay aware of changes within the field.

Integrating Information Literacy Skills Across the Curriculum

Librarian's Role in Integrating Information Literacy

The learning and technology standards set forth by the AASL and the ISTE, respectively, make the school librarian responsible for integrating information literacy across the curriculum. A librarian can do this independently in library studies or collaboratively with classroom teachers depending upon the school's scheduling format. Using a variety of research and information problem-solving models, librarians should guide students of all ages and grade levels through inquiry in order to develop the information literacy skills of sourcing, validating, and effectively using information. By doing this and aligning educational goals with the AASL and ISTE standards, librarians will help students develop the information literacy skills needed to be successful in all facets of education.

Designing Collaborative Instruction

The most important aspect of collaboration is communication. Clear, open communication will allow for both parties to feel that their educational goals for students are heard, understood, and ready to be met. It also allows for the assignment of roles and responsibilities within the partnership. This is vital in making sure the workload in these activities is split evenly and fairly. Maintaining this communication throughout will ease the process for all involved. Establishing the type and degree of collaboration is next. While it is easy to view collaborative instruction as strictly research projects or reading reports, it can also be as simple as providing resources or book lists for the teacher to use with students outside of the library. Lastly, librarians need to be aware of the curriculum they are supporting. They should become familiar with the standards in the content area they are collaborating on.

Obstacles to Collaborating with Teachers

One major barrier to collaboration is teachers' beliefs or misunderstandings about the librarian's role, abilities, and purpose within the school. To overcome this, it is first vital to make sure teachers understand what librarians can offer and how they can assist in students reaching their educational goals. This can be accomplished through many different forms of outreach, and it will make teachers more willing to take the time to collaborate. This leads to another common obstacle for planning—time. As with most collaborative projects, time is often a constraint when attempting to work with teachers as a librarian. Because time is a commodity and cannot be produced, creative solutions, like collaborative documents for planning, can be used to work together asynchronously. Librarians should also consider advocating for protected time during the day to collaborate with teachers. Another barrier is the librarian's potential lack of knowledge of the content area he or she wishes to assist in. To mitigate this, the librarian should familiarize him- or herself with the standards used to guide instruction in that area. This will provide the background knowledge needed to most successfully collaborate.

Assessing Student Work on Collaborative Assignments

Throughout the learning process, both the librarian and teacher should collect data as students traverse inquiry-based work. This data should pertain to a student's ability to find, evaluate, and use information to construct new knowledge. To do this, both formative and summative assessment data should be used. **Formative assessments** are small, ongoing assessments that occur while learning is taking place. These may look like checklists, self-assessments, peer reviews, or conferences with the librarian. This allows for students to receive regular feedback throughout the process and for librarians and teachers to assess their effectiveness. **Summative assessments** are more formal. Typically, they are the product that was created as a result of completed research, such as a paper, speech, book review, or presentation, but they can also come in the form of tests, quizzes, or exams. They are used to determine student success as well as the success of the instruction that took place. The role and use of assessments conducted in the library and the classroom will vary between school districts and classrooms.

Standards for Learners, School Librarians, and School Libraries

The third Shared Foundation in the AASL Standards is Collaborate. For school librarians, the Collaborate Competencies involving other educators focus on facilitating collaborative opportunities, demonstrating the importance of collaborative tools, and sharing responsibilities. By facilitating collaborative opportunities, librarians are able to work with teachers to produce meaningful learning opportunities for students that neither adult could create alone. This enhances student learning while also meeting the instructional goals of both the librarian and teacher. By demonstrating a personal use of collaborative tools, librarians build opportunities to extend collaboration regardless of time and space constraints, which are some of the most often-referenced obstacles in collaboration. In sharing educational responsibilities, librarians can bridge the gaps across disciplines. It is also best practice to share with all stakeholders what collaboration is taking place and what impact it has so that the community is aware. This adds value to the library and serves as a way to promote collaboration.

Disseminating Research Findings

It is well known that students with access to an adequately staffed school library program generally perform better on standardized tests across all subjects. It is the responsibility of school librarians to use this information to advocate for themselves and their programming, and they can do this in multiple ways. First, librarians may have the opportunity to speak directly to staff to explain their offerings and the benefits they have. They should also create easy-to-distribute informational materials that demonstrate the impact school libraries have on learning that they can pass out while speaking to staff or at other times. It is also highly recommended that librarians have an elevator pitch always prepared so they are able to verbally advocate for themselves if the opportunity arises. In doing so, librarians form partnerships with teachers and administrators, and they can form relationships with students that lead to success for all involved.

Analyzing and Evaluating Data to Plan and Implement Modifications

Changes made to the school library program are typically data-driven. This can be quantitative or qualitative and related to circulation and usage, student achievement, or any other desired library behavior or quality. The type of data will depend on the type of changes and outcomes that are desired. The librarian should establish a goal and use collected data as a baseline that will be compared later to determine the success of any changes. The librarian should also use action-based research and existing professional information and resources to develop his or her plan to make modifications to the library's space or programming. Once the changes have been implemented, updated data should be collected as it relates to the goal and analyzed to see if growth occurred. For example, the librarian may be looking for an increase in circulation, student performance on library activities, or overall patronage. Growth indicates successful changes, while a lack of growth indicates the modifications were not successful and need to be revisited.

Chapter Quiz

Ready to see how well you retained what you just read? Scan the QR code to go directly to the chapter quiz interface for this study guide. If you're using a computer, simply visit the online resources page at **mometrix.com/resources719/nbptslibmecya** and click the Chapter Quizzes link.

Integration of Technologies

Digital Resources

Web-Based, Networked, and Stand-Alone Resources

Digital resources do not necessarily share the same point of access. For web-based resources, they are on websites that anyone with an internet connection can access. Networked resources also require an internet connection but are limited only to those who share the network. Accessing the network allows for research sharing, which enables schools to expand the breadth of information in a cooperative manner. Stand-alone resources are a collection of files such as articles or pictures specifically uploaded to a library webpage or database for research. If a library offers stand-alone resources, an internet connection is not necessary to access those resources. Using a digital device, a student can search and view digital material that has been saved to files.

Providing Digital Resources

For students and faculty to use digital resources in the LMC or remotely, the LMS must ensure they have access by doing the following:

- Report internet outages or network disruptions to the IT department immediately.
- Post links on the library webpage to all digital resources. Links should be tested periodically for connectivity. If a broken link is identified, the LMC should troubleshoot with the assistance of the IT department or vendor.
- Keep track of database and e-book subscription renewal dates to avoid a lapse in service. This may include working with the business office by submitting purchase orders and ensuring payment in a timely manner.
- Apprise students and faculty of current usernames and passwords when necessary.

These measures help build confidence in the LMC.

Teaching Students to Locate Information Digitally

The LMS will teach search strategies as part of information literacy classes. This starts with elementary concepts such as basic terminology (e.g., keyword, search bar, browser) and simple keyword searching. As students progress and research needs deepen, the LMS will introduce new vocabulary (e.g., Boolean Operator, filter, platform, advanced search) and platforms and demonstrate how and when to use them. By modeling searches in catalogs, databases, and e-books, the LMS can empower students to choose the best platform for their research needs and teach them how to narrow results using advanced search functions and filters.

Criteria to Consider When Evaluating Information

To ensure students are using the most relevant, reliable, and accurate information, the LMS should encourage them to evaluate sources using the following criteria:

- Why is this information valuable for my research? With so many resources available, students can choose the information that best suits their research needs.
- When was the information published? Students should be encouraged to use the most current information for research.
- Who is responsible for the information? Students should check the credentials or reputation of the author or publisher responsible for the information.

- Where does the information come from? The information should come from a reliable website or academic journal.
- What does the site state as the purpose for offering the information? Students can determine if the information is biased.

Uploading and Downloading Files

Uploading and downloading files refers to the sending and receiving of information. An internet connection is necessary to successfully upload and download files. Uploading is electronically sending information from locally stored files. An upward-facing arrow icon usually denotes the upload function. Downloading is receiving files from elsewhere. A down-facing arrow usually indicates the download function, and the files are often automatically stored. Files which have been downloaded can be recalled and viewed without an internet connection; however, any edits would be saved solely on the downloaded version. Uploaded and downloaded files are used often in research for saving or sending useful information or creating stand-alone libraries.

Promoting Netiquette

Netiquette is a term that concerns proper etiquette over the internet. The LMS will remind students to demonstrate the same level of respect virtually as they do in person. This is an age-appropriate concept that needs to be revisited each year, and it includes searching, sending, and receiving appropriate materials; using acceptable language; and treating others respectfully. As part of information literacy, the LMS will promote responsible digital use by teaching classes on using sources legally. Students will learn how to avoid plagiarism by properly paraphrasing, quoting, and summarizing, as well as knowing how and when to cite sources.

Encouraging Habitual and Adequate Use of Information Resources

In order to best use resources and information from the library, students will require direct instruction. Research projects using an established inquiry-based research model are the most prominent way to give this instruction. When posed with a question or when posing their own question, students should be able to identify the information needed to address the question. In order to best prepare students for locating information, the librarian should provide instruction on using both the physical and digital resources available in the library. This starts with accessing the catalog and using keywords to find resources. Locating these resources requires instruction on navigating the physical library space, like helping students find the nonfiction section or access virtual resources. The next step is assessing the validity of a resource. Students should be taught to consider the source, context, relevancy, and currency of the resource they are using to ensure it is valid. Resources should not be used if they are taken out of context, are outdated, or not from reliable sources. Once information has been pulled from resources, students can use it to connect ideas and draw conclusions to answer the aforementioned questions. Completing this process allows for students to grow comfortable with accessing resources and ensures they are able to do so successfully.

Ethical Information Use

Ethical information use provides writers and creators with credit for their works and protects the individual referencing them from any legal repercussions of plagiarism. Students should be taught how to properly use and cite information used in their writing in order to protect their academic integrity, and the school librarian is often responsible for covering this process in his or her instruction. When it comes to finding resources, students should be taught to evaluate their credibility by determining if they come from a reliable source, if they are current, and if they provide accurate information. Once credibility has been established, students should analyze the writing and establish what information is usable for their work. When doing this, students should ensure the content from which they are gathering their information is relevant to the subject they are researching. Using primary sources is often best. Ethical use comes in the way the students use these resources in their own work. In order to ensure proper and legal usage, students need to be taught proper citation, quotation, and paraphrasing in their writing and research projects.

Digital Resource Terms

- **Keyword:** A searchable word that best summarizes the desired content. In most cases, the main topic is the initial keyword.
- **Boolean Operator:** Words such as AND, OR, and NOT used in a search to narrow or broaden results.
- **Sort:** A search tool designed to target results by reorganizing them by relevance, date, or alphabetical listing.
- **Filter:** A search criteria checklist that allows for more relevant results.
- **Platform:** A particular technology, such as a search engine, database, or catalog, chosen to perform a search.
- **Advanced search:** A tool using Boolean Operators to allow for a multiple keyword search to narrow or broaden search results.

How Search Engines Work

The most popular search engine is Google, hence the phrase "Google search." Search engines are not the most effective digital research tool, and regardless of which search engine a student chooses, he or she is bound to be overwhelmed by the scope of results. Search engines, using keyword data, search the internet for related information and offer results in the form of websites, images, and social media posts. The results are not screened for accuracy or even validity, which passes that burden on to the student. Some offer advanced search functions and commands by which a student can manipulate the results. A Boolean type search can be conducted when AND, NOT, or OR are used with keywords. To put quotation marks ("") around a keyword phrase limits the results to the exact phrase. Many search engines also understand truncation, which is placing an asterisk (*) at the end of a root word so as to not limit search results to just one form of a word.

Directories

Directories are compilations of subject-specific resources students can use for research. They are sometimes known as pathfinders. Since the files in directories have been collected by an LMS, teachers, and others who are interested in promoting student achievement, the information can usually be trusted as a valid source. Directories can include links and references to both print and nonprint items. Print references are usually books, identified by bibliographical information. Digital items usually include a URL link. The LMS can prepare a directory by conducting a subject search of library catalogs and databases. The information is compiled into a list and then uploaded onto the library webpage or printed and kept at the circulation desk.

Managing Email

In addition to communicating with individuals, the LMS will want to connect through email with larger groups. This may be accomplished by creating or joining an email list called a Listserv. A Listserv is a collection of email addresses that is managed through one central address and designated to a particular group. An LMS might be included on a Listserv with other professionals or could create one for book club members. Groups can be named so emails will target the proper recipients. Listservs can also be used to communicate only one way. An LMS can choose to join a prescribed Listserv that only sends out information and does not accept replies. This is common when subscribing to newsletters. If the email group is large enough to justify the cost, it can be managed through businesses such as Mailchimp, ConvertKit, or Constant Contact.

Criteria for Validating Information

Most research information comes from outside sources and should be validated before being submitted or presented. The information should be checked for bias and accuracy. Bias refers to information that attempts to affect the reader's opinion on the subject or only provides one point of view. This is most common when researching controversial topics. One way a user can avoid citing biased information is to closely examine the source. Most legitimate sites will offer a page that describes the identity and mission of the authors. With that information in mind, the user can better determine whether the information may be skewed. To validate accuracy, the user must consider the credentials of the author. Most research articles will offer references to information that can be verified. Information that differs significantly from other sources should especially be checked.

Web 2.0

Web 2.0 is a term coined to describe the state of the current digital capabilities available to 21st-century learners. It replaced Web 1.0, with the main difference being broader internet access due to greater worldwide connectivity, which enabled more widespread sharing and collaboration. In Web 1.0, information could be researched but not easily shared. In our Web 2.0 world, much more information can be made available through many different platforms. This creates both positive and negative experiences because while a wider resource pool is overall a good thing, it can also be overwhelming. The LMS can make searching the Web 2.0 more manageable with information literacy lessons designed to teach students to narrow and evaluate results.

Digital Library

A digital library, also known as a paperless library, offers all its resources in a digital format. The resources may be scanned copies of print resources or links to databases, articles, and e-books. Students have many options for accessing these resources. Usually they can be read from any device, downloaded, emailed, or printed. The resources in a digital library represent the most current information on a topic because publishers can replace or update information as necessary. Unless the student is accessing a stand-alone library, an internet connection is necessary.

Online Collaboration Tools

Web 2.0 technology offers students the ability to share information with a variety of collaboration tools. For example, email allows students to send documents back and forth for composition and editing. Most students have an email address, and email is free to use, making this a popular option. Another free tool for collaborating is an online, collaborative word processing service like Google Docs. Some institutions subscribe to software that offers an online collaboration space that multiple students can use remotely and simultaneously to work together. For the LMS, these tools are useful for emailing research articles or uploading them to a group collaboration space for student use. Using Web 2.0 tools also offers the opportunity for positive social interactions because, when collaborating, students can practice sharing ideas and respecting others' contributions.

Online Textbooks and Notebooks

Digital textbooks and notebooks are electronic resources that are growing in popularity. These take the place of print textbooks or paper notebooks as curriculum aids. Online textbooks are digital or scanned versions of print textbooks. Since students are provided textbooks by their school district, there is no need for the LMC to purchase them, but the LMS can still be helpful by instructing students on how to use them effectively. Online textbooks are similar to e-books and offer tools that are helpful when studying that would not be allowed in print textbooks, like underlining and highlighting. Some software packages, like Microsoft, offer an online notebook that enables students to organize their work under tabs. Teachers can upload information and assignments to the notebook, and the LMS can upload resource links.

Remote Access

Remote Access Tools

As a core resource offered by the modern library, **remote access** allows users to access and use **e-resources** from anywhere they can access the internet. Once a user's online identity is verified by logging in with his or her library credentials—typically a username and password—the patron will have access to the library's available digital resources. These resources may sometimes be limited or differ to what is available in or through the library due to licensing and user agreements with vendors and publishers. Most commonly, the available resources include databases of electronic information for research, e-books, video resources, and access to the circulation system.

Remote access is a beneficial tool in distance learning as it eliminates the need to be present to gain access to needed resources. Additionally, remote access increases library resource usage because patrons don't have to physically access the library and can access resources at any time.

Online Catalogs

Online catalogs are electronically accessible bibliographic databases that organize all materials available in and through a library, including both physical and digital resources. Using search terms and filters, patrons can search the collection to find resources and information to suit their needs. The procedure following the selection of a resource will vary based on the resource type.

For physical resources available in the library, there are two options. Patrons may use the location information to find the resource in the collection themselves or they may place it on **hold.** Placing a resource on hold notifies the librarian via the library management system that the material has been requested and should be located, pulled, and reserved for this patron. Holding a resource through the catalog requires patrons to log in and verify their identity using their library-assigned credentials.

Digital resources are available for immediate access. Patrons will once again verify their identity using their library-assigned credentials and can then access the resource online or download where applicable.

Databases

Databases are collections of electronically stored information and are accessible through a library's website. They organize and provide quick retrieval of information for users. In school libraries, databases are most commonly used for research and require the library to have a subscription to their service. Users must verify their online identity in order to access information. Because information needs will vary among students due to factors such as grade level, interests, or assigned topics, it is important that the librarian select the database most appropriate for the student's needs. Some databases provide more controlled searches by allowing only predetermined terms to be entered into the search bar, while other databases allow searches of any keywords as well as the ability to use Boolean search methods to narrow down desired results. It is the responsibility of the librarian to select the most appropriate database(s) and provide instruction on how to appropriately and effectively interact with it.

WEB LINKS

Web links, synonymous with **hyperlinks**, are clickable words or images that link the user to a website or additional resource, typically providing access to information. Their primary functions are to provide direct links to sites and sources referenced in writing. They can also be used to provide access to publicly available resources that may be useful in completing research or other assignments. Web links are commonly used in pathfinders**. Pathfinders** serve as pathways to more information on specific topics and use web links to provide direct access to information. They provide guided and controlled access to information on the web. Web links may also be embedded. By embedding a link in an image, information and resources become more easily accessible to those with limited reading abilities. This allows for usage across grade and content levels.

DISTANCE LEARNING

Distance learning, also sometimes referred to as **distance education,** is the process through which lessons and materials are presented to an audience who is not physically present in the room with the teacher. This is sometimes done in the event of school closures, but some programs use it as the standard form of education. Libraries are equipped to assist both students and teachers with distance learning in a variety of ways. Primarily, they function as a resource bank and access point. Both students and teachers can remotely access a variety of digital resources online through the library, such as e-books, databases, pathfinders (also commonly referred to as LibGuides), homework help, and many others. For teachers, resources for professional development are typically available through the library to help provide adequate distance-learning lessons and activities. Librarians can create tool kits of resources for teachers to use based on grade level, skill, content, or learning goal.

Materials and Resources

MATERIALS AND RESOURCES THAT ENHANCE STUDENT LEARNING AND ENGAGEMENT

INSTRUCTIONAL MATERIALS AND RESOURCES

The careful selection of instructional materials and resources for lesson plans is an integral component of enhancing student engagement and the overall learning experience. Lesson materials should be relevant to students' interests so as to facilitate personal connections to learning and ultimately, deepen understanding. In building positive relationships with students by educating themselves on students' backgrounds and interests, teachers can effectively locate and implement varied instructional materials and resources that are relevant to students and foster motivation for learning. Additionally, interactive materials, such as manipulatives or other hands-on learning resources, enhance learning and engagement through encouraging participation. Similarly, cooperative learning materials encourage student participation and engagement through fostering collaboration. Teachers can also enhance learning experiences through incorporating authentic materials that are relevant to instruction such as maps, brochures, historical documents, or similar materials that enhance student engagement and learning.

TECHNOLOGICAL RESOURCES

Technology is integrated in nearly every aspect of life as a tool to enhance and assist in daily activities. This notion also applies in the classroom, as technological resources are an excellent method of increasing student engagement and interest, supporting students in their individual learning needs, and enhancing learning. The use of computers, tablets, smartphones, and other technological resources serve to improve understanding of classroom instruction, foster relevancy and personal connections, and scaffold instruction to address diverse learning styles and needs. Additionally, teachers have myriad digital resources available in the form of interactive websites, videos clips, and apps that can be implemented to enrich lessons and increase development across all subject areas. Often, these resources accommodate students' individual learning needs through providing increasingly challenging activities based on individual skill level, and the teacher can utilize these resources to tailor instruction to address individual student needs. Technological resources can also add authenticity to learning experiences, making them more engaging and enhancing student learning. Virtual field trips or science experiments can provide real-world connections to instruction by recreating authentic learning experiences without students having to leave the classroom.

Community Resources

Community resources are beneficial in enriching instruction to foster engagement and enhance student learning. They provide students the opportunity to connect and apply what they learn in the classroom with the real world. This ultimately makes learning more authentic, as students are able to see the relevancy of what they are learning. This enhances learning by making it more engaging. Through field trips, teachers can incorporate community resources such as museums, art exhibits, science centers, and even local areas such as parks or historical sites into curriculum to accompany material learned in class. Additionally, if access to field trips is limited, teachers can take advantage of community outreach programs that bring learning experiences to classrooms. Reaching out to members of the community that are relevant to topics being covered in class, such as scientists or local historians, can be beneficial in allowing students to understand how what they are learning is applicable outside of the classroom. Locating and implementing community resources enhances student learning and engagement through making learning authentic, relevant, and applicable in the real world.

Developmentally Appropriate Materials and Resources

To create engaging and effective learning experiences, instructional materials and resources must be developmentally appropriate. Teachers must have a solid understanding of the general cognitive, physical, social, and emotional developmental levels of their students as well as individual differences in skills and abilities to properly select developmentally appropriate materials. The age and developmental level appropriateness of instructional resources can be determined by considering the material's size, height, and level of difficulty for students. Whether materials accommodate individual differences in skill level, ability, or interest can be determined by their versatility. If a resource can be used in multiple ways, it will appeal to a variety of learning needs and interests and support development across domains. Developmentally appropriate materials are reflective and considerate of students' diversities. Teachers can determine this by using their knowledge of students' backgrounds to select materials that incorporate and are sensitive to their students' cultural differences to support development by fostering personal connections to learning.

Technology Use in the Classroom

Significance of Technology in Instruction

Rapid advancements in technology systems and operations require the teacher to actively educate themselves on new developments to effectively plan, organize, deliver, and evaluate instruction. Most students are **digital natives**, meaning they have grown up accustomed to using technology in their daily lives and are familiar with its functions. As such, the teacher must be proficient with current technology and how to effectively incorporate it into daily instruction to create a relevant, interesting, and engaging learning environment. Understanding how to utilize and implement new technology resources improves a teacher's effectiveness in planning, organizing, and delivering differentiated instruction, as it enables them to derive material from a multitude of resources that appeal to students' individual needs and interests. In addition, it improves the teacher's ability to collaborate with other teachers for instructional planning and communicate with students, families, and colleagues. This ultimately enhances the learning experience by providing individualized, student-centered, and interactive instruction to promote engagement and support academic success. Additionally, understanding the functions of current technology systems and operations enhances the planning, organization, and evaluation of instruction by enabling the teacher to effectively utilize relevant digital productivity tools.

Incorporation into Daily Classroom Activities

Numerous educational technology resources are available to enhance all aspects of daily instruction. Digital tools can be highly beneficial in increasing student engagement, participation, and understanding, as well as addressing a variety of learning needs. Technology resources such as presentation slides, video clips, or audio books, can be used to introduce new topics or supplement instruction. Teachers can also create an **online classroom** in which they deliver instruction as well as provide students opportunities to collaborate in a digital workspace, ask questions, participate in discussions, turn in assignments, and receive feedback. Online activities such as WebQuests or digital scavenger hunts are valuable in allowing students to explore new concepts or research information while interacting with authentic digital resources. Teachers can also incorporate **total participation activities** to conduct formative assessments using technology resources, such as online surveys, polls, or games (such as word clustering games). In addition, students can prepare for assessments by utilizing resources such as online flashcards, quizzes, or review games. **Educational experiences** can also be supplemented using technology resources. For example, digital science experiments can reinforce concepts learned in the classroom. Additionally, virtual field trips allow students to explore locations they may otherwise be unable to visit.

Safe and Appropriate Use of Technology

Issues That May Be Encountered

Technology provides valuable learning tools, yet the teacher must be mindful of issues that may arise regarding safety and appropriateness when planning, organizing, delivering, and evaluating instruction. When using the internet, social media, and digital resources, students may be vulnerable to inappropriate or unsafe content. The teacher must assess all digital material when planning and organizing instruction to ensure that content, advertisements, and search engine results are **safe**, **instructionally applicable**, and respectful of **students' privacy**. Student misuse of technology is a common issue that may be exacerbated when students are permitted to bring their own devices to class. **Misuse** includes using technology for off-task activities, accessing inappropriate websites, apps, or social media, and engaging in cyberbullying. It is important that the teacher establish clear expectations for the use of personal devices and take proper measures to block access to non-instructional material to ensure students engage with technology appropriately. Students may encounter individuals online that subject them to harmful or inappropriate communication. In addition to ensuring that students remain on task, the teacher must frequently monitor students' technology use to ensure they are not engaging with individuals or materials that may ask them to divulge personal details or compromise their safety.

Importance of Educating Students on Appropriate Technology Use

Educating students on appropriate technology use establishes a focused, engaged, and safe learning environment. When teachers **model** and **instruct** students on appropriate and responsible practices, they develop an awareness of the immediate and future implications of their online behavior. This ultimately teaches students to make informed decisions that protect their safety and privacy when using digital resources both within and outside of the classroom. Establishing clear procedures and expectations for technology discourages misuse, as it helps ensure that students are focused, on task, and engage appropriately with technology as a learning tool to enhance instruction. In addition, it teaches students how to interact with others online safely and responsibly using proper **digital citizenship**. It also teaches students how to respond if they encounter inappropriate content or behavior. When the teacher effectively educates students on proper technology use, it becomes an efficient and valuable instructional resource that enhances the overall learning experience.

Privacy Guidelines

To establish a safe learning environment in which all students are protected, it is imperative that teachers consistently adhere to strict privacy guidelines. Teachers must ensure that all of their actions and practices within and outside of the classroom align with **FERPA** as well as state and district laws regarding student privacy. Additionally, teachers must be well informed on and follow the privacy policies of their individual schools. Students' **personal information**, including grade histories, attendance and discipline records, medical histories, special needs, addresses, birthdays, and any other sensitive details must remain confidential. In an increasingly digital learning environment, it is important that teachers make sure photographs, video recordings, or names of students are not shared online or on social media without proper consent. When students interact with digital resources in the classroom, their data is often collected and recorded, so teachers must be cognizant of what information is shared, select technology resources appropriately, and instruct students not to divulge any personal information about themselves online. Following strict privacy guidelines is necessary in protecting all students' rights to confidentiality.

Copyright Laws

When creating, planning, and delivering instruction, teachers must consider copyright laws before selecting or distributing materials and resources to ensure they do not infringe upon the creator's rights. While teachers are often given flexibility regarding the **Copyright Law** under the **Fair Use Doctrine**, they must be mindful to ensure that accessing, copying, and utilizing unpurchased materials, content, resources, or images falls under this doctrine to avoid copyright infringement. Teachers must make certain that all resources are used explicitly for instructional purposes and avoid reproducing and distributing entire works for individual student use. Teachers should, instead, copy or display excerpts. To avoid potential copyright infringement when planning and delivering instruction, teachers can either ask creators for permission to use their work or ask their schools, districts, or students to purchase the material. Teachers can further protect themselves by citing the source of all retrieved and distributed content. Utilizing free instructional material that is not covered under the Copyright Law, including facts and resources within the **public domain** or **Creative Commons**, as well as government records, pictures, and maps, allows teachers to avoid copyright infringement when creating, planning, and delivering instruction.

Fair Use Doctrine, Public Domain, and Creative Commons

Fair Use Doctrine	• The Fair Use Doctrine allows educators to use, reproduce, and redistribute copyrighted materials for educational purposes so long as they adhere to specified guidelines. These guidelines are typically categorized as: • **Purpose**: Materials must be used for educational, nonprofit purposes to achieve a specific learning objective. • **Nature**: The nature of the work refers to the type of copyrighted work being reproduced (fictional/nonfictional, consumable) • **Amount**: Reproduction and redistribution must be limited to a small portion of the creator's work, such as an excerpt from a book. • **Effect**: Reproduction and redistribution may not interfere with the creator's ability to substantially profit from his or her work in the future.
Public Domain	Materials in the public domain are not protected under copyright laws and are free for use, reproduction, or redistribution. This includes government or historical documents, speeches, ideas, or facts and works published before March 1, 1989 that do not have an official copyright license. Copyrighted works in the United States enter the public domain 70 years after the death of the original creator.
Creative Commons	Creative Commons is an organization in which creators can reserve partial copyrights to their original works while relinquishing others to allow for public use, reproduction, and redistribution. This organization is intended to provide educators with access to learning materials, resources, and original works to incorporate into their classroom.

Acceptable Use Policies

Acceptable use policies are integral to establishing a classroom environment in which all students and staff engage with technology safely and appropriately. An acceptable use policy is an **agreement** between students, families, the school, and the district to ensure users are **accountable** for their use of technology and online behavior. These policies outline specific guidelines and **expectations** to make users aware of safe and responsible practices regarding technology use in the classroom and help to prevent inappropriate behavior by defining clear **consequences** for violating the terms. In addition, acceptable use policies are beneficial in informing students, staff, and families of the actions taken to protect students' privacy and safety when using technology in the classroom, such as blocking access to inappropriate or non-instructional websites. When acceptable use policies are successfully implemented and followed, students, teachers, and families are protected while interacting with digital materials in the classroom, ensuring a safe and appropriate learning environment.

Review Video: Benefits of Technology in the Classroom
Visit mometrix.com/academy and enter code: 536375

Digital Etiquette

Digital etiquette refers to a set of guidelines for **appropriate** and **responsible** interaction with technology and individuals online. These guidelines emphasize the importance of engaging with individuals online politely and respectfully in a considerate manner, just as they would in face-to-face communication. This includes using appropriate language, respecting others' opinions, and avoiding engaging in harmful interactions or content online. In addition, digital etiquette outlines how to adjust communication styles based on one's audience to ensure proper and professional interactions. Digital etiquette also defines proper measures for protecting oneself and others when engaging online. This includes avoiding potentially harmful situations such as providing personal information about oneself or others, communicating with individuals whom one does not know, and carefully considering the present and future implications of one's online behavior. As a teacher, following and instilling these guidelines in students is integral to establishing a positive learning environment in which students safely and responsibly interact with technology. Digital etiquette provides teachers and students with a framework for acceptable technology use and online behavior that is necessary for success in an increasingly digital world.

Effective Incorporation of Technology in Instruction Process

To enhance the quality of the overall instructional process, teachers must thoughtfully consider a variety of aspects regarding which technology resources will be most valuable in increasing efficiency and effectiveness. Teachers must determine **desired learning outcomes** and evaluate which technologies will be most beneficial in planning, organizing, delivering, and evaluating instruction. They must evaluate the **efficacy** of the resource in supporting students as they achieve learning targets. This includes ensuring that technology resources are current, relevant, and effective in enhancing the delivery of comprehensible and engaging instruction. When determining which technologies to implement for student use, teachers must assess the **developmental appropriateness** of the technologies as well as whether the resources are **adaptable** to individual differences, learning needs, and interests. Additionally, it is important that teachers ensure that technology resources foster **interaction** and **active learning** among students so as to support curiosity and engagement in learning. As **equity** issues regarding technology may exist within the classroom, the teacher must consider what supports may need to be implemented to properly support students in achieving learning targets. Students' safety and privacy when utilizing technology is paramount; therefore, the teacher must be certain that selected digital resources protect students from harmful content.

Developmentally Appropriate Selection of Technology for Instruction

Student learning and achievement is maximized when the teacher applies knowledge of **developmentally appropriate** practices, activities, and materials to selecting technology resources that enhance instruction. Teachers must understand the characteristics and needs of developmental stages, including age-related and individual learning differences across domains. This knowledge enables the teacher to implement technology that supports achievement when planning and delivering instruction. Effectively applying this knowledge requires the teacher to incorporate digital resources that provide **age** and **individually appropriate** challenges to facilitate developmental growth. This includes integrating technology that supports instruction by stimulating engagement, curiosity, and exploration. Developmentally appropriate technology provides appropriate levels of difficulty, interaction, and active learning opportunities based upon students' developmental stage while accommodating individual needs, interests, and abilities. Additionally, in developmentally appropriate practice, the teacher integrates technology resources to accompany instructional activities for a length of time that is beneficial to students relative to their developmental stage to maximize learning benefits.

Integrating Technology to Promote Creativity and Innovation

The availability of digital resources allows the teacher to provide students with multiple opportunities to develop their creativity and innovation in all areas of instruction. When integrated to accompany learning, technology is highly beneficial in allowing students to navigate new ways to **construct knowledge**, **generate ideas**, and **create products**. Effectively incorporating technology for these purposes requires the teacher to consider the instructional topic, specific skills they intend to develop, desired learning outcomes, and students' individual needs and interests. This knowledge enables the teacher to determine which digital resources are most engaging, applicable, and beneficial in providing a learning environment that enhances creativity and innovation among students. For example, digital storytelling resources are effective in enhancing creative writing in language arts, virtual labs can enhance science instruction, and digital drawing apps can enrich artistic creativity for creating new ideas and products. During instruction, assuming the role of facilitator while allowing flexibility for appropriate student choice is an effective strategy for allowing the expression of creativity as students manipulate digital tools for the development of knowledge, ideas, and products. It is important to note, however, that technology in the classroom should be used intentionally to enhance, rather than replace, instruction.

The effective integration of technology into instruction is invaluable in promoting creative thinking and innovation among students when constructing and generating knowledge, new ideas, and products. With the vast array of available technology for instructional use, the teacher can select from a multitude of resources on a variety of topics to enhance instruction and accommodate students' varying learning styles, needs, and interests. The incorporation of technology facilitates the creative and innovative process while promoting **critical thinking** and **problem-solving** abilities by allowing students to explore, manipulate, and learn the functions of digital tools in a way that is relevant to them. This encourages students to employ **higher-order thinking** skills as they make connections between the capabilities of digital resources and their application in solving problems and creating new ideas and products. Using technology to support instruction increases engagement and enhances the overall learning experience. Students' understanding is deepened as they construct knowledge using technology resources.

Equity Issues in the Classroom Related to the Use of Technology

The integration of technology to enhance learning is a valuable and increasingly prevalent component of instruction; however, equity issues related to the use of technology pose significant impacts on teaching and learning. Schools in **rural** or **socioeconomically disadvantaged** districts may lack the necessary funding to provide all students with technology devices for classroom use. Economically underprivileged students may lack internet access, computers, and digital devices at home or access to a public library, thus impeding their ability to complete assignments outside of class that require technology use. During instructional activities that require students to bring personal digital devices for participation, students without their own devices face inequity that hinders their ability to engage in learning. In addition, students who lack access to digital resources often face challenges in the classroom, as they may not have developed the same knowledge regarding technology use and functions as classmates with more experience. Equity issues related to technology access and use can negatively impact academic achievement. It is imperative that teachers are mindful of potential inequities that exist within their classrooms when planning instruction to properly address them and support student success.

Identifying and Addressing Issues

As technology becomes increasingly integrated into daily life, inequities among students are more apparent and pose significant impacts to achievement. Identifying disparities related to technology is integral to applying equitable practices to ensure that students are supported. To properly identify digital equity issues, teachers must recognize some of the **causal factors**, including socioeconomic status, race, and geographic location, and determine the presence of these factors in their districts. Additionally, teachers must be aware of individual students' backgrounds and needs to identify potential inequities regarding technology. Applying **equitable practices** to address these issues ensures all students have equal academic opportunities. It cannot be assumed that all students have devices or access to computers and the internet at home, so teachers should avoid requiring technology use outside of the classroom when possible. If the school is financially able, students can be issued equipment such as devices and hotspots to establish equity. Teachers can also provide alternative, paper assignments that achieve the same outcomes as the technology-based version if school devices are unavailable. In the classroom, teachers can provide time during, before, and after the school day for technology use as well as provide available school-issued devices for activities.

Effectively Addressing Equity Issues

Access to technology and familiarity with its functions is vital for success in the modern-day classroom. Implementing appropriate measures for addressing inequities among students regarding technology use is imperative in supporting and facilitating academic achievement. By consciously applying **equitable practices**, teachers and staff ensure that all students are provided with the necessary support for access to technology and digital resources for instructional use. In addition, promptly identifying and addressing equity issues ensures that students are able to keep pace with their peers in regard to understanding how to utilize digital resources to maximize their learning. Applying equitable practices to support students that lack access to technology helps close the achievement gap by providing all students with equal opportunities for academic achievement.

Chapter Quiz

Ready to see how well you retained what you just read? Scan the QR code to go directly to the chapter quiz interface for this study guide. If you're using a computer, simply visit the online resources page at **mometrix.com/resources719/nbptslibmecya** and click the Chapter Quizzes link.

Access, Equity, and Diversity

Equal Access to Services and Programs

Americans with Disabilities Act

The **Americans with Disabilities Act (ADA)** is a 1990 federal law designed to prevent discrimination against disabled individuals. Compliance with ADA standards is meant to increase accessibility and decrease inequity for the disabled community in public spaces. In regard to the school library setting, these standards impact the design of the physical space, assistive technology, and the collection itself.

To increase accessibility of physical spaces, it is required that doorways be 32 inches wide to accommodate wheelchairs and that floors be kept clear and spacious enough for mobility aid users to approach and maneuver within the area. Table height must also be able to accommodate mobility aids when students are seated or working at the table. Assistive technology in the library, such as text readers or magnifiers, should be kept easily accessible. Additionally, tools used to access digital resources should be equipped with adaptive technology such as screen readers, zooming tools, and high-contrast settings. The library collection should also represent the disabled community. Fiction books with disabled characters and nonfiction books covering the topic of disabilities should be available.

Library Bill of Rights

Adopted by the American Library Association (ALA) in 1939, the **Library Bill of Rights** is a set of principles meant to uphold First Amendment rights as they relate to libraries. It serves to protect access for patrons in all libraries, and these protections extend to the school library.

In adherence to the Library Bill of Rights, school library materials should not be excluded on the basis of views pertaining to them, the background or origin of the materials, or personal opinion. Materials expressing multiple viewpoints should be made available where appropriate and should not be censored outside of appropriateness for age. Regarding further censorship, it is the responsibility of the library to challenge attempts of censorship from any sources, including but not limited to parents, political groups, and religious organizations. The Library Bill of Rights also protects the privacy of students and any information regarding how they use the library.

Accommodations for Patrons with Visual Impairments

Appropriate accommodations should be made to increase accessibility for visually impaired patrons, such as including assistive technology, modifying existing physical spaces and signage, and adjusting the library collection. **Assistive technology** is any item or tool used to increase the accessibility of an existing resource. For visually impaired individuals using online or digital resources, this usually consists of screen readers and high-contrast or zoom settings. When using physical resources, these technologies may include magnifiers or the addition of tactile markers in books. It is best practice to maintain the aforementioned resources as well as any adapted, braille, or large print books in such a way they are easily movable and able to be delivered closer to the student as needed (e.g., a cart of adapted resources). Assistance with circulation procedures, such as checking in or out and scanning barcodes, should be provided as required by individual impairments. Individuals using mobility aids such as canes should be able to move safely and freely within the library space. This means maintaining large, clear areas around the collection. The size and contrast of signage within the library can be increased to improve readability where needed, such as on collection markers.

Accommodations for Patrons with Physical Impairments

While the ADA mandates physical layout requirements, other accommodations can be made where appropriate to best fit the physical needs of patrons. Some examples include the size and placement of the circulation desk; the height of shelves; and the size, height, and placement of tables. Both the digital and physical collection should be representative of and meet the needs of patrons with physical disabilities. This can include adding audiobooks, which eliminate the need to hold a book and turn pages, as well as adding tools like book holders and page turners to make books already in the collection more accessible.

Not all students with physical disabilities will be able to access the library space in person, so it is vital to consider them when making decisions on digitally accessible resources. For students who can visit, additional assistance can be provided by storing adapted resources in easy-to-access ways, such as on a cart or in movable storage that can be pushed to the students where they are seated or to an area with ample clear space. If the circulation system is not easily accessible or moveable, students can be assisted by having a peer helper or the librarian check their books in or out.

Accommodations for Patrons with Sensory Processing Disorders

Sensory processing disorders impact the way an individual's brain processes external stimuli. These stimuli can include lights, sounds, smells, visual cues, textures, or any other stimulation revolving around the senses. Most often, students with sensory disorders will bring their own aids to assist in coping with their responses to stimuli; however, there are steps that can be taken to prevent overstimulation in the library when the librarian is aware of these sensory considerations in their patrons.

Visual schedules of activities and routines set to take place that day help students to see and understand the flow of programming and help to prevent them from becoming overwhelmed. Keeping the library dimly lit (or at least not overwhelmingly bright) and devoid of overstimulating colors and patterns in decor will prevent overstimulation in students with visual concerns. For patrons with auditory concerns, consider the use of white noise in addition to maintaining an overall low volume in the area. To prevent decision fatigue and overstimulation when selecting books for checkout, a small, curated collection of books can be offered to students individually.

Specific Learning Needs

A **specific learning need** is any academic, physical, or behavioral concern or difference in an individual that impacts learning. This includes learning disabilities, difficulty or inability to see or hear, behavioral disorders, or communication disorders. Students with these needs require modified instruction. Students with visual impairments may benefit from media available in large print or audio versions and the availability of magnifying devices. Students with hearing impairments will need a written form of any audio media used, which can be a transcript or captioning where available. Physical impairments are addressed in a variety of ways but may require the use of modified media tailored to the specific student. For example, writing utensils, scissors, and other supplies may be modified to create the appropriate grip for the student. For students with behavioral concerns, modified instruction may be required. This often requires the use of multiple forms of media, like video or audio, to meet their individual learning needs. Communication disorders are often addressed through media containing imagery in two-way communication.

Assessing Student Reading Levels

While it is not typically the responsibility of school librarians to assess student reading levels, they should be knowledgeable of the methods their school uses and know how to interpret those results in order to best serve their students. Depending on the testing program used, students are typically given an assessment that determines their ability to read and comprehend and then equates their ability with a Lexile level, a Developmental Reading Assessment level, a Guided Reading level, or a particular grade level and month within that grade level that reflects what a student should be able to comprehend at that time. By understanding the process and the meaning of these levels, librarians can more adequately recommend books for their readers to use independently. It may also be necessary for the librarian to modify library assignments for students based on their individual reading levels. Lower reading levels may be caused by documented learning disabilities. As such, it is imperative librarians be aware of Individualized Education Programs (IEPs) or 504 plans for their students and modify instruction to meet needs. Librarians may enrich instruction for students with higher abilities by providing books written on a higher reading level that still contain age-appropriate content.

Resources for Multilingual and Multicultural Populations

Multilingual and multicultural students are an integral part of many school communities and need to be served in ways that meet their specialized needs. Students learning English may need access to language dictionaries or devices that allow them to access translation software throughout their day at school and potentially at home to complete school-related work. In the library specifically, it is important to maintain an up-to-date section of the collection with books, both classics and current popular titles, in students' home languages. Not only does this allow students to independently use library resources, but it also allows teachers access to translated literature to use in the classroom. Multicultural students should also be represented in the collection. Fiction and nonfiction titles available in the collection should be free of any stereotypes and biases, and they should be representative of all students.

Equal Access

As the term implies, **equal access** describes an ideal scenario in which every individual has the same full access to resources and information as his or her peers. In a library setting, this means equal access to resources and facilities. While there are a variety of barriers to consider, some of the most common are physical, visual, auditory, or mental impairments, language barriers, and socioeconomic concerns. Adjustments can and should be made to the physical space of the library to accommodate students. The addition of tools and technologies to assist students in accessing the existing collection will be necessary in some cases, like magnifiers, screen readers, or text-to-speech devices. It may also be necessary to add resources to the collection in the form of audio and large print books. For students with language barriers, it may be necessary to add titles in students' primary language, especially for popular and high-demand titles. Consider reducing or eliminating fees and fines for overdue and lost books. Requiring students to pay to continue accessing information creates a socioeconomic barrier and further prevents equal access. Accommodations look different in every library to best meet the needs of the population being served.

Chapter Quiz

Ready to see how well you retained what you just read? Scan the QR code to go directly to the chapter quiz interface for this study guide. If you're using a computer, simply visit the online resources page at **mometrix.com/resources719/nbptslibmecya** and click the Chapter Quizzes link.

Ethics

Legislation Related to the School Library

Children's Internet Protection Act

Congress enacted the **Children's Internet Protection Act (CIPA)** in 2000. The overall purpose of CIPA is to ensure that children are protected from exposure to explicit internet content, such as anything considered obscene as defined by Miller v. California, anything considered harmful to children, or pornography. While it has previously been deemed unconstitutional for the federal government to limit access to particular topics in school libraries, Congress used the Universal Service Fund (USF) to force compliance. The USF provides telecommunication subsidies, and any school using the USF to receive discounted rates on internet services is required to install internet filtering software to prevent access to obscene sites and materials in order to be in compliance with CIPA. The filters must remain active during all searches conducted by minors. Failure to adhere to these standards can result in loss of access to the USF funds.

Children's Online Privacy Protection Act

Enacted in 1998 and effective in 2000, the **Children's Online Privacy Protection Act (COPPA)** is a federal law meant to protect the privacy rights of children under the age of 13. This was done in part to address internet marketing that specifically targeted young children as consumers. Under this law, sites that collect information from visitors must obtain parental consent before collecting any personal information from children under the age of 13, and parents and guardians retain the right to revoke these permissions and request all information collected be deleted. This law also addresses social media. Because of the work that must be done to verify permission, many websites and social media platforms do not allow access to their content to anyone under the age of 13. Failure to comply with COPPA can and has led to multimillion dollar fines for internet content creators and the platforms they use. Due to the restrictions COPPA has enacted, many sites will not be available for use by students in order to maintain the students' privacy. It is important that educators check the data collection and permissions of a website before having children visit it, even for educational purposes.

No Child Left Behind Act

Signed into law in January 2002, the **No Child Left Behind Act (NCLB)** was meant to support standards-based reforms to learning. As such, the act required that all states develop and administer standardized assessments as a measure for student knowledge. Additionally, it was meant to hold school districts accountable for bridging the gap between learners that were considered low performing and learners that were considered high performing based on testing data. Results from standardized tests were used to determine if a school had reached Adequate Yearly Progress (AYP). Schools that continually failed to meet AYP were sometimes required to submit corrective action plans, offer tutoring services to students, implement new curriculum, terminate a significant portion of staff, or possibly be closed or turned into a charter or similar school. Compliance with the act ensured access to funds that could be used to help meet these goals by covering the expenses of professional development and educational technology. The amount of money granted to each school was based on student enrollment. NCLB was replaced by the **Every Student Succeeds Act (ESSA)** in 2015.

Individuals with Disabilities Education Act

The **Individuals with Disabilities Education Act (IDEA)** was signed into law in 1990. It has six main components: Individualized Education Program (IEP), Free Appropriate Public Education (FAPE), Least Restrictive Environment (LRE), appropriate evaluation, parent and teacher participation, and procedural safeguards. An IEP is a document stating a child's disabilities, how they impact his or her school experience, and what accommodations must be made for this child. It is the duty of all educators to be aware of their students' IEPs and adhere to them. FAPE refers to the right that ensures all students with disabilities are given the proper accommodations at no cost to the student or family. The LRE part of IDEA outlines regulations for students with disabilities regarding what type of class they should be in, whether it be a general education class, a self-contained class, or some other type of class that best supports their needs. Appropriate evaluation requires students to be properly evaluated by a team of educators and service providers before receiving services. Parent and teacher participation outlines the requirements for keeping parents abreast of any changes regarding their child's status as it relates to IDEA and emphasizes the importance of parents and teachers working together. Lastly, procedural safeguards protect the rights of parents and teachers to challenge decisions related to services.

Section 504 of the Rehabilitation Act

The **Rehabilitation Act of 1973** is a federal law meant to protect the rights of individuals with disabilities, specifically in employment and education, through affirmative action, nondiscrimination, and "reasonable accommodations." **Section 504** of the Rehabilitation Act requires that "reasonable accommodations" be made for students or employees as deemed necessary by their disability. In a school setting, these accommodations can include extended testing times, additional breaks during testing, the use of assistive technology, unlimited access to the restroom, or any other accommodation needed for a student to successfully complete a required task. When a student's disabilities do not require an individualized instruction through an IEP, he or she is typically given a 504 Plan to ensure his or her needs are being met to ensure success. A 504 Plan covers a broader range of disabilities and impairments than an IEP plan, and it is also less detailed and structured.

USA Patriot Act

The **USA Patriot Act**, often referred to as the Patriot Act, was enacted in 2001 in response to the September 11th terrorist attacks and subsequent anthrax attacks. The purpose was to strengthen national security with a heightened focus on foreign terrorism. It included increased surveillance (e.g., wiretapping), increased penalties for crimes of terror, and easier resource sharing between government agencies. Regarding its impact on schools, the passing of the Patriot Act amended the Family Educational Rights and Privacy Act (FERPA) and made it possible for legal authorities to gain access to otherwise private student information without consent. The act was intended to be temporary and needed to be renewed each time the expiration date approached in order to remain in effect. The Patriot Act has been extended many times since its initial inception; however, in 2020, the House of Representatives did not pass a bill extending it, so it is no longer active.

Family Educational Rights and Privacy Act

The **Family Educational Rights and Privacy Act (FERPA)** is a federal law that was passed in 1974 with the purpose of protecting the privacy of students enrolled in school while also allowing parents to access student records. This law applies to any school, including universities, receiving federal funding. FERPA allows parents and guardians to request to see school records and documentation as it relates to their child at any time. They may also request documentation be amended as appropriate. In terms of privacy, FERPA disallows the disclosure of any information related to a child that could be considered an educational record. For example, a school may divulge contact information to create a directory; however, it may not attach any information regarding grades or coursework to this. FERPA also does not allow for adults within a school to discuss with students any educational records about other students. FERPA requires consent be given by parents of minor students or by students themselves if they are of age before any educational records may be released to any entity.

Major Court Cases Relating to the School Library

Island Trees v. Pico

Island Trees v. Pico refers to the landmark case that stemmed from an incident in which a group of students contested the removal of books deemed inappropriate from their school library. In the fall of 1975, a group of parents submitted a list of books available in the high school and junior high libraries that they felt were inappropriate. The school board agreed with the parents and removed the titles a few months later in 1976. Steven Pico, a 17-year-old student, along with four other students, argued that this removal was a violation of their First Amendment rights. The students felt the books were removed as part of personal and/or political agendas of decision-makers, and they took legal action to contest the removal. The US District Court for the Eastern District of New York sided with the decision of the school board to remove these books; however, the students appealed this, ultimately landing the case in the Supreme Court. It was decided in 1982 that the First Amendment places some limits school decision-makers from removing content from libraries, as doing so infringes on the rights of students. This is known as the first Supreme Court case to ever address information access in a school library as a right.

Tinker v. Des Moines

The **Tinker v. Des Moines** case is best known for protecting the right of nondisruptive freedom of expression within schools. In an effort to express their feelings about political and warfare action regarding Vietnam, a group of public school students in Des Moines in 1965 planned to begin wearing black armbands. Principals within the district announced that any students who chose to participate would be asked to remove their armband immediately and be suspended should they not comply. The students chose to contest this decision as they felt their First Amendment rights were being violated. The case came before the Supreme Court, and in 1969 it was decided that both students and teachers were to maintain their First Amendment rights within schools; as such, it was decided that so long as these expressions were not disruptive or interfering with the learning environment, the rights of students and teachers to express themselves were protected. In order to request students or teachers to remove any clothing they are using to make their statement, a school must be able to prove they are requesting the removal for reasons other than avoiding being uncomfortable with the opinion being expressed.

United States v. American Library Association (ALA)

Prior to the **United States v. American Library Association (ALA)**, the Children's Internet Protection Act (CIPA) was passed, stating that schools and libraries that received credits from federal funding to pay for internet must implement filtering software on internet-enabled devices used by students in effort to protect them from obscenities. The ALA felt that this act was a violation of First Amendment rights and challenged the law. The ALA won in the US District Court for the Eastern District of Pennsylvania, which determined that CIPA was indeed a violation of rights; however, the US government appealed this decision to the Supreme Court. In 2003, the Supreme Court reversed the decision of the district court and determined that CIPA was not unconstitutional and that the use of internet filtering software in schools and libraries was not a violation of First Amendment rights. As such, schools receiving the aforementioned federal assistance in paying for internet access are required by law to use filtering software or forfeit federal funding.

Reno v. American Civil Liberties Union (ACLU)

Reno v. American Civil Liberties Union (ACLU) was the first case that addressed the regulation of materials on the internet. Prior to this case, the **Communication Decency Act (CDA)** was passed in 1996 in an effort to protect minors on the internet by criminalizing the transmission of any obscene, indecent, or offensive materials or writings to anyone under the age of 18. The ACLU argued that this type of filtering was unconstitutional and would infringe on the rights of adults, leading them to file for a preliminary injunction. The injunction was granted; however, it was appealed and led to Reno v. ACLU landing in front of the Supreme Court in 1997. During the same time period, the ALA filed a similar suit against the Department of Justice, which was consolidated with Reno v. ACLU. The Supreme Court established that the CDA was unconstitutional as it would suppress freedom of speech while attempting to protect minors, thus impeding the First Amendment rights of internet users.

Impact of Court Cases Pertaining to Copyright

The aspect of copyright most often addressed in schools is fair use. **Fair use** allows for reproduction and/or distribution of copyrighted materials for educational purposes without gaining permission from the creator so long as it meets the fair use conditions. These conditions were a result of Folsom v. Marsh (1841), in which the publication of copied letters from President George Washington was questioned as copyright infringement, and the ruling in that case created some fair use guidelines that were ultimately codified in the **Copyright Act of 1976**. The conditions that must be considered before reproducing work are as follows: the purpose and character of use, the nature of the work, the amount of the work being reproduced, and the effect on the market or value of the work being reproduced. So long as these conditions are balanced, a work may be legally and ethically reproduced. As such, portions of literature and other resources used in or needed for academia may be reproduced and disseminated for use in school.

Chapter Quiz

Ready to see how well you retained what you just read? Scan the QR code to go directly to the chapter quiz interface for this study guide. If you're using a computer, simply visit the online resources page at **mometrix.com/resources719/nbptslibmecya** and click the Chapter Quizzes link.

Outreach and Advocacy

Promotion of Programs, Resources, and Services

Promotion

Promotion is the process of notifying various library stakeholders of the programs and resources available through the school library. The purpose of promotion is to advertise library services to people who may not be aware of them. By increasing the number of people who understand the variety of library offerings, librarians and staff can increase program participation, volunteers, donations, and stakeholder buy-in. For programs particularly, promotion is key to ensure they are well attended. The best programs in the world will fail if no one is aware of them.

Different Promotional Strategies

By considering the wants and needs of the various library stakeholder groups, librarians and staff can reach them with appropriate messaging through familiar channels. Some of the most important stakeholder groups to consider promotion toward include students, parents, teachers, and administrators. Each of these groups has a particular set of needs regarding library programs, and each is best reached using their preferred communication channels. **Students** may care about how fun or helpful programs are for them, and they can generally be reached via classroom or library announcements, handouts, or direct communication with their parents. **Parents** may care about students' educational needs being met by programs, and they can be reached by student handouts, PTA meetings, and email. **Teachers** may want programs that attract and retain students while providing good educational opportunities. They can generally receive library promotions directly from the library staff or through staff channels like meetings and email. **Administrators** are likely to be concerned with the cost and scope of programs, how they further educational objectives, and how they promote the mission of the school. They can generally be reached via personal conversations and formal presentations.

Relation of Promotion of Programs and Resources to Library Budgeting

Library budgets are determined in many cases by the number and kind of programs and resources that the library offers. Many resources and programs may go unnoticed without proper promotion and personal librarian advertisement. Properly promoting library offerings can help those who fund the library to see it as being worth the money being spent, and it can encourage more donations. For school administrators, it is critical that library operations can be promoted in a way that emphasizes their importance and demonstrates specific needs for funding and staffing. Informally, promotion to local school communities can assist with budgetary needs by attracting donors and volunteers to reduce the need for direct library funding from the school.

Promoting New Acquisitions and Services to the Community

Identifying Users and Nonusers

Circulation data provides up-to-date information regarding library users. With this data, the librarian can tell which students are accessing library resources, the type of resources used, and for how long. This data clearly identifies which students are and are not using circulated resources; however, circulation is only one way in which students use the school library. The library is often used as a space for independent or small group study. Collecting data on which students are using the library for this purpose can be done by requiring students to sign into the space for study. This data may show the librarian that students who are not circulating resources are indeed still using the library space. Students who do not check out or access resources are considered **nonusers**. There are several commonly used methods to increase patronage within the school library. Collaboration with teachers provides the librarian with access to students, and it also provides the students with access to the library during a time that fits within their schedule. Developing reading programs offers students incentives to read and visit the library. Outreach, whether direct to nonusers or schoolwide in the form of promotional materials, helps to spark student interest in library offerings.

Increasing School Library Use Among Students

Getting students excited about reading is often cited as a way to increase student engagement in the library. There are a variety of methods to achieve this. Hosting events like guest speakers, author visits, or interactive learning opportunities tends to pique student interest in the library schoolwide. Day-to-day opportunities to increase engagement include the addition of makerspaces, reading programs, and up-to-date and interesting book displays. For students unable to physically access the library, increasing their accessibility by ensuring they are knowledgeable about what can be accessed remotely allows them to use the library consistently on their own terms. Collaborating with teachers to ensure students are visiting the library during class time also leads to an increase in usage. Students who visit with their class are more likely to visit again independently, especially in schools with flexible scheduling.

Library Brochures

Creating a brochure is a quick and easy way to promote everything the **library media center (LMC)** has to offer. There are many online document tools that can be used for this. Brochures share practical information with the school community such as the mission statement, staff names and contact emails, hours of operation, and directions on how to obtain the login information for password-protected databases. Resource information in a brochure should include fiction and nonfiction collection statistics, available e-resources, audiovisual materials, and types of technology (e.g., computers, printers, charging stations) housed in the library. Stating circulation guidelines in the brochure is also a good idea. Miscellaneous details about joining a library club or using a makerspace can also be included. Because brochures are essentially handouts, they can be displayed throughout the school and included in promotional initiatives.

Scheduling Library Orientation

Students can become familiar with all their LMC has to offer by attending a library orientation workshop. Resource needs change as students progress through elementary, middle, and high school, so having workshops at different levels to introduce new resources is important. During an orientation, an LMS explains how library resources are available to help students achieve. An orientation should involve a tour of the physical space to point out where genres of interest and newly acquired titles are located, along with a grade-appropriate demonstration of how to access electronic resources. The students should also be reminded of general rules and library etiquette.

Arranging orientations can be challenging depending on class schedule structure, but they are important and rewarding because yearly content updates foster fresh excitement about learning.

Encouraging Students to Use Library Resources

Even when students know the school library offers useful resources, they will often bypass the library and search the internet for the information they seek. While it's true that finding library resources sometimes involves a time-consuming visit to the LMC, the time thought to be saved by doing an internet search instead is often lost when the students have to verify the authenticity of a source. An LMS can encourage students to choose the library resources by building an organized collection of print and electronic resources that students can easily access and trust to cover their curricular needs. When students are successful, they are more likely to return for their next project and promote the library resources to their classmates.

Prominent Placement of Library Information on the School Website

Most students will know where in the building their LMC is located, but it is also important for students to know where on the internet their library resources are kept. A school library webpage is a good place to showcase all the resources the library has to offer, and it's important to include instructions on how to access them. One way an LMS can guide traffic to the library webpage is **to advocate for a convenient link on the school homepage menu.** Contacting the school information technology (IT) department, the person who usually handles such matters, with this request is important because most library resources are funded by the school or district, and the school or district can reserve funding if usage statistics do not support the investment. Thus, making it easier for students to access resources is very important.

Showcasing New Acquisitions

Every school library should have a physical display and a virtual display to showcase newly acquired items. The physical display should be an eye-catching arrangement near the library entrance and visible from the hall to draw in passing students and faculty. All item types and genres can be part of the display. The LMS can promote new acquisitions virtually by creating a slideshow using a presentation tool. The slideshow can then be added to the library webpage or shown on a monitor. Many library automation systems also have a feature that displays newly cataloged items on the homepage. Scheduling a book talk for fiction is a great way to build excitement about new releases and visiting classrooms is another way to highlight new subject-specific resources.

Students Promoting New Material

Students who like to read might be interested in joining a library book club. Club meetings usually include first choosing a book and then chapter discussions. Forming an advisory group as an extension of the book club is a great way to get students involved in promoting new acquisitions. Often, students are promoting the books or other resources that they have suggested or recommended. After reading a book, students can post reviews on social media and/or write book reviews for the school newspaper. Students can get creative with their recommendations by designing posters using art supplies or online design software. Students can also help by creating displays around the library. In schools that serve elementary and middle school students, older children can promote new materials by visiting primary grades to do book talks.

Relaying New Acquisitions to Faculty

Library media specialists can keep fellow faculty members apprised of new materials by creating bibliographies. The bibliography could be subject-specific or include all items added to the collection within a certain timeframe. Some schools only receive new items once a year and others add to the collection continuously, so the LMS can decide how often to produce an updated bibliography. Most automation systems will create the bibliography for the LMS with only a few clicks after the preferred format settings have been selected. By sharing these bibliographies with other teachers, the LMS is demonstrating an interest in each discipline, and library staff may be more likely to be invited into the classroom to deliver an information literacy lesson or have the teacher promote the library to the students.

ATTENDING DEPARTMENT MEETINGS TO PROMOTE NEW MATERIALS

Collaboration between the teachers and the LMS is very important to student success. The LMS should include the teachers in collection development by soliciting their input when ordering. When the library receives new materials, an LMS can request to share the new titles with faculty at their department meetings where all teachers of the same discipline are present. Here, the LMS can also learn about upcoming projects planned for different grade levels in which the new acquisitions could be useful and, with the faculty members, devise strategies for library support. These strategies could include scheduling a classroom visit or cocreating a **pathfinder,** a directory with project-specific resources, with the new arrivals included. By requesting to attend department meetings to promote new materials, the LMS is affirming the commitment to helping the students achieve.

SHARING LIBRARY INFORMATION IN SCHOOL NEWSLETTERS

An LMS should be a regular contributor to a school newsletter. Newsletter recipients include students, faculty, administration, parents, and alumni, thus providing an opportunity to reach all the school stakeholders at the same time. These are usually distributed once a month and are a great place to showcase new acquisitions. This can be done in the form of book reviews or blurbs. In addition to sharing new items, the LMS can highlight library resources by sharing class visits and research projects and promote upcoming library events such as author visits and book fairs. Book cover images and pictures of displays and special collections foster interest and are easy to include in newsletter submissions as most article information is compiled electronically.

Advocating for the Library

ADVOCACY

Advocacy is any action showing support for a particular goal or asking an individual or organization for assistance with a particular goal. One of the primary topics of advocacy in the school library is the budget. Due to the increasing costs of technology and curriculum materials, elective course budgets are often lowered, leaving the librarian responsible for filling in the gaps through advocacy efforts. Opportunities for collaboration between the librarian and teachers are also not very often available, and creating this time requires advocacy at the school level. Literacy advocacy, speaking out about the needs of students as they relate to reading, is another key component of advocacy within the library. This requires librarians to not only ensure their spaces are stocked with the resources required to meet the needs of students, but to also share those resources and their knowledge with educators throughout the building in order to best help students develop their reading skills. Far too often, school librarians are also left to advocate for their own jobs, usually in the face of budget cuts or staff reduction efforts. Lastly, school librarians should also be prepared to advocate for the rights of students, such as their right to access information, their right to read, and their First Amendment rights as they relate to library access.

PLANNING ADVOCACY STRATEGIES

Data is a key tool librarians can use to support the needs they're advocating for, as it is typically irrefutable proof of a need. To demonstrate the importance of adequately staffed libraries, data may be pulled from a plethora of studies that proves that students attending schools with staffed libraries perform better on standardized tests and show higher rates of achievement overall. For budgeting and fundraising purposes, there is data related to per pupil spending, average spending in years prior, or the cost of materials lost or damaged that need to be replaced. Forming relationships with school stakeholders in the community provides a librarian with paths for advocacy, as such relationships can lead to donations. Regarding advocacy concerning the rights of students, school librarians should be aware of any legislation or changes to legislation that impact students and their accessibility in the library. This includes laws related to book banning and other First Amendment-related rights. Librarians must be able to speak out for the protection of the rights of students within the library.

Advocating for the Library to School Staff

Time and time again it has been proven that students who are able to participate in library programming with qualified staff perform better overall on standardized tests and are better prepared to participate in life beyond school. As such, it is important that librarians spread this information and do their part to ensure that they are participating in the education of all students. This may require a librarian to advocate for adequate instructional time with students. With classroom teachers, librarians should ensure that they are aware of the advantages librarians can provide and collaborate to develop programming to support education goals. With administrators and other decision-makers, librarians will need to share the same information and also work with the administrator to create a schedule conducive to learning goals. By advocating to all members of the staff the benefits of library programming, librarians will be able to best support students.

Library Advocacy in the Community

Community partnerships are a vital part of school libraries. Organizations are able to provide funding and support that may not be available otherwise. This can include things like donations and grants, visits from community members, and a number of other experiences for students to participate in. In order to gain these partnerships, the librarian must advocate for his or her programming. Advocating within the community typically starts with some form of outreach from the librarian to the entity with whom he or she desires a relationship, such as an email, phone call or letter. When planning to meet with an organization, group, or individual within the community, the librarian should consider how their goals align with the goals of the library and how a partnership can benefit both parties, and the librarian should be prepared to share a concrete plan that can demonstrate the mutual benefit they will both receive.

Chapter Quiz

Ready to see how well you retained what you just read? Scan the QR code to go directly to the chapter quiz interface for this study guide. If you're using a computer, simply visit the online resources page at **mometrix.com/resources719/nbptslibmecya** and click the Chapter Quizzes link.

Reflective Practice

Research and Reflective Practice

Reflective Practice

In education, to be a reflective practitioner means to reflect on one's own actions and processes as they relate to the education and programming one is providing as well as the roles one is playing within the school community. Educators are expected to take time to analyze their actions and assess them for effectiveness. If educators find that their current actions are ineffective, they will then assess the situation to establish what obstacles exist within their control and what changes they can make in their practice to eliminate those obstacles. Educators will then initiate these changes and repeat the process. This self-reflection ensures that educators are providing students with effective lessons that meet curriculum goals. As with any educator, this is an important practice for librarians. As society and technology change, it is imperative that the thought processes and practices of librarians also change to ensure patrons are receiving an education and access to a collection that is valuable and representative of themselves.

Using Journals and Portfolios

Journals and portfolios play a vital role in being a reflective practitioner, as they provide regular documentation of ongoing events, practices, and candid thoughts. **Journals** typically consist of written anecdotal notes over a certain time period. These notes may be reflections on a lesson plan recorded daily or a few times over the course of a unit. The purpose is for the educator to have information to look back on when reflecting on the effectiveness of his or her lessons and actions so that proper changes can be made. **Portfolios** vary slightly from journals in that they should feature examples of what the educator is reflecting on in addition to notes, like student work samples and examples of the expected materials and outcomes. What an educator chooses to use as a reflective tool is typically a personal choice, but in some cases the type may be mandated by the administration in alignment with professional development goals. However, the end goal of both journals and portfolios is the same, which is to provide an opportunity for in-depth reflection.

Self-Assessments and Peer Assessments

Self-assessment is a large component of being a reflective practitioner. It provides an educator with the opportunity to assess his or her strengths and weaknesses in his or her role. There are premade self-assessment tools for educators in which they assign themselves a grade or score for a proposed facet of education; however, educators may choose to make their own tools based on their professional development goals. **Peer assessment** shares the same goal but varies in that it is completed with another individual or group of individuals in the same or similar role(s). The most common peer assessment for school librarians is observation, after which the participants conference to provide feedback on what they saw, what they commend, and what they think needs changing. The overall goal of both types of feedback is to provide the librarian with the information needed to make the appropriate adjustments to best enhance and deliver learning opportunities.

Incident Analysis

Incident analysis is a process that strives to find the root cause of an incident and prevent it from happening again. An **incident** can be defined as any unexpected or unplanned event that occurs. This will often be used in education in partnership with classroom management. The educator will reflect on an incident involving student behavior, like frequent outbursts or general inattentiveness, and do his or her own investigation to find the root cause of the issue. If there is an external cause, the educator should work on resolving it, and if it is an internal cause, more investigation will need to occur with the student to establish a solution. In addition to this, the school librarian may use incident analysis to address organizational issues. Because organization is a key component of the library, it is important to have a reliable system and address any incidents that arise within that system. By reflecting on these incidents and making proper adjustments, the librarian can better serve students.

Critical Friends

A **critical friend** is someone who provides support and feedback while remaining honest and unbiased. Unlike a mentor, a critical friend is not in a position of authority over the individual that he or she is supporting. Critical friends are meant to encourage individuals while challenging their thinking and processes with the goal of making them more successful in their field. For a librarian, his or her critical friend will likely be another librarian who he or she identifies as a peer. Critical friends may develop as a partnership between two individuals or as a small group of individuals similar to a PLC; however, the difference in such a group when compared to a PLC is the intentional use of a critical lens that is used to work on reflective practices as opposed to a focus on broader issues unrelated to one's self and one's own practices. The overall goal of a critical friend or critical friend group is to ensure educators are reflecting and making changes to their practices as needed.

Independent Research

Independent research is a process through which one poses a unique question and does a lot of research using a variety of resources to answer that question. Librarians should be well-versed in this for a variety of reasons. Due to the nature of many school libraries, school librarianship can be a lonely role. As such, it is important for a librarian to be able to answer his or her own questions through independent research. Doing this enables librarians to find solutions to any problems they may be experiencing, and it leads to librarians who are well-informed, adhere to best practices, and are able to make the most beneficial decisions for their library. Librarians are also expected to teach independent research skills to their students, which makes the ability to do independent research themselves vital. In order to best lead students in research, a librarian must be able to effectively use research tools and complete the steps needed to acquire, vet, and use information.

Committees and Task Forces

At the school level, librarians can serve on a variety of committees. By doing so, they will have advocacy platforms through which they may ensure that the library's needs and the students' best interests as they relate to the library are being represented. Examples of committees that school librarians may serve on include, but are not limited to, parent-teacher organizations, faculty advisory committees, curriculum committees, and fundraising committees. They may also serve on task forces that establish rules and procedures within the school. By playing an active role in the school through participation in these committees, librarians are ensuring that the aforementioned needs are at the forefront of the minds of decision-makers and stakeholders. Beyond the school level, there are opportunities for librarians to serve on committees that vote on book awards at the local, state, and national level, serve as members of advocacy groups through broader organizations, and participate in research related to school libraries.

Action Research

In education, **action research** is a process in which educators seek to improve their practices by performing a theory-supported investigation within their own professional context. The educator begins by **identifying** a problem area, gathering **data** related to the problem, and performing a literature review to find existing research on the topic. Using the data and theoretical background, the educator then develops a **plan** to address the issue before **implementing** changes. The educator then collects more data and **reflects** on the results to see if and how the results changed. This process should be documented and **recursively** repeated to work on optimizing any changes that might affect the outcomes. **Reflection** often leads to identifying new areas in which improvements are needed, making this a continuous cycle in pursuit of better practices. Because action research is usually performed on a small sample and is informal, the results are limited in their applicability to all contexts. Due to the informality of action research, there is rarely an ethics review board involved in establishing the process. Educators engaging in action research must, therefore, maintain transparency and caution in the scope of their research practices as the results have a direct impact on students and other professionals. Despite action research's limitations, documentation of the process and findings can still be broadly useful as other educational contexts may benefit from such information.

Chapter Quiz

Ready to see how well you retained what you just read? Scan the QR code to go directly to the chapter quiz interface for this study guide. If you're using a computer, simply visit the online resources page at **mometrix.com/resources719/nbptslibmecya** and click the Chapter Quizzes link.

NBPTS Practice Test

Want to take this practice test in an online interactive format?
Check out the online resources page, which includes interactive practice questions and much more: **mometrix.com/resources719/nbptslibmecya**

Multiple Choice Questions

1. Several new fiction novels have been added to the library's collection. Which of the following is the LEAST effective way to promote these books to students?

a. Shelve new books for early circulation.
b. Create eye-catching book displays.
c. Hold book talks to discuss the new additions.
d. Display signage about the new books in the school hallway.

2. A librarian wants to support distance learning efforts. Which of the following skills would be most beneficial for distance learners?

a. Validating sources
b. Coding skills
c. Citing sources
d. Remotely accessing databases

3. Which of the following scenarios would be best addressed by using the library's professional collection?

a. A teacher is looking for new methods of assessment for her math course.
b. A student wants to learn more about the pathways to becoming a nurse.
c. A staff member is curious about the written expectations of his position.
d. A guidance counselor needs resources to help students pick a trade to enter.

4. Which of the following is NOT an example of folk literature?

a. Legends
b. Fables
c. Myths
d. Dramas

5. A librarian is working on her collection policy. In the section regarding weeding, she has stated she will eliminate any books that are damaged, not circulated within that school year, superseded (and the updated copy is in the collection), or inaccurate based on new findings. Which of these criteria should be reconsidered?

a. Damaged
b. Not circulated within the school year
c. Superseded
d. Inaccurate based on new findings

6. Which of the following is NOT permitted under fair use policy?

a. Directly quoting a speech in a paper
b. Parodying a movie for a film class project
c. Sharing a PDF of a novel for students to read leisurely
d. Reproducing a passage from a novel to analyze in class

7. A librarian has received a book order following a purchase completed with a purchase order. Which of the following is the correct next step?

a. Sort and appropriately catalog the new books.
b. Compare the purchase order, packing slip, and contents of the box.
c. Update the library budgeting information to reflect the amount spent.
d. Call the vendor and confirm the package has been delivered.

8. A librarian is helping a student create a slide show presentation that he is going to give to his classmates and teachers. Which of the following concepts would not be helpful for the librarian to bring to the student's attention as he creates his slide show presentation?

a. Design
b. Content
c. Audience
d. Graphics creation

9. A librarian is looking for book reviews backed by the American Library Association. Which of the following sources should she refer to?

a. *Kirkus Reviews*
b. *The Horn Book Magazine*
c. *Booklist*
d. *School Library Journal*

10. Which of the following best describes the purpose of acceptable use policies?

a. They outline the appropriate and expected use of technology available to students.
b. They ensure students are aware of the proper book care techniques.
c. They explain to people who may use the library for meetings the proper way to handle equipment.
d. They notify parents of damage to a book caused by their child mishandling it.

11. Which of the following is a clear violation of the ALA Code of Ethics?

a. The librarian accepted a donation from a local organization that required him or her to spend a portion of the money on books covering a specific topic.
b. The librarian accepted a book donation that required students to vote on their favorites and submit feedback.
c. The librarian accepted a donation from a local organization that was contingent on the removal of controversial titles.
d. The librarian discarded a large portion of donated books without first consulting the donor.

12. A student is looking for the publisher and publication date of a book to use in a citation. What section of the book should the librarian refer the student to?

a. Imprint
b. LCCN
c. Preface
d. Author main entry

13. The library has recently acquired several new nonfiction resources. What is the most effective way to share these offerings with the school's teaching staff?

a. Attend a staff meeting with the books to share.
b. Create and share a bibliography of the new books.
c. Display the new books in the library.
d. Post a slideshow on the library's website homepage.

14. A teacher approaches the school librarian with a lesson plan in Language Arts that will involve student research use several types of sources, including encyclopedias, biographies, and the Internet. How can the librarian best help the teacher achieve the goals of the lesson plan?

a. Ask the teacher to give students the assignment and then schedule a time to bring the class to the library. Directly teach students research techniques for print materials and for the Internet. Show them how to locate internet databases that will meet their needs and how to coordinate information from several sources
b. Give the teacher a list of appropriate databases, show her where biographies and encyclopedias are shelved in the library, and ask her to schedule a time for her class to come in and do their research under her supervision
c. Schedule a time to visit the teacher's classroom and answer any questions students may have about doing this type of research
d. Assemble a cart for the teacher to check out for her classroom with encyclopedias and select biographies

15. You have noticed students are not circulating novels from a particular section of the collection. Which of the following would best address this concern and spark interest in those novels?

a. Reading workshops
b. Book talks
c. Mini-lessons
d. Reading incentive programs

16. A picture book recently added to the school collection was the subject of a challenge initiated by a student organization. Which of the following is NOT required in the challenge proceedings as part of due process?

a. A notice of decision be sent to all students in the school
b. The concerns be addressed promptly by the appropriate stakeholders
c. The decision regarding removal be made by impartial individuals
d. An opportunity for involved parties to share concerns

17. The librarian creates a computer "scavenger hunt." Students work at computers to find items on a list of computer resources. The first student to successfully find all the items and write down the websites where they are located is declared the winner, the "Champion Computer Researcher." This activity promotes which of the following state goals for library media centers?

a. The ethical use of information resources
b. The appreciation of diversity within a student group
c. Effective oral and written communication
d. Integrating technology into the library program

18. Students are working on a long-term project and should be completing research at school and at home. Which of the following can the librarian review with them to provide the most assistance?

a. The hold process
b. The renewal process
c. How to navigate the nonfiction section
d. How to remotely access research databases

19. A librarian and teacher are collaborating on student research problems. Their goal is stated as "students will demonstrate proficiency in using online research tools to answer questions." Which of the following examples best enhances their original goal?

a. By the end of the unit, students will demonstrate they have both the skills and proficiency necessary to use online research tools to answer questions.
b. Students will learn the skills needed to operate online research tools.
c. By the end of the unit, 80 percent of students will demonstrate proficiency in using library databases to answer questions by creating a research presentation.
d. Students will demonstrate proficiency in using online research tools by creating a visual presentation of their findings.

20. What makes the I-Search model different from other research models?

a. It was designed to be cyclical.
b. It was designed to allow for reflection.
c. It was designed to focus on the inquiry process.
d. It was designed to support student autonomy.

21. Which of the following does NOT demonstrate curriculum support within the library?

a. Purchasing new copies of classic books solely to update their cover art, even though existing copies are in good condition
b. Subscribing to new research databases for student use
c. Purchasing assistive technology for students with disabilities
d. Adding popular titles in multiple languages to the library collection

22. The ALA asserts which of the following?

a. Circulation records should be made accessible to parents without needing to request them.
b. Children and youth are entitled to privacy regarding their circulation records.
c. Teachers may access student circulation records if it is done in an effort to better support them.
d. Law enforcement has the right to immediate access of student records if there are concerns for student well-being.

23. Students are working on research projects in their science class. Where should the librarian refer them for up-to-date information written by field specialists?

a. Magazines
b. Search engines
c. Newspapers
d. Academic journals

24. Which of the following best explains the reasoning for transitioning from Anglo-American Cataloging Rules to Resource Description and Access?

a. To simplify listings for books in shared catalogs
b. To better catalog in digital environments
c. To make online catalogs easier to browse
d. To reduce inaccuracies in the collection catalog

25. A librarian completes an inventory and notices a large portion of the collection is missing from the shelves. She then notices over time that many titles are being returned by the students who were using them without being checked out. Reviewing which of the following with her students would benefit her the most?

a. Acceptable use policies
b. Interlibrary loan procedures
c. Circulation procedures
d. Reconsideration policies

26. Which of the following is not a component of the International Society for Technology in Education's standards?

a. Local collaboration
b. Digital citizenship
c. Computational thinking
d. Innovative design

27. Which activities below would it be best for a beginning librarian NOT to engage in right after arriving at a new school?

a. Weeding and schedule changing
b. Staff meetings on preventing plagiarism
c. Fund raising activities such as book fairs
d. Reorganizing the library furniture

28. Shared decision-making regarding libraries requires a committee of stakeholders. Which of the following stakeholders should be consulted most when one is deciding on the filtering software to purchase for use on student devices?

a. IT professionals
b. Library support staff
c. Administrators
d. Parents

29. Which of the following stages of the Stripling Model is NOT correctly defined?

a. Wonder: students develop questions and make predictions.
b. Construct: students begin to develop a product from their findings.
c. Investigate: students evaluate information to answer their questions.
d. Express: students apply what they have learned to new contexts.

30. In a school with a fixed library schedule, a classroom teacher asks the librarian if she could bring her class for two consecutive periods next week instead of the usual one. She has assigned her students to work in teams on different aspects of the US Revolutionary War and feels that they will need more than just one class period to complete this research. What realistic but helpful response may the librarian give?

a. Regretfully tell the teacher she has no extra time in her schedule. The school is on a fixed schedule and there are no "free periods." Suggest that small groups come to library on their free time at recess and lunch period
b. Respond that the library will be overcrowded if everyone in the class is looking for materials simultaneously. Suggest that the students come in shifts to do their research, perhaps team by team
c. Juggle the schedule, trading one teacher's period for another if necessary, to allow for the one-time-only extra time period and offer to start the class off by teaching some Internet research techniques and showing students where relevant books are located in the library
d. Decline the double period request because of the fixed library schedule but offer to pull a cart of relevant books instead and deliver these to the classroom

31. Which of the following problems would be best addressed with a short-term goal?

a. School administration wants to see a schoolwide increase in student reading comprehension through a partnership between teachers and the librarian.
b. The school librarian wishes to genrefy the novel section of the school's collection to make it easier for students to find what interests them.
c. School board members have approved major library renovations that will be guided by the choices of the librarian.
d. The school librarian wants to implement a needs assessment-based purchasing plan for the picture book and nonfiction book collections.

32. A teacher has asked the librarian to assist with providing intrinsic motivation for students in reading and writing. Which of the following is the best choice for doing so?

a. A guest author visit
b. A reading reward program
c. Intensive writing lessons
d. Consequences for failing to write

33. A group of librarians is working together to develop curriculum documents for its district. What organization should the group refer to as the primary basis of learning standards and objectives?

a. AASL
b. LOC
c. ALA
d. OCLC

34. A new school librarian is having difficulty getting everything done on time. Which of the following would be the BEST first step for her to take to solve her problem?

a. Supervise the media clerk more closely and assign that person more tasks
b. Ask the principal to hire more help in the library than the library has traditionally had
c. Make comprehensive daily, weekly, and monthly plans listing what needs to be done, the deadline for completing each task, and the person responsible for handling the task
d. Put in overtime hours as necessary to complete all tasks on time

35. A librarian is drawing up a plan for a lesson on creating a slide show presentation. The class she is going to instruct contains several students for whom English is a second language. What is the best way for the librarian to handle the potential difficulties these students may have in understanding her?

a. She should inform these students that if they feel they will not understand what she is saying, they are excused from the lesson and may spend the time browsing the library's collection
b. Since a slide show is a visual medium, she should take advantage of that and show what to do rather than lecturing about it. She can invite students to try some of the techniques she is teaching and make the lesson as hands-on as possible so that its content will cross the language barrier
c. She should assign each ESL student a student partner who will sit with them and help explain what she is saying
d. When she gives her lecture, she should speak very slowly and clearly and periodically stop to ask for anyone who does not understand the lesson to raise his or her hand

36. Which of the competencies for a beginning librarian did the librarian fulfill in the following conversation?

Librarian: Juan, how can I help you today?
Juan: I need something about World War II.
Librarian: Are you going to write a report about World War II?
Juan: Actually, no. We are going to have a debate.
Librarian: About the whole war?
Juan: No, just about the US dropping that bomb on Hiroshima.
Librarian: Which side will you take in the debate, Juan?
Juan: I am on the side that will argue that the bombing was justified.
Librarian: I know just the materials you want. We have some books over here. One is the autobiography of a man who was on that bombing flight. Over there, we have some DVDs with films of the aftermath and also an interview with President Truman during which the president explains his reasoning for giving the order to drop the bomb. And I'll write a list of websites where you can find more information.

a. Effectively interviews patrons to determine information needs
b. Applies bibliographic and retrieval techniques for organizing and using information sources
c. Employs a variety of techniques to guide the development of independent readers
d. Understands the role of the school library program as a central element in the intellectual life of the school

37. Which of the following goals is written in the clearest and most measurable way?

a. Kindergarten students will increase their attention span length by 25 percent during group reading time.
b. In the fall semester, we will increase the circulation of novels among intermediate students by 15 percent by using lessons that expose students to appropriate novel choices.
c. Students will circulate more graphic novels that support classroom curriculum over the course of the school year.
d. Volunteer hours will increase by using social media to promote parent involvement.

38. A teacher has brought his class to the library for instruction and book exchange. The teacher participates in the instructional session with the librarian, but when students are excused to look for books and disperse to different areas in the library, the teacher ignores their behavior. Two boys are chasing each other around a shelf of books. The teacher does not correct them. What should the librarian do?

a. Point out the behavior to the teacher
b. Ignore the behavior
c. Speak to the boys firmly about proper library behavior
d. Call for the principal to handle the problem

39. Which of the following technological duties would NOT be part of the librarian's job description?

a. Housing and maintaining computer labs
b. Producing the daily televised school announcements
c. Monitoring student use of cell phones
d. Maintaining the school's website

40. A librarian is developing a new mission statement for the school library. Which of the following pieces of information is NOT necessary in the mission statement?

a. A clear, well-explained goal
b. Why the mission is important
c. The method by which a goal will be achieved
d. Current key interests of the library program

41. Which of the following is the most appropriate first step when analyzing how to allocate the book budget based on current collection use?

a. Refer to the curriculum guideline to ensure purchases directly support learning.
b. Consult a student advisory committee for suggestions.
c. Survey staff for information regarding how the library's collection can best support them.
d. Pull historical circulation data that provides a detailed view of resource usage.

42. A librarian has reorganized the fiction section so that books are grouped together based on their content. Which of the following best describes this shelving method?

a. The *Sears List of Subject Headings*
b. Genrefication
c. Dewey Decimal Classification
d. Library of Congress Classification

43. A weekly block of library time is assigned to a seventh grade class in a middle school. The librarian could best use this time with students by:

a. Instructing them in effective ways to do research on the Internet and in efficient use of library reference materials and books on the library bookshelves
b. Allowing this time to be a "free" period for students when they can return books, select others, and ask the librarian for help and guidance when they see a need for it
c. Introducing them to new materials in the library's collection by reading short passages from new books and showing brief previews of new DVDs and audio books
d. Asking them to be "library aides" during this period so that they can assist younger students who are looking for materials and also reshelf books

44. Which of the following responsibilities should NOT be assigned to a library volunteer?

a. Reshelving picture books when they are returned
b. Organizing the series section of the fiction collection
c. Assisting students in retrieving books of choice
d. Using circulation statistics to complete a library needs assessment

45. A student wants to use a news website as a source for information in an essay. Which of the following is the most important factor he should investigate to determine the validity of the source?

a. Currency
b. Age
c. Relevance
d. Bias

46. What federal regulation requires doorframes to be a minimum of 32 inches wide?

a. CIPA
b. FERPA
c. ADA
d. Title IX

47. Which theory suggests that learning is a product of interactions with one's environment?

a. Cognitivism
b. Humanism
c. Behaviorism
d. Constructivism

48. Which of the following is NOT a benefit of a well-trained library staff?

a. The library collection is organized more effectively.
b. Students receive better services from highly qualified individuals.
c. There is little need to provide professional development opportunities.
d. Stakeholder concerns are adequately addressed.

49. A librarian is seeking feedback on her library collection from an informed but unbiased party. Which of the following people best fits this description?

a. Lead librarian
b. Critical friend
c. Administrator
d. Classroom teacher

50. Which of the following pieces of information would be found in the physical description field of a MARC entry?

a. Description of the cover art
b. Considerations for care of a physical resource
c. Number of pages in a book
d. Publication information

51. A librarian is hosting an event in which she wants students to engage with community members and gain exposure to opportunities outside of school offerings. Which of the following will she likely plan?

a. A family read-aloud event
b. A speech from a local guest
c. An illustrator visit
d. A writing workshop with guest editors

52. Which of the following is required for schools to continue receiving credits for internet services from the Federal Communications Commission?

a. Signed acceptable use policies from all students
b. Notifying families of the use of credits
c. Using verified vendors for purchases
d. Installing content control software on school devices

53. A teacher is concerned that some students in his class who were researching a topic through databases found some biased, incorrect information and unknowingly included it in their reports. What is the first action the librarian should take to prevent this from happening again?

a. Have a staff meeting to discuss the problem of unreliable resources that may be biased. Ask teachers to help solve this problem
b. Obtain a list of suspect databases from the concerned teacher and evaluate each one carefully to see if the information is accurate, reliable, and unbiased. Remove these sources from the library's collection
c. Ask the concerned teacher to visit the websites himself and report to the librarian his opinion of the information he finds there
d. In your next period with this class, explain how to examine information obtained from the Internet for accuracy

54. A group of librarians is developing the district's new reconsideration policy. Which of the following areas should be included?

a. Annual budgeting information
b. Student circulation policies
c. Acceptable use agreements
d. Book challenge procedures

55. A librarian accesses some research models to help students find information for a report. Next, she shows students how to find these research models and tells them why they are more helpful than Google. What reasons does she give?

a. The research models are not as commercial as Google is
b. Students can gain more detailed information from specific research models
c. Her school district recommends this research model
d. These research models are easier to use than search engines

56. Which would be the most appropriate way for a librarian to instruct students in Internet research skills?

a. Assign classes that come for their library period to choose a topic, locate information on the Internet and write down the website where they located it. When time is up, the librarian should call classes together to share
b. Prepare a slide show presentation that demonstrates the process of locating information on the Internet and present this program to all classes that come to the library
c. After conferring with each classroom teacher about his or her current curriculum, demonstrate separately to different classes how to use the Internet to find information on the topic each class is presently studying
d. Prepare a display of books about using the Internet and use class time to show these books to students, urging them to check out the books and read for themselves about ways to find information online

57. A high school librarian has been granted funds to attend a conference hosted by a division of the ALA. Which of the following conference opportunities will she benefit from the most as it relates to her position?

a. ACRL
b. YALSA
c. RUSA
d. PLA

58. Why should the librarian periodically review online databases?

a. To make sure students are not plagiarizing from them
b. To verify that the subject matter is accurate and covers student needs
c. To make sure nothing inappropriate for students is on the database
d. To assess the difficulty of the reading levels on the database

59. Which of the following types of poetry is defined by the presence of a plot and a clear beginning, middle, and end?

a. Lyric
b. Narrative
c. Dramatic
d. Ode

60. Which of the following scenarios demonstrates a teacher practicing cognitivism?

a. A teacher scaffolds instruction and breaks down the content into more manageable pieces.
b. A teacher ensures that the social-emotional needs of all students are met before beginning instruction.
c. A teacher implements both positive and negative consequences as reinforcement in his or her classroom.
d. A teacher guides students in collaboratively constructing understanding through authentic problem-solving.

61. Though biographical narratives are nonfiction, what portion of information may be inaccurate?

a. The subject's date of birth
b. Dialogue between two parties
c. Significant events in the subject's life
d. Accomplishments of the subject

62. A group of librarians meet to complete a peer assessment. What are they most likely assessing?

a. A librarian's lesson delivery
b. Current district guidelines related to the library
c. The age of the library's collection
d. Budgeting guidelines

63. Which of the following is NOT a responsibility of a school librarian?

a. Scheduling classes
b. Reporting statistics to administrators
c. Circulating library materials
d. Critiquing books

64. Which of the following would be best addressed by a long-term financial goal?

a. Reducing the overall amount spent on replacing lost books and reallocating some of those funds to digital resources
b. Increasing the number of diverse titles available in the picture book section of an elementary library
c. Updating flexible seating choices for leisure reading time in a middle school library
d. Adding new databases to the library's collection to support schoolwide learning goals

65. Which of the following best describes the purpose of a reflective journal?

a. A compilation of work samples and lesson plans an educator can use to look back on.
b. A set of questions requiring the educator to reflect on his or her practices.
c. A collection of anecdotal notes over time focused on analyzing lessons that have taken place.
d. An investigation into an event that is accompanied by an analysis on how to prevent further related events.

66. A librarian notices there are several gaps in the nonfiction collection. To figure out her next steps, she inventories the nonfiction collection and determines what topics are not covered. Which of the following terms best defines the steps she has taken?

a. Loss prevention
b. Purchase planning
c. Needs assessment
d. Program implementation

67. A class of freshman students is working on history projects. Which of the following will best ensure equal access to the resources needed to complete the projects?

a. Partnering the students to share assigned resources
b. Compiling resources on a cart for the class to use
c. Allowing students to reserve what they need
d. Allowing students to renew resources as many times as needed

68. A parent contacts the school librarian to request a particular novel be removed from the school's collection because it contains content the parent views as obscene. Which of the following is the most appropriate first step in the book challenge procedure that will follow?

a. The librarian will remove the book from the shelf and refrain from circulating it until a decision has been made regarding the challenge.
b. The librarian will meet with his or her administrator to discuss the content of the book and its appropriateness for the ages of students in the school.
c. The librarian will request that the parent read the book in its entirety and submit a book challenge form.
d. The librarian will consult with district lawyers to discuss the rights of students as they pertain to the school library.

69. A librarian has just purchased new software for the library's computers that will make research easier and more effective. After the software is installed and she has become familiar with it, what should she do next?

a. Hold a brief staff meeting to instruct teachers and library staff in using the new software.
b. Circulate a memo explaining the changes and how to use the new software.
c. Instruct each class that comes to the library on how to use the new software.
d. As students enter the library to do research on the computer, instruct them individually on how to use the new software.

70. A new librarian discovers that her predecessor had a fixed-schedule program that allowed classes to visit the library at assigned times every week, leaving little time open for other activities. The library did not host specials events such as book fairs, Battle of the Books, student reading clubs, etc. The new librarian's vision for her media center includes all these activities, as well as flexible scheduling to allow students more individual library time. What is the FIRST step she should take to accomplish these goals?

a. Announce her plans for flexible scheduling at the next staff meeting and implement them immediately. Time should not be wasted on outdated kinds of schedules
b. Discuss her plans for change with the principal and get his/her input about the concept and affordability of flexible scheduling, as well as potential costs to the library in hosting special events
c. Do nothing at the present because the staff and principal seem very content with the way the library functioned in the past and postpone the idea until next year
d. Discuss with teachers, either at a staff meeting or individually, the advantages of flexible scheduling and plan to begin a flexible program with a few classes from each grade

71. A student can solve a math problem using the method learned in class. What stage of Bloom's taxonomy is that student working in?

a. Remember
b. Understand
c. Apply
d. Analyze

72. A librarian is working on the MARC annotations for audiobooks in her collection. Which of the following pieces of information will NOT be included in the annotation field?

a. Summary
b. Abstract
c. Playing time
d. Review

73. Which of the following does NOT demonstrate information literacy skills in a classroom context?

a. A student uses the skills he or she learned in the library to access an article with firsthand accounts of a historical event for use in a social studies research paper.
b. A student decided to further research the writer of an article that he or she wanted to quote and used the information gathered to determine the writer was not credible and the source should not be used.
c. A student entered a question into the search bar of a database to find information needed to complete an academic inquiry.
d. A student used a direct quote in a paper and used proper citation techniques to provide credit to the writer quoted.

74. A librarian is evaluating her paraprofessional staff. Which of the following tools will she likely use only in the formal evaluation?

a. Notes recorded during a walk-through
b. A checklist of professional expectations
c. Performance notes from throughout the year
d. Data-based levels of performance

75. The following are all components of research-based reading programs. Which component addresses the reader's ability to read texts accurately with appropriate expression and speed?

a. Vocabulary
b. Phonemic awareness
c. Fluency
d. Phonics

76. Which of the following was determined by research conducted by Keith Curry Lance?

a. Information literacy is a vital part of student success and should be included in library programming.
b. Inquiry-based learning processes are best for student learning gains.
c. Students cannot be adequately served by librarians who must also perform warehousing tasks.
d. There is a positive correlation between standardized test scores and adequately staffed libraries.

77. A middle school librarian is planning a book club program for families that will occur after school, and he needs to promote it to parents. Which of the following promotion methods will likely yield the lowest parent turnout?

a. Partnering with the parent-teacher organization for social media posts
b. Prompting the students to tell their parents
c. Directly contacting parents through email lists
d. Sending fliers home in parent contact folders

78. Which of the following is NOT an example of a librarian protecting the intellectual freedom of students?

a. The librarian advocates for the school collection to continue housing diverse titles.
b. The librarian uses lessons that are meant to explore student interests.
c. The librarian strictly adheres to district policy when a book is challenged for removal.
d. The librarian reorganizes the fiction collection by age appropriateness.

79. Which of the following is NOT an outcome of a positive learning environment?

a. An increase in academic performance
b. A decrease in student learning mistakes
c. Better student attendance rates
d. More student motivation

80. Which of the following is NOT a Standard for the 21st-Century Learner according to the American Association of School Librarians?

a. Inquire, think critically, and gain knowledge
b. Share knowledge and participate ethically and productively as members of our democratic society
c. Pursue personal and aesthetic growth
d. Demonstrate mastery of research and communication skills

81. A good way for a school librarian to assess students' performance is to:

a. Start each lesson with a pop quiz on the last lesson
b. Point out student errors during discussion so that they will not repeat them
c. Incorporate unacceptable behavior into the grades she gives
d. Enlist the help of students in creating an evaluation system so that they understand and have some ownership of it

82. A librarian wants to provide students with a story-based experience that encompasses cultural awareness, listening skills, and new vocabulary. Which of the following individuals should he host?

a. Guest readers from the community
b. Speakers from a local company
c. Storytellers from a neighboring area
d. Authors on a book tour

83. Which of the following best describes the purpose of a subscription service?

a. Allowing regular contact with students and families who subscribe to the library email list
b. Maintaining an up-to-date, refreshed collection
c. Providing access to books from outside libraries
d. Delivering books to home for students

84. Which of the following was developed by Eisenberg and Berkowitz?

a. Student autonomy and the I-Search model
b. Metacognitive scaffolding and the Big6 model
c. Whole student-based processes and the Information Search Process
d. Inquiry-based learning and defined library curriculums

85. A student has performed a search with the term NOT in order to exclude information. What is this an example of?

a. Using Boolean operators
b. Sorting search results
c. Filtering search results
d. Using a computational search engine

86. Which of the following would NOT be an appropriate way to obtain additional funding for a school library?

a. Hosting a book fair in the library
b. Collaborating with a parent-teacher organization for a fundraiser
c. Asking individual staff members for monetary donations to purchase library materials
d. Applying for grants related to the library's programming

Refer to the following for question 87:

A school librarian is preparing her first monthly report to the principal. She is new to both this school and to her job.

87. In a library media center that follows a flexible schedule, it is important for the librarian's monthly report to include what other kinds of information besides statistics?

a. Problems with staff and students
b. Collaborative projects with teachers
c. Future plans for library growth
d. Budget requests

88. A librarian wants to effectively and efficiently communicate the updated library goals to all staff members. Which of the following is the most appropriate method to accomplish this goal?

a. Sending out a text message that highlights the key goals
b. Presenting the goals at the next faculty meeting
c. Sharing an explanatory presentation to all staff via email
d. Attending grade-level meetings to share more information

89. Following a budget cut, a librarian wants to increase patron access to resources while decreasing spending. Which of the following would be the most effective way to do so?

a. Enforce higher overdue and lost book fees.
b. Enter a consortium with other libraries.
c. Host creative fundraisers in the community.
d. Transition to more subscription-based services.

90. A librarian is purchasing updated computers for the library. Which of the following components should he look for in a computer to ensure that the type he purchases will continue to have equitable access for all students?

a. Ongoing support from the company after purchasing
b. The ability to add software and connect hardware after purchasing
c. How closely company privacy policies align with school policies
d. The size and portability of the devices

Refer to the following for questions 91–92:

A student comes to the library and you observe him wandering confusedly in the library's section of science books.

91. What is the first thing you should do to help him?

a. Ask the student what his assignment is and what kind of books he is looking for
b. Tell the student that books are shelved by the author's last name and let him have the opportunity to use this information to find the books he is looking for
c. Find an opportunity later on to ask his teacher what the assignment is so that if he has difficulty locating materials the next time he comes to the library, you can help him
d. Send another student from his class over to help him, as they both have the same assignment

92. You interview the student and he tells you that he has been assigned to write a paper on the annual migration of Monarch butterflies from North America to Mexico. Which of the following would you suggest that the student do first?

a. Look for books in the Dewey Decimal System with the number 590, Zoology
b. Put "butterflies" into an Internet search engine
c. Use OPAC to find MARC entries about Monarch butterfly migration
d. Consult the Readers' Guide to Periodical Literature for articles on the topic

93. A first-grade teacher is inquiring about authors to use in her instruction for early readers. Which of the following award-winning authors would you recommend that she consider?

a. Lois Lowry
b. S.E. Hinton
c. Harper Lee
d. Eric Carle

94. Which of the following is NOT a benefit of interlibrary loans?

a. Decrease in spending for libraries
b. Extended borrowing periods for patrons
c. Maximized use of available resources
d. Increased access for patrons

95. Which of the following is NOT most likely to be determined by evaluating a budget?

a. It is decided books for the after-school book club will be borrowed from the public library and not purchased this school year.
b. Various sections of the library are weeded and reduced by 15 percent in the biography, fairy tale, and sports sections.
c. The librarian develops a purchasing plan for diverse titles in order to enhance the nonfiction collection.
d. The principal determines the library is entitled to the remaining funds from office purchasing.

96. Which of the following is NOT a method to use for more accurate results when using a search engine?

a. Putting quotation marks around information to ensure results contain those key phrases
b. Adding an asterisk behind words when the spelling may be incorrect
c. Entering a question as it would be posed to another person
d. Using AND, NOT, and OR in searches to limit results

97. The librarian has established the need for new furniture and has received funding for it. This is a large project that requires bids from multiple vendors in order to proceed. Which of the following is the next step?

a. Develop sample contracts for the vendors to review.
b. Write and share a request for proposal.
c. Cold-call vendors to check for interest in the project.
d. Develop a purchasing plan that outlines when purchases will take place.

98. Several new books focused on families have been added to the library. How can the librarian best reach parents to promote these offerings?

a. Display a banner on the circulation system's homepage.
b. Create a popup for the school's website.
c. Have the information added to the weekly school newsletter.
d. Run a campaign on the morning announcements.

99. A librarian is helping a student cite her sources for an English paper. Which style of citation is most appropriate in this scenario?

a. Chicago style
b. APA style
c. Turabian style
d. MLA style

100. A librarian is in the process of selecting a new vendor to work with. Which of the following should he or she do first?

a. Submit the vendor to the purchasing department for approval.
b. Cross-reference prices of various books with other major retailers.
c. Establish the overall estimated cost of titles to be acquired.
d. Ensure the availability of the desired titles.

Constructed Response

1. A class of sixth-grade students is learning how to write a research paper. Each student has been assigned an endangered animal topic, and the students must explore that animal's identifying qualities, behaviors, native habitat, as well as the reasons for its endangered status. The teacher of the class has asked you to teach a lesson on the types and characteristics of print, non-print, and electronic resources, and how they should be utilized in this project.

- Explain how you would structure this lesson and what information and suggestions you would include.
- Describe the advantages and limitations of each kind of resource as they pertain to this age group and assignment.

Answer Key and Explanations

Multiple Choice Questions

1. A: Immediately adding new books to the shelves usually causes them to blend in with older books and does not help promote circulation. Creating book displays (B) is a great way to get attention and help the books stand out. Book talks (C) promote interest in the new additions by sharing what the books are about. Signage throughout the school (D) sparks interest in students who may not typically visit the library.

2. D: Providing students with the skills needed to access databases gives them an entry point to a plethora of information even if they are not able to physically access the library. Validating sources is a key library skill but is not most helpful to students participating in learning remotely, and this also applies to coding skills and citing sources.

3. A: Professional collections are meant to be sources of professional development for teachers and other staff members. This includes books on teaching and assessment strategies, manipulative kits, and curriculum support. Student queries about professions (B) can best be answered in the nonfiction section or through database research. Similarly, this is likely how a guidance counselor would address the same queries (D). While information about behaving in a professional manner may be found in some of the resources in a professional collection (C), that is not the collection's main purpose.

4. D: Folk literature is a style of story typically derived from tales passed down orally through generations. Legends (A), fables (B), and myths (C) all began this way. Because folk literature is derived from tradition, there is no known singular author. As a result, there tends to be varied forms of the same story. Dramas began as written plays meant to be performed by actors and are generally written by one distinctive author, distinguishing them from folk literature.

5. B: While a school year may seem like a long time for a book to remain uncirculated, best practice is to wait five years before considering it for weeding based on the lack of circulation alone. While books that are damaged (A) can sometimes be repaired, it may be necessary to weed books that have multiple repairs preventing them from being read or that have pages missing. A book is considered superseded (C) when a new edition is released. While this does not warrant immediate weeding, the older edition can be weeded after the newer edition has been added to the catalog. As technology and science progress, so will the related information and findings. As such, it is important to weed out any books that are no longer factually accurate (D).

6. C: Sharing a PDF of a novel for students to read for their own entertainment fails to satisfy fair use criteria. Fair use allows for portions of work belonging to others to be used for educational, reporting, research, critical, or other scholarly purposes. Directly quoting a speech in a paper is acceptable under fair use so long as the quote is correctly cited to give credit to the person who is being quoted. Parodies are often considered acceptable under fair use. Reproducing a small portion of a work for the purpose of teaching is permitted and not considered copyright infringement.

7. B: Upon receiving any kind of purchased materials, the librarian should assess the contents. The purchase order, packing slip, and contents of the box should match exactly. The packing slip then needs to be sent to the individual responsible for paying for the order so that he or she may complete the process. Sorting and cataloging should not occur until after all expected contents have been accounted for and payment has been confirmed. Updating the library budget should occur after payments have been processed. Calling the vendor to confirm delivery is not necessary with available package tracking.

8. D: A slide show is for creating visual presentations, not graphic design. A slide show presentation needs to be organized with a specific design, a plan for content delivery, and a direction toward a certain audience. The librarian can guide the student to create this kind of organization for a presentation.

9. C: *Booklist* is a publication from the ALA that reviews a variety of books for all readers. It provides highly detailed, unbiased reviews as well as related award information. The reviews in *Kirkus Reviews* (A) are written by writers and editors and are not ALA affiliated. *The Horn Book Magazine* (B) reviews children's and young adult books and staffs a variety of reviewers. The *School Library Journal* (D) is similar to *Booklist* but is not published by the ALA.

10. A: Acceptable use policies outline expectations and guidelines for student use of technology. In most cases, these policies must be signed by students and their families before the students are allowed to use school-owned devices. Proper book care (B) must be taught to students using direct instruction during library programming. Preparing a handbook for using library equipment (C) may be beneficial for others who occasionally operate within the space, but it is not an acceptable use policy. Communication with parents is a key component of library management when it comes to working with children directly (D), but like answer C, it is not an acceptable use policy.

11. C: The ALA Code of Ethics states that librarians will not advance the private interests of others while limiting access to patrons. Accepting money for removing controversial titles does just that: limits access and advances private interests. While choice A is similar in that it has a contingency, it does not remove anything from the collection. Instead, it only adds new titles. Book donations that require an action such as student voting (B) are a popular way to gain free books and do not cross any ethical boundaries. While discarding donated books may seem unethical (D), it is common practice and necessary for library maintenance.

12. A: The imprint of a book lists the publisher, the publication date, and the location of the publisher. This information is useful in some citation methods. The Library of Congress Control Number, or LCCN, is a number assigned to records in national databases and would not be pertinent in this scenario. The preface provides background information the reader needs to know before beginning to read. The author main entry field is the MARC field that provides the name of the book's author.

13. B: Sharing a bibliography of new acquisitions with staff will present them with the new offerings while also describing the content, making it easier for them to find the books that align with their curriculum. While sharing the new books at a staff meeting will bring attention to them (A), it does not allow teachers a thorough look into what is available. Displaying books in the library (C) will likely not reach all teachers as many are unavailable to peruse the collection. Posting a slideshow on the library homepage (D) is not the most effective way as it requires the teachers to go to the website to see this information.

14. A: Ask the teacher to give students the assignment and then schedule a time to bring the class to the library. Directly teach students research techniques for print materials and for the Internet. Show them how to locate internet databases that will meet their needs and how to coordinate information from several sources. Answer A provides the best way for students to learn research techniques, especially since they will be interested because of the assignment. Answer B puts the entire burden on the teacher with no real assistance from the librarian. Answer C may not be possible unless the library has a media clerk who can be present if the librarian leaves the library. Also, it is really not necessary because the teacher can bring the class to the library. Answer D is also incorrect because another one of the answer choices is more appropriate.

15. B: Book talks allow librarians to share the general content of a book in a way that is meant to spark interest in readers. A reading workshop is a classroom framework for independent reading that usually begins with a mini-lesson before students read independently and then share what they learned or how they applied a skill or reading strategy. Mini-lessons are a component of instruction defined by their short period of direct instruction, typically 5 to 10 minutes. These lessons are then followed by some type of supporting activity. Beginning a reading incentive program does not outline what section of the library students will check books out of; therefore, it may not lead to an increase in circulation in that section.

16. A: While due process requires notices to be sent to involved parties regarding updates on the matter, it does not require any large groups be informed of the decision. Prompt response (B) is ensured by the promptness required by due process. Due process requires that decisions be made by individuals who are impartial and unbiased to the challenge at hand (C). This ensures only factual information and rights are considered when making a decision. Allowing individuals involved to voice concerns provides the opportunity to be heard as is required in due process (D).

17. D: Integrating technology into the library program. By creating an interesting activity that prompts students to discover the functions of various computer programs, the librarian is integrating computer technology into the library program. Answer A, ethical use, does not apply here, as nothing is copied or plagiarized during the search. Answer B also does not apply because diversity is not an issue. Everyone is equal when using a computer. Answer C does not apply because the students are not using oral or written communication.

18. D: Learning how to remotely access research databases will best benefit students in this situation as they will learn the proper skills to access the information they need regardless of where they are. The hold and renewal processes will allow students to reserve books they need for their work and retain them for longer periods; however, the needed information from these books likely could be found in a database, which eliminates the limitations a physical copy has, such as time constraints and waiting for others to return it. The ability to navigate the nonfiction section would allow students to find physical resources more easily, but students will still encounter the aforementioned constraints with physical copies.

19. C: Answer C provides a specific goal that is achievable and realistic by stating 80 percent of students will show success and that this success will be measured by their final product of a research presentation. The timeliness is highlighted by the "end of the unit" statement. Answer A would be improved by adding the number of students they expect to be proficient and the tool they will use to measure them. While answer B states the desired ability of students, it lacks any detail and specificity that would make the goal practical. It would need the desired level of achievement, the method that will be used to get students to that point, and an explanation of how proficiency will be measured. Answer D fails to outline how many students are expected to succeed, but it is well written outside of that.

20. D: The I-Search model was developed by Ken Macrorie specifically to allow students to choose their own research topics while learning the stages of inquiry. This was done to prevent negative feelings toward the whole research process. The Stripling Model is cyclical. Both the Stripling and I-Search models end in an opportunity for reflection. All research models are meant to focus on the inquiry process by intentionally guiding students through it.

21. A: Purchasing new copies of classic books solely to update their cover art does not demonstrate curriculum support because it does not improve student learning, access, or instructional use of the collection. Since the existing copies are in good condition, this action does not meaningfully enhance the library's ability to support the curriculum. Providing access to new databases (B) would extend student access to a variety of information, thus supporting the curriculum in many areas. The addition of assistive technology (C) extends access of existing resources to more students, making the current collection better able to support learning for all. Adding popular titles used in teaching in languages other than English offers multilingual learners the opportunity to better participate in learning experiences.

22. B: The American Library Association Bill of Rights asserts that children and youth are entitled to private records regarding their circulation history. This means that their records are protected from others, such as parents and teachers. While these records can be given to parents at their request (A), it is not required to provide them with immediate or remote access. The ALA does not support automatically making minors' circulation records accessible to parents without a specific, justified request; doing so would undermine the child's right to privacy. Law enforcement must follow the process established in its jurisdiction in order to obtain student records (D). School librarians should be familiar with this policy to ensure they adhere to it. Providing teachers with access to circulation records (C) is a direct invasion of student privacy.

23. D: Academic journals are a compilation of resources written by field experts. Magazines and newspapers are usually more general-interest-based and not strictly academic. Search engines may be able to direct students to journals but will not present the information directly.

24. B: Resource Description and Access (RDA) replaced Anglo-American Cataloging Rules, Second Edition (AACR2) in 2010. The primary difference between these two sets of rules is that RDA established in-depth guidelines for cataloging digital resources, something that was becoming more common in libraries at the time. Removing Anglo-American from the name was meant to show that these rules did not only apply to US or British libraries and could be used globally. While adhering to these guidelines can make the other answer choices true, those answers were not the sole reasons for the transition.

25. C: In this situation, it seems students are picking books from the stacks that they would like to read but not checking them out using the library circulation system. In order to best prevent this, the librarian should start by reviewing and reteaching the circulation procedures in place. Reviewing the acceptable use policy (A) would be more appropriate if there were issues with students abusing or misusing school technology. Interlibrary loans (B) allow students to gain access to books not available in their school's library and is not applicable to this situation. Reconsideration policies (D) outline the steps to take following a book challenge. This would apply to a situation in which a student raises a concern about a book he or she felt was not appropriate for the school collection.

26. A: One of the ISTE Standards for Students is 'Global Collaborator,' which includes working in teams both locally and globally. However, there is no separate standard titled 'Local collaboration,' so choice A is not a component name of the ISTE standards. Other standards include being empowered learners, digital citizens (B), knowledge constructors, innovative designers (D), computational thinkers (C), and creative communicators.

27. A: Weeding and schedule changing. Librarians need to know the library's content thoroughly before deciding what materials to weed and what to acquire. If a librarian discards a teacher's favorite materials, she will lose a supporter of the library. The librarian should wait awhile before weeding. Answer B should be done early in the year so that staff members understand that plagiarism is widespread, sometimes inadvertent, and what teachers can do about it. Answer C is always a good idea whenever the librarian can find time in the school and library schedule. Answer D, reorganizing the furniture, can be done right away. The arrangement of the librarian's space should reflect her personal philosophy and competency.

28. A: In this scenario, IT professionals will be the most knowledgeable committee members. They will be able to determine which software is most closely aligned with what the school needs. Library support staff (B) may be able to explain the purpose and function of the software but likely lack knowledge of the choices. While administrators (C) should be consulted and will likely have the final say, they too likely do not have the background knowledge necessary to make the best-informed decision. Parents (D) should be aware of the use of filtering software but do not need to be consulted on what type is purchased.

29. B: The Stripling Model was designed as a cyclical inquiry. There are several stages that connect back to one another as students work through research. The definition of construct is actually students constructing new understandings and making connections to previous knowledge. Wonder (A), investigate (C), and express (D) are all correctly defined.

30. C: Juggle the schedule, trading one teacher's period for another if necessary to allow for the one-time-only extra time period and offer to start the class off by teaching some Internet research techniques and showing students where relevant books are located in the library.

Even on a fixed schedule, there are a few free periods for students to come to the library and exchange books. The librarian could trade periods with another teacher (with that teacher's permission) who is normally scheduled for the period before or after one of those free periods. Prior to the scheduled time period, the librarian and teacher can discuss and plan relevant instruction in research skills for this class. Answer A is too inflexible and discounts the possibility of juggling schedules. Answer B is unlikely, because a whole class at a time is usually in the library, especially if the schedule is fixed. Answer D offers to provide some help to the teacher, but not as much as in answer C.

31. B: Short-term goals are typically defined as those taking six to 12 months, while long-term goals are any that require more time than that. Genrefying a library can be done within a year and will likely take less time. Seeing a schoolwide increase in reading abilities (A) will require implementation of common teaching practices that can take at least a year to simply adopt. It will then require testing of students and modified teaching. This more closely aligns with a schoolwide three-year plan. Major renovations are timely (C) and can require more than a year, especially in this situation in which school board members are asking for librarian input. Purchasing plans (D), especially those that require a needs assessment, often require three to five years to complete due to budget constraints.

32. A: Guest author visits have been shown to motivate students to read and write more. This has a cross-curricular impact and will help inspire students in many areas of learning. Reading reward programs (B) can provide extrinsic motivation through prizes and acknowledgement. Writing lessons (C) provide students with the lessons, guidance, and structure needed to complete writing assignments but do not address motivational issues. Giving students consequences (D) for failing to write may motivate some students who prefer to avoid those consequences, but it is not the best or most effective way to motivate all students.

33. A: The American Association of School Librarians (AASL) is the only national association dedicated to school librarianship. It has developed learning frameworks for use in libraries to ensure student success. The Library of Congress (LOC) is the US research library and does not establish standards related to school libraries. Though it is the parent organization of the AASL, the American Library Association (ALA) outlines expectations of librarians with no emphasis on the school library role. The Online Computer Library Center (OCLC) focuses on data management systems within libraries.

34. C: Make a comprehensive daily, weekly, and monthly plan listing what needs to be done, the deadline for completing each task, and the person responsible for handling the task.

Making a detailed plan of goals, needs, assigned times, etc. will clearly lay out for the librarian what her tasks are. She can estimate the time required for each and assign a date and time for completion of each item. Answer A would not be the best first step, because after making the plan, it may be evident that the media clerk is already performing all that he/she can handle. Answer B might be a good second step, but it is not a good first step. If the library has traditionally managed with the number of employees it presently has, then the problem is more likely to be time management than the need for more help. After the beginning librarian has made her plans, she can show the principal item by item what the problems are and ask for his help if it turns out that her workload is indeed excessive. Answer D, putting in overtime hours, may be necessary but that fact will not be clear until the planning takes place. An exhausted librarian will not be efficient, so that option is not the most desirable.

35. B: Since a slide show is a visual medium, she should take advantage of that and show what to do rather than lecturing about it. She can invite students to try some of the techniques she is teaching and make the lesson as hands-on as possible so that its content will cross the language barrier. All students enjoy a hands-on lesson, and by giving one, the librarian is making sure that ESL students are not derided or embarrassed by their language difficulties. Answer A singles them out and excludes them from learning something they would benefit from knowing. Answer C is not feasible because the partner would not be understood any more than the librarian. Answer D is apt to embarrass ESL students, although speaking slowly and clearly is a good idea.

36. A: Effectively interviews patrons to determine information needs. Note that in the beginning of the conversation between Juan and the librarian, he is at first vague and general about his topic. The librarian asks a series of skillful questions to narrow down the subject area and is then able to help Juan. Answer B would apply to the librarian's knowledge of appropriate materials, but her primary action in the conversation is to determine Juan's information needs. Answer C is incorrect because Juan is not trying to improve his reading skills. He is looking for information. Answer D deals with the librarian's philosophy and not with her ability to discover a patron's needs.

37. B: Goals established in schools should follow SMART goal suggestions, meaning they should be specific, measurable, achievable, realistic, and timely. Answer B is specific in that it states what the library staff plans to do, how much it wants to increase circulation based on data, and what student group the library wants to see the increase in. The goal can be measured by comparing circulation data, it is achievable and realistic based on the lesson information provided, and it is timely because it outlines the period in which the goal is trying to be accomplished. While answer A provides a specific percentage increase that is desired, it is not realistic nor is it truly measurable in the library. Answer C lacks specificity by excluding how much of an increase in circulation the library wants to see and what group of students it wants to see the change in. Answer D also lacks specificity by not outlining the number of volunteer hours the library wants to reach and over what period it wants to increase them in.

38. C: Speak to the boys firmly about proper library behavior. Since the students are in the library, they are on the librarian's territory, and she has as much responsibility as the teacher to see that they behave correctly. The teacher has had a chance to correct these boys but has not done it. Speaking to him about their behavior might embarrass the teacher or make him resentful. He might continue to ignore it. After it is clear that the teacher is aware of the behavior and is choosing not to intervene, the librarian should corral the unruly students and remind them how to behave in the library. Answer D is not necessary because the problem can be handled by the librarian without the need to hand it over to someone else.

39. C: Monitoring student use of cell phones would not be a part of the librarian's job description. Student cell phone use is not part of the librarian's technological skill areas. The responsibility for students who bring cell phones to school belongs to the school, if it has regulations regarding cell phones at school, and if not, to the classroom teacher. Responsibilities described in answers A, B, and D are increasingly becoming part of the school librarian's job description.

40. D: An explanation of key interests of the library is part of a philosophy, not a mission statement. A well-written mission statement consists of a goal, a reason for the goal, and the methodology that will be used to reach the goal. Stating the goal as well as the reasoning for it provides clarity and highlights importance for library stakeholders. By providing the methods that will be used, the librarian is sharing the process through which the mission will be met.

41. D: Circulation data provides detailed information about the specific types of resources used, including by what grade levels and for how long. This should be used as a first step to ensure the librarian is allotting the appropriate amount of money and attention to each category in a way that best serves students. Using curriculum information to guide purchasing (A) is helpful when buying books specifically for that purpose, but those books may not be needed based on what the collection currently has and on whether those resources are being utilized. This also goes for supporting the staff via purchasing requested materials to help support the curricular needs (C). A student advisory committee (B) provides insight on what students are interested in and will actually read; however, purchasing leisure reading titles may not be in the library's best interest at that time if there are other gaps to be filled.

42. B: Genrefication is a rapidly growing library trend in which a fiction section is organized by the genres of books rather than in alphabetical order by the author's last name or other standard methods. The Library of Congress Classification system (D) uses a combination of letters and numbers to represent the bibliographic information for resources. Books are then shelved according to the numerical order assigned to them. The Sears List of Subject Headings (A) is a simplified list of subject headings, often used with the Dewey Decimal Classification in smaller libraries to provide subject access, but it is not a shelving or classification system like LCC or DDC. The Dewey Decimal Classification (C) is the most common in school libraries. It provides detailed information on organizing the nonfiction section of a library but has fiction sections organized by the author's last name.

43. A: Instructing them in effective ways to do research on the Internet and in efficient use of library reference materials and books on the library shelves. Answer A fulfills both the librarian's responsibilities and the students' needs. Instruction of this sort can be tailored to ongoing classroom projects and individualized to meet the needs of students who need support, as well as students who can work on their own. Answer B does not produce any educational results. Part of assigned library time should be set aside for exchanging books, but not all of it. Answer C is like a "story time" for older students, although making students aware of new materials should be part of the librarian's instructional plans from time to time. Although answer D is very helpful to the librarian, it is of little educational value to the students.

44. D: Analyzing circulation information to complete a needs assessment in order to make decisions for the library is the role of the librarian. The lead librarian should be responsible for any major decisions, such as those regarding library needs, budgeting, and purchasing. Volunteers should assist in tasks with minimal impact to the overall program. Allowing trained volunteers to shelve books (A) does not impact library lesson times and helps to create more time for planning for the librarian. Organizing books (B) similarly has minimal impact on day-to-day library lesson times and creates more time for the librarian. Assisting students in retrieving books (C) increases access for children by reducing the wait time required for them to get assistance.

45. D: Many news sources can be biased in order to remain relevant to their target audiences. This is something that should be assessed before quoting a site in an academic writing assignment. The currency (A) and age (B) of a news site should be up-to-date given the nature of news outlets. In this scenario, relevance (C) refers to whether or not the information in the article pertains to the topic, and it most likely will because the student located it in his query. While any of these choices could potentially invalidate a source, the potential bias would be the criteria most likely to invalidate this resource for use in this student's project.

46. C: The Americans with Disabilities Act (ADA) was designed to protect the rights of individuals with disabilities by ensuring equal access to resources and facilities. It requires doorframes to be wide enough to fit standard wheelchairs. The Children's Internet Protection Act requires that internet filtering software be used in schools that receive federal credits for internet services. The Family Educational Rights and Privacy Act protects the privacy of students enrolled in a school by limiting the creation of and access to education records. Title IX was implemented to prohibit sex-based discrimination in schools.

47. C: The theory of behaviorism suggests that learning is an outcome of interactions with one's environment, and thus, it is the responsibility of the educator to create an environment conducive to learning. Cognitivism (A) focuses on how the brain retains information through organizing it. The theory of humanism (B) revolves around self-actualization and the hierarchy of needs. Constructivism (D) suggests that synthesizing new knowledge requires building upon prior knowledge.

48. C: Though the staff is adequately trained at the time, that does not mean further and ongoing professional development is not needed. Library processes and procedures and trends in reading change often; thus, in order to adequately maintain a library, it is vital that continuing education opportunities be available. A library collection maintained by trained staff will be more organized (A) than one managed by untrained individuals who lack understanding of the organization methods used. Highly qualified staff will have the background knowledge needed to offer quality programming to students (B). Knowledgeable staff members are better able to address any concerns or questions posed by stakeholders using what they have learned in their training (D).

49. B: A critical friend is a peer who provides support and critical feedback on an educational situation. He or she is not in a position of authority and voluntarily provides feedback as it is asked of him or her. In this case, it will likely be another librarian. While a lead librarian in a school or district is qualified to give feedback and input, he or she is considered a biased party as a stakeholder in the school system who likely has his or her own vision for how the library should be run. An administrator is not likely to be qualified to give feedback and is also biased as a stakeholder in the school. While classroom teachers may have advice to offer on pedagogy or classroom management, they are not best suited to provide feedback on how to best run a library.

50. C: The physical description of a resource lists the extent, meaning the length in pages if it's a book or the running time if it's an audio or video resource. It also details the dimensions of physical resources and other related information like if it contains nonbook companion items or illustrations. Cover art description (A) would be found in the annotation field and publication information (D) would be found in a book's imprint. Considerations for care of resources (B) is not something listed in standard cataloging practices.

51. B: Hosting a guest speaker will be the best event for students to learn more about community offerings as it will offer an opportunity to speak with a community member in a way not often available to students. A family read-aloud event would be better suited to address a goal related to library usage or overall interest in reading. A visit from an illustrator or writer will likely spark student interest in the content being covered but won't provide them with information about community offerings. A writing workshop also does not provide students with community offering information.

52. D: In order to increase accessibility, the Federal Communications Commission (FCC) established the E-Rate program, which subsidizes the cost of internet for schools. Internet credits provided by the FCC are contingent upon schools using internet filtering software to protect the safety and privacy of students. Families are not required to be notified of the acceptance or use of these credits (B). Acceptable use policies (AUPs) are documents that outline the expected and appropriate use of school devices. It is typically required that students and parents sign these before using any devices (A). There is currently no requirement regarding what vendors libraries receiving E-Rate credits can use (C).

53. B: Obtain a list of suspect databases from the concerned teacher and evaluate each one carefully to see if the information is accurate, reliable and unbiased. Remove these sources from the library's collection. The librarian is the person responsible for assessing information from databases for accuracy and/or bias. Answer A, asking busy teachers to help with the problem, is asking them to do something they may not know how to do or have time to do. Answer C also puts the burden on the teacher when the responsibility for determining accuracy is the librarian's. Answer D is a good follow-up after the librarian has assessed the databases, but it is not the first step to take.

54. D: The primary purpose of a reconsideration policy is to provide transparency and guidance on how complaints or formal challenges regarding library materials will be resolved. These policies outline book challenge procedures as well as the First Amendment rights that protect access to books for students. Budgeting information would be found in annual budget reports created by the body that determines funding within a school or district. Student circulation policies would most likely be developed at the school level and be available from the librarian by request. Acceptable use agreements are most often district-created documents that outline the expected use of school-owned technology.

55. B: Students can gain more detailed information from specific research models; if school districts recommend or require the use of a specific research model, teachers and students will have the same framework for evaluating student projects. Answer A is not relevant because the financial backing of a particular research model does not reflect its relevance or the significance of its information. Answer C does not restrict the librarian to district-recommended materials. Answer D may or may not be true, but the importance of the task lies in the results, what students can find out by using these research models.

56. C: After conferring with each classroom teacher about his or her current curriculum, demonstrate separately to different classes how to use the Internet to find information on the topic each class is presently studying. Teaching different classes to find materials they can use best supports the specific projects of each class. Students are more likely to pay attention to a demonstration if it involves something they need to do. A is incorrect because it leaves students on their own to blunder around trying to use an unfamiliar process. B is a good idea, but it takes the "one size fits all" approach to instruction. D is not the best approach because it encourages students to figure out a process by themselves, without teacher instruction or help.

57. B: The Young Adult Library Services Association hosts annual conferences as well as other events that provide librarians who serve young adults opportunities for professional development as it relates to their field. The Association of College and Research Libraries (A) hosts events targeting librarians who serve adult patrons with academic focuses. Offerings from the Reference and User Services Association (C) focus on reference-related topics. The Public Library Association (D) offers professional learning opportunities to those who serve in public libraries.

58. B: To verify that the subject matter is accurate and covers student and teacher needs.

Through this review, the librarian may discover that some subjects are not properly covered in the database, and she may need to purchase others. Answer A is incorrect because a review of the database will not reveal student plagiarism. Answer C is incorrect because a filter prevents students from accessing inappropriate sites. This information is not found on a database. Answer D is incorrect because students with a variety of reading skills will access each database.

59. B: Narrative poems are known for their plotlines and story-like structure. Lyric poems (A) are often song-like and meant to express emotions, while ode poems (D) are a subcategory of lyrical poem. Dramatic poems (C) are meant to be read as a monologue or acted out, and they usually rhyme or contain some type of rhythm.

60. A: Cognitivism focuses on how learners process, store, and retrieve information; teachers often scaffold learning and break it into manageable chunks so students can more easily incorporate it into their existing schema. Ensuring social-emotional needs are met (B) falls under the theory of humanism. Behaviorism suggests students need to interact with their environments and learn from the related consequences in order to best learn (C). Guiding students through collaborative, authentic problem-solving is more characteristic of constructivism, which emphasizes knowledge construction through experience (D).

61. B: Dialogue between parties in biographical narratives may not be completely accurate because the exact dialogue may not have been known. There may be several reasons for this, such as the time the conversation took place, the lack of witnesses for the conversation, or the lack of documentation for the conversation. The subject's date of birth (A), significant life events (C), and accomplishments (D) are all usually thoroughly documented and able to be verified.

62. A: Peer assessments are completed within a group in order to provide members with feedback. This most often takes place in the form of observation followed by a debrief in which feedback is shared. Discussing library guidelines (B), collection ages (C), and budget information (D) may all take place during professional learning community meetings; however, these are not considered peer assessments.

63. D: Critiquing books. The librarian should remain neutral about books and other materials in the library's collection, recognizing that there are many points of view on an issue and many writing styles. The librarian is responsible for scheduling classes and library-related events, reporting on the functioning and collection of the library, and maintaining and facilitating circulation of the library's materials.

64. A: Long-term financial goals are ones that take longer than a school year to meet, while short-term goals can be met within a year or less. In order to reallocate funds for something new, the spending in another area must be minimized. In answer A, the librarian must first implement a plan to reduce the amount spent on replacement books before he or she can set aside those funds for reallocation. Doing so will likely take a few school years to build up funds and use them as stated, making this a long-term goal. Increasing the number of titles available and updating furniture options can be achieved within one fiscal year so long as the librarian budgets appropriately. Adding new database options is a quick process once they have been paid for.

65. C: A reflective journal is best defined as a collection of notes concerned with reflecting on the librarian's current practices. A portfolio is a compilation of student work samples (A) that can be used to demonstrate student growth and proficiency and the aligned effectiveness of the librarian. A set of questions used to assess oneself (B) is considered a self-assessment and usually has an associated score evaluating effectiveness. Investigations into any incidents (D) that are then used to guide changes are considered incident analyses.

66. C: A needs assessment is a systematic process for identifying gaps between current resources (such as collections, services, or programs) and patron needs. In this case, the librarian notices and wishes to fill gaps in the collection. To do so, she must assess what is present and what needs to be added. Loss prevention (A) may have prevented the books that filled these gaps from going missing; however, it does not help replace them at this point. Loss prevention usually entails good cataloging practices or clear circulation policies. While the librarian will likely use this information to guide purchasing in the future (B), that is not the goal at hand. Program implementation (D) is more aligned with lesson planning and instruction.

67. B: When a large group or entire class of students is working on the same assignment, it is best to have the students share resources within the class. This is best accomplished by creating a class resource cart for them to use. Partnering students to share assigned resources (A) limits access by preventing students from using resources that are available to other pairings. Allowing students to reserve what they need (C) prevents other students from accessing materials that are on hold. Allowing endless renewal (D) also prevents access to students who need the resource and are waiting for it to be returned.

68. C: Book challenge procedures are initiated by book challenge requests. These requests are highly detailed and meant to ensure the party challenging the book has done its own due diligence. Requesting the parent read the book and submit a form will give the librarian a better understanding of the reasoning for the challenge. This process also acts as a deterrent for individuals who are just challenging books as part of mass political movements or statements. Removing books from circulation at the request of the parent impedes on the First Amendment rights of other students. Removing the book (A) should not be done unless the decision made following the challenge deems it must occur. While meeting with the school administrator will be necessary at some point during the challenge process (B), it does not need to occur until a formal challenge has been filed. Similarly, the district lawyer may become involved in the process (D) but contacting him or her is not the first necessary step.

69. A: The librarian should hold a brief staff meeting to instruct teachers and library staff in using the new software. If the staff knows how to use the software, they can assist individual students right away, even before students receive instruction from the librarian during their next scheduled library visit. Also, staff members should become familiar with all new technology. Choice B risks that not all teachers will read the memo and be able to help their students use the software. Choice C is the second action the librarian should take, but since she cannot meet with every class in one day, informing the teachers first is more important. Choice D would carry individualized instruction to an extreme. The librarian would be unable to perform other tasks if she attempted to show students one at a time how to use the software.

70. B: Discuss her plans for change with the principal and get his/her input about the concept and affordability of flexible scheduling, as well as the potential costs to the library of hosting special events. There is likely to be a financial component to making these changes. In some school settings, having a flexible schedule means that the school must hire someone to give the teachers the prep periods they formerly had during a fixed schedule. Hosting special events can require extended hours for a school's custodial staff, along with additional electrical and heating expenses. The librarian needs to find out from the principal if the school budget can handle these changes. Also, as a matter of diplomacy, obtaining the principal's support for a change in practice is a good management technique. Answer A could cause dissension among staff members and bring criticism from an uninformed principal. Answer C is the easy way out, but it will not result in achievement of the librarian's goals. Answer D is a good second step for the librarian to take after she has obtained the support of the principal.

71. C: In Bloom's taxonomy, apply refers to the ability to use what has been learned in new situations. Remember is the lowest level of the taxonomy and is the ability to recall facts and concepts. Understanding allows the learner to explain ideas. Analyze focuses on the ability to make connections among ideas.

72. C: MARC annotations contain information about the general contents of a resource. The summary (A) briefly explains what the resource is, reviews (D) give a short snippet expressing how others feel about the resource, and abstracts (B) provide a more detailed explanation of the contents (these are typically found on the back or inside jacket of books). Information on playing time of an audiobook (C) would be found in the physical description of a MARC tag.

73. C: When using databases to access information, students should use keyword or Boolean search methods. This provides a return of the most accurate information and is considered an overall best practice. By accessing a resource using a library database (A), a student is showing proficiency in the sourcing component of information literacy. By completing further research to assess the credibility of a source (B), a student is demonstrating the validation component of information literacy. In using proper citations for quoted materials (D), a student is demonstrating awareness of information literacy's copyright and ethics component.

74. D: Data-driven information is a key component of formal evaluation. Using data provides quantitative reasoning to determine effectiveness. Walk-throughs (A) are a type of informal evaluation in which the evaluator very briefly observes a person or space, typically for five to 10 minutes, and records what he or she sees during that time on a document or form established by the walk-through program used in the school. Checklists (B) are another informal tool that allow an observer to do a quick assessment. Performance notes (C) are a type of anecdotal notes, or notes taken spontaneously as interesting incidents occur. Anecdotal notes may be helpful in forming a general idea of incidents, but they are not comprehensive or standardized enough to be used as a formal measure. Choices A, B, and C may be used to help provide feedback in formal evaluations, but data-based information is the key component to a formal evaluation.

75. C: Fluency is defined as the ability to read accurately with appropriate expression and speed. In reading instruction, vocabulary (A) refers to words the reader can recognize in the text. Phonemic awareness (B) addresses the individual parts of words that make sounds, which are called phonemes. Phonics (D) is applying phonemic awareness to decode an unfamiliar word.

76. D: Research conducted by Lance determined that students with access to school libraries with certified librarians performed better on standardized tests. Paul G. Zurkowski pioneered the term "information literacy" and focused much of his studies on its importance. Ross J. Todd's research focused on the impact of inquiry-based learning processes. David V. Loertscher determined that students learning from librarians who also needed to perform warehousing tasks could not be adequately served.

77. B: While guiding students on how to explain the book club to their parents may be beneficial, depending on them to communicate to their parents is the least likely of the choices to be successful. Having the parent-teacher organization share information about the book club (A) allows for an easy way to reach parents on a platform with which they are already engaged. Contacting parents directly through email lists (C) eliminates a dependency on any other sources and provides the opportunity for direct contact back. Sending home informational fliers (D) will have similar success, specifically by placing them in a folder seen regularly by parents rather than sending them home loosely.

78. D: Organizing a collection by age will restrict the access of certain patrons to particular titles, thus impeding on both their rights and their intellectual freedoms. By housing diverse titles (A), the librarian is allowing students to explore several cultures, belief sets, and other facets of the world. Allowing students to explore their own interests (B) supports intellectual freedom by providing time for students to personalize their own enriched learning experiences. Ensuring book challenge procedures are adhered to (C) prevents any unnecessary removal of books or resources from students who would like to use such materials for their own enjoyment or educational needs.

79. B: Students are not guaranteed to make fewer learning mistakes in a positive learning environment. On the contrary, they may make more mistakes as they will feel more supported and more willing to take risks in their learning. Studies focusing on positive learning environments have shown that overall academic performance improves, staff and student attendance rates improve, students feel more motivated to learn and participate in learning experiences, violence among students decreases, and there is better teacher retention.

80. D: Demonstrate mastery of research and communication skills is not a component of the AASL's Standards for the 21st-Century Learner. The four standards featured are inquire, think critically, and gain knowledge (A); draw conclusions, make informed decisions, apply knowledge to new situations, and create new knowledge; share knowledge and participate ethically and productively as members of our democratic society (B); and pursue personal and aesthetic growth (C). These standards are meant to support the educational development of well-rounded and competitive learners.

81. D: Enlist the help of students in creating an evaluation system so that they understand and have some ownership of it. The best way to evaluate students is to let them know the criteria from the beginning so that they understand the librarian's expectations. If they have been involved in drawing up the criteria, they will be more accepting of the librarian's evaluation of their progress. Answer A, start each lesson with a pop quiz, would not be practical because some students might have missed the lesson. Also a quiz tests only knowledge, not performance. Answer B, point out student errors, requires the librarian to be careful not to alienate students by embarrassing them and does not foster change. Answer C, incorporate unacceptable behavior into grades, would make the grades too ambiguous. The librarian should evaluate growth in library skills. Generally, most reporting forms have a section where the evaluator can indicate a need for behavior improvement.

82. C: By definition, a storyteller is someone who verbally recalls stories for audiences. Most of the stories are culturally based and revolve around topics the audience may not yet be familiar with. Because these stories are told from memory, there is an increase in audience engagement and the listening skills required. Guest readers would read a book to the audience, and although they may engage with the audience while reading or choose a book with a specific cultural orientation, these topics are not as intuitive in this scenario as they are in storytelling. This same information pertains to authors doing a read-aloud. Speakers would provide an experience that is not necessarily story based.

83. B: Library subscription services are the parts of the collection that continually renew offerings and grant access to subscribers. Examples include e-book and audiobook vendors, databases, and magazines. These subscriptions allow access to up-to-date information and new materials and resources. Contacting families through an email list (A) does not align with this definition of subscribing as it is not a service that provides access to resources. Delivering books to students (D) also does not align with this meaning of subscription. Providing access to books from other libraries (C) requires the library to be part of a consortium of libraries and participate in interlibrary loans.

84. B: Eisenberg and Berkowitz focused on student-led inquiry and related metacognitive processes. Doing so allowed them to develop the Big6 research model that provides students with the guidance and skills needed to support their own inquiries. Ken Macrorie developed the I-Search model to support student autonomy (A). Carol Kuhlthau's Information Search Process is meant to take a whole student-based approach to learning and highlights the potential feelings of students as they work through research (C). Many researchers and library figureheads, such as Keith Curry Lance and David V. Loertscher, have helped to better define library curriculums and refine inquiry-based learning processes (D).

85. A: Terms like AND, NOT, and OR are examples of Boolean operators. They are used to narrow or broaden a search by including or excluding particular phrases in search results. Sorting search results (B) would allow the student to organize the results by categories like age, relevancy, or alphabetical. Filtering results (C) would allow the student to remove results based on his or her chosen criteria, usually the same used in sorting. A computational search engine (D) provides statistics as opposed to search results from a standard web crawler-based search engine.

86. C: Pressuring staff members into making donations can strain working relationships and is unprofessional. Book fairs are one of the most common forms of fundraising for school libraries. Typically, the library earns a percentage of the overall profit. Collaborating with a parent-teacher organization for fundraising benefits both parties financially, and both parties can share the planning and hosting responsibilities. Grants for library programming and reading initiatives are another popular way to obtain funding, and they require applications that explain how the funds will be used.

87. B: Collaborative projects with teachers. The primary purpose of the monthly report is to inform the principal how productive the library has been. This productivity includes more than circulation statistics. It includes projects the librarian has worked on with classroom teachers. Answer A is not a good choice because interpersonal problems, or infractions of the rules, are best dealt with informally and verbally. If written down, they may start conflicts or inflate concerns. Answer C is something to include in an annual budget request. A report details past events, not future plans. The same reasoning applies in Answer D. The monthly library report is not the proper venue for budget requests, although it is possible to write the report in such a way that it hints at future needs.

88. C: Sharing an explanatory presentation to all staff via email is the most effective and efficient method because it ensures that all staff members receive the same detailed information at the same time. It allows staff to review the goals at their convenience and provides a consistent reference that supports clarity and efficiency. While sending out a text message (A) is a quick way to reach all parties, it does not express the importance of the topic and is easy to ignore or forget about. It also does not address the goals in-depth, which will likely lead to more questions than answers for those who read the message. Presenting at a faculty meeting (B) allows for immediate questions and discussion, but it may not reach all staff members and does not provide an easily accessible reference afterward. Like a faculty meeting, a grade-level meeting (D) provides an audience in a setting conducive to covering the needed content but is ultimately inefficient because of the number of meetings that the librarian would need to attend.

89. B: A consortium is a cooperative group of libraries that share resources. In this situation, entering a consortium would increase access and reduce spending by providing patrons with access to resources available in other libraries without requiring the home library to purchase them. Enforcing or increasing fees (A) has been shown to lead to decreased patronage as some individuals are unable to pay and thus cannot check out more materials until the fees are addressed. A decrease in circulation can lead to a decrease in funding if that data is used to make financial decisions. While hosting fundraisers (C) can bring in money, a consortium is a better solution as it provides access to resources that already exist and have been paid for. Subscription-based services (D) are likely to cause an increase in spending as they are billed at regular intervals.

90. B: The ability to add software and connect hardware after purchasing is critical to being able to modify devices so that they are usable for all. This may include screen readers, dictation programs, modified controllers, and other tools that increase accessibility. Ongoing support (A) from the company is helpful when any issues arise and may be helpful when adding the aforementioned technology and tools, but ongoing support does not increase access on its own. Ensuring the privacy policies of all parties align (C) is necessary when purchasing new technology and keeps students safe, but it does not increase access. While size and portability may seem to be the easiest way to increase access (D), these qualities do not address all disabilities. Only by allowing continuous modifications can all disabilities be addressed.

91. A: Ask the student what his assignment is and what kind of books he is looking for.

Before the librarian can effectively help the student, she must interview him about his needs. If his answer is vague, such as, "Well, I have to write this science paper," she should ask him a series of questions until she understands his exact need. Then, she can assist him in finding appropriate materials. Answer B assumes that the student knows what book he wants and does not know how to find it. This may not be the case. He may not know what book will help him. Answer C puts the problem off until another time, and the student may have a deadline to complete his assignment. Answer D takes valuable library time away from the student assigned help, and that student will not know as much as the librarian does about available materials.

92. C: Use OPAC to find MARC entries about Monarch butterfly migration. The student clearly needs guidance in locating research materials. OPAC is a computerized catalog that will help narrow his search to appropriate materials. The Dewey Decimal System has been replaced in most libraries with computerized catalogs like OPAC. B might be a helpful suggestion, but the topic is so broad that too many responses would probably be generated. D, the *Readers' Guide to Periodical Literature*, is another outdated print resource now generally replaced by online data resources.

93. D: Eric Carle is the only author from these answer choices that writes for beginning readers. His works include *The Very Hungry Caterpillar, The Grouchy Ladybug,* and *Brown Bear, Brown Bear, What Do You See?* Lois Lowry is best known for *The Giver Quartet* and *Number the Stars.* S.E. Hinton authored the young adult book *The Outsiders.* Harper Lee wrote the award-winning *To Kill a Mockingbird*, which is often used in middle grades and high school.

94. B: Books or resources borrowed through interlibrary loan (ILL) services will still typically have hard deadlines for when they need to be returned to the library that owns them. This is done to ensure equal access to resources is maintained, especially for patrons of the library that owns the resources. ILL services allow libraries to provide access to resources for patrons without having to purchase each resource, creating a decrease in spending (A). By being in a library consortium, a library can provide patrons with access to resources that includes the offerings of all consortium members. This leads to an increase in circulation of resources, thus maximizing the use of resources (C). Similarly, this increases access to patrons (D) by allowing them to borrow and use resources not available directly from their home library.

95. B: Weeding in libraries is usually driven more by circulation data and the quality and relevance of books than by budgeting information. Choosing to borrow books from another library (A) reflects the lack of funds available to purchase books, something one would notice when evaluating the budget and determining the most appropriate cuts to make. While enhancing a collection (C) seems to be aligned with library goals, in this situation the librarian has created a purchasing plan based on information gained from evaluating the budget. The principal determining the library is entitled to funds (D) shows that the school is aware of a deficit in the library or that it needs funding, both of which would have been discovered in an evaluation.

96. C: Entering full questions into a search engine does not assist in finding a direct answer. Instead, students should use key terms and phrases to return the most helpful results. Inserting quotation marks (A) ensures that the results presented will contain those terms or phrases as written. Using an asterisk with words that may be spelled differently (B) allows the engine to return results with similar spellings that match the other information searched. AND, NOT, and OR (D) are Boolean operators and are used to limit results to better fit what the searcher is looking for.

97. B: A request for proposal (RFP) is the first step in requesting bids from vendors and outlines the needed goods and services being sought. Vendors respond to an RFP with proposals that outline how they can fulfill its needs. From those proposals, a vendor is selected. Sample contracts (A) are not something a librarian would create; the contracted work would be outlined in the vendor proposal. Cold-calling vendors (C) is likely not necessary to gain interest in the project. A purchasing plan (D) would better align with smaller projects, such as book and resource purchasing, but not with something that requires bids.

98. C: Having this information added to the weekly newsletter ensures it will reach most families. Because parents are expecting this document regularly, they are more likely to see this information than with the other methods offered here. A banner on the circulation system's homepage (A) would require the parents to access the system, which is not something they do often. School websites are hubs of information (B) but not something parents tend to browse for leisure, so they may not see the popup until much later than the librarian would hope. Running a campaign on the morning announcements (D) would put the responsibility to share information on students, which is far less effective than direct and expected contact.

99. D: MLA (Modern Language Association) style citations are most appropriate in this scenario as they are most commonly used in the humanities, including English and literature. Additionally, MLA is the most-used citation method in high schools. Chicago Style citations (A) are used by professional scholars and are more popular for works pertaining to history. Turabian Style (C) is a modified version of Chicago style meant for students. APA stands for American Psychological Association, and APA citations (B) are used in the social sciences like psychology, anthropology, sociology, and education.

100. D: The initial step in selecting a vendor is to ensure it stocks the desired resources because many vendors are age and content specific. After ensuring availability, the librarian may choose to move forward with purchasing; however, he or she may continue this process with other vendors and compare costs (C). Cross-referencing prices with other retailers (B) gives the librarian a frame of reference for price expectations. Once the librarian verifies the vendor he or she wishes to work with, he or she may need to send that information to the finance or purchasing department for approval before submitting a purchase order (A). This should be done only after it has been fully established that the vendor is able to provide what is needed.

Constructed Response

1. Essay question graders commonly look for the following elements in a strong response: strong content knowledge, clear organization, and effective arguments or examples. Language and usage are not usually strictly graded, but they can make a big impact on the clarity of your ideas.

Please use the provided rubric to make sure your response meets these common criteria. Try to have a friend or family member grade your response for you or take a break after writing your response and return to grade it with fresh eyes.

CONSTRUCTED RESPONSE RUBRIC

Domain	Description
Content Knowledge	• The response directly addresses every part of the prompt. • The response demonstrates independent knowledge of the topic. • The response discusses the topic at an appropriate depth.
Organization	• The response introduces the topic, usually with a thesis statement or by restating the prompt. • The response directly addresses the prompt by providing a clear and concise answer or solution. • The answer or solution is supported by logical arguments or evidence. • The response restates the main idea in the conclusion.
Arguments and Examples	• The response provides a reasonable answer to the prompt. • The answer is supported by strong reasoning or evidence. • The response develops ideas logically and connects ideas to one another. • The reasoning and evidence provided act to support a unified main idea.
Language and Usage	• The response demonstrates effective use of grammar and uses varied sentence structure throughout the response. • The response demonstrates correct use of spelling, punctuation, and capitalization. • The response demonstrates strong and varied use of vocabulary relevant to the topic and appropriate for the intended audience.

How to Overcome Test Anxiety

Just the thought of taking a test is enough to make most people a little nervous. A test is an important event that can have a long-term impact on your future, so it's important to take it seriously and it's natural to feel anxious about performing well. But just because anxiety is normal, that doesn't mean that it's helpful in test taking, or that you should simply accept it as part of your life. Anxiety can have a variety of effects. These effects can be mild, like making you feel slightly nervous, or severe, like blocking your ability to focus or remember even a simple detail.

If you experience test anxiety—whether severe or mild—it's important to know how to beat it. To discover this, first you need to understand what causes test anxiety.

Causes of Test Anxiety

While we often think of anxiety as an uncontrollable emotional state, it can actually be caused by simple, practical things. One of the most common causes of test anxiety is that a person does not feel adequately prepared for their test. This feeling can be the result of many different issues such as poor study habits or lack of organization, but the most common culprit is time management. Starting to study too late, failing to organize your study time to cover all of the material, or being distracted while you study will mean that you're not well prepared for the test. This may lead to cramming the night before, which will cause you to be physically and mentally exhausted for the test. Poor time management also contributes to feelings of stress, fear, and hopelessness as you realize you are not well prepared but don't know what to do about it.

Other times, test anxiety is not related to your preparation for the test but comes from unresolved fear. This may be a past failure on a test, or poor performance on tests in general. It may come from comparing yourself to others who seem to be performing better or from the stress of living up to expectations. Anxiety may be driven by fears of the future—how failure on this test would affect your educational and career goals. These fears are often completely irrational, but they can still negatively impact your test performance.

Elements of Test Anxiety

As mentioned earlier, test anxiety is considered to be an emotional state, but it has physical and mental components as well. Sometimes you may not even realize that you are suffering from test anxiety until you notice the physical symptoms. These can include trembling hands, rapid heartbeat, sweating, nausea, and tense muscles. Extreme anxiety may lead to fainting or vomiting. Obviously, any of these symptoms can have a negative impact on testing. It is important to recognize them as soon as they begin to occur so that you can address the problem before it damages your performance.

The mental components of test anxiety include trouble focusing and inability to remember learned information. During a test, your mind is on high alert, which can help you recall information and stay focused for an extended period of time. However, anxiety interferes with your mind's natural processes, causing you to blank out, even on the questions you know well. The strain of testing during anxiety makes it difficult to stay focused, especially on a test that may take several hours. Extreme anxiety can take a huge mental toll, making it difficult not only to recall test information but even to understand the test questions or pull your thoughts together.

Effects of Test Anxiety

Test anxiety is like a disease—if left untreated, it will get progressively worse. Anxiety leads to poor performance, and this reinforces the feelings of fear and failure, which in turn lead to poor performances on subsequent tests. It can grow from a mild nervousness to a crippling condition. If allowed to progress, test anxiety can have a big impact on your schooling, and consequently on your future.

Test anxiety can spread to other parts of your life. Anxiety on tests can become anxiety in any stressful situation, and blanking on a test can turn into panicking in a job situation. But fortunately, you don't have to let anxiety rule your testing and determine your grades. There are a number of relatively simple steps you can take to move past anxiety and function normally on a test and in the rest of life.

Physical Steps for Beating Test Anxiety

While test anxiety is a serious problem, the good news is that it can be overcome. It doesn't have to control your ability to think and remember information. While it may take time, you can begin taking steps today to beat anxiety.

Just as your first hint that you may be struggling with anxiety comes from the physical symptoms, the first step to treating it is also physical. Rest is crucial for having a clear, strong mind. If you are tired, it is much easier to give in to anxiety. But if you establish good sleep habits, your body and mind will be ready to perform optimally, without the strain of exhaustion. Additionally, sleeping well helps you to retain information better, so you're more likely to recall the answers when you see the test questions.

Getting good sleep means more than going to bed on time. It's important to allow your brain time to relax. Take study breaks from time to time so it doesn't get overworked, and don't study right before bed. Take time to rest your mind before trying to rest your body, or you may find it difficult to fall asleep.

Along with sleep, other aspects of physical health are important in preparing for a test. Good nutrition is vital for good brain function. Sugary foods and drinks may give a burst of energy but this burst is followed by a crash, both physically and emotionally. Instead, fuel your body with protein and vitamin-rich foods.

Also, drink plenty of water. Dehydration can lead to headaches and exhaustion, especially if your brain is already under stress from the rigors of the test. Particularly if your test is a long one, drink water during the breaks. And if possible, take an energy-boosting snack to eat between sections.

Along with sleep and diet, a third important part of physical health is exercise. Maintaining a steady workout schedule is helpful, but even taking 5-minute study breaks to walk can help get your blood pumping faster and clear your head. Exercise also releases endorphins, which contribute to a positive feeling and can help combat test anxiety.

When you nurture your physical health, you are also contributing to your mental health. If your body is healthy, your mind is much more likely to be healthy as well. So take time to rest, nourish your body with healthy food and water, and get moving as much as possible. Taking these physical steps will make you stronger and more able to take the mental steps necessary to overcome test anxiety.

Mental Steps for Beating Test Anxiety

Working on the mental side of test anxiety can be more challenging, but as with the physical side, there are clear steps you can take to overcome it. As mentioned earlier, test anxiety often stems from lack of preparation, so the obvious solution is to prepare for the test. Effective studying may be the most important weapon you have for beating test anxiety, but you can and should employ several other mental tools to combat fear.

First, boost your confidence by reminding yourself of past success—tests or projects that you aced. If you're putting as much effort into preparing for this test as you did for those, there's no reason you should expect to fail here. Work hard to prepare; then trust your preparation.

Second, surround yourself with encouraging people. It can be helpful to find a study group, but be sure that the people you're around will encourage a positive attitude. If you spend time with others who are anxious or cynical, this will only contribute to your own anxiety. Look for others who are motivated to study hard from a desire to succeed, not from a fear of failure.

Third, reward yourself. A test is physically and mentally tiring, even without anxiety, and it can be helpful to have something to look forward to. Plan an activity following the test, regardless of the outcome, such as going to a movie or getting ice cream.

When you are taking the test, if you find yourself beginning to feel anxious, remind yourself that you know the material. Visualize successfully completing the test. Then take a few deep, relaxing breaths and return to it. Work through the questions carefully but with confidence, knowing that you are capable of succeeding.

Developing a healthy mental approach to test taking will also aid in other areas of life. Test anxiety affects more than just the actual test—it can be damaging to your mental health and even contribute to depression. It's important to beat test anxiety before it becomes a problem for more than testing.

Study Strategy

Being prepared for the test is necessary to combat anxiety, but what does being prepared look like? You may study for hours on end and still not feel prepared. What you need is a strategy for test prep. The next few pages outline our recommended steps to help you plan out and conquer the challenge of preparation.

Step 1: Scope Out the Test

Learn everything you can about the format (multiple choice, essay, etc.) and what will be on the test. Gather any study materials, course outlines, or sample exams that may be available. Not only will this help you to prepare, but knowing what to expect can help to alleviate test anxiety.

Step 2: Map Out the Material

Look through the textbook or study guide and make note of how many chapters or sections it has. Then divide these over the time you have. For example, if a book has 15 chapters and you have five days to study, you need to cover three chapters each day. Even better, if you have the time, leave an extra day at the end for overall review after you have gone through the material in depth.

If time is limited, you may need to prioritize the material. Look through it and make note of which sections you think you already have a good grasp on, and which need review. While you are studying, skim quickly through the familiar sections and take more time on the challenging parts.

Write out your plan so you don't get lost as you go. Having a written plan also helps you feel more in control of the study, so anxiety is less likely to arise from feeling overwhelmed at the amount to cover.

STEP 3: GATHER YOUR TOOLS

Decide what study method works best for you. Do you prefer to highlight in the book as you study and then go back over the highlighted portions? Or do you type out notes of the important information? Or is it helpful to make flashcards that you can carry with you? Assemble the pens, index cards, highlighters, post-it notes, and any other materials you may need so you won't be distracted by getting up to find things while you study.

If you're having a hard time retaining the information or organizing your notes, experiment with different methods. For example, try color-coding by subject with colored pens, highlighters, or post-it notes. If you learn better by hearing, try recording yourself reading your notes so you can listen while in the car, working out, or simply sitting at your desk. Ask a friend to quiz you from your flashcards, or try teaching someone the material to solidify it in your mind.

STEP 4: CREATE YOUR ENVIRONMENT

It's important to avoid distractions while you study. This includes both the obvious distractions like visitors and the subtle distractions like an uncomfortable chair (or a too-comfortable couch that makes you want to fall asleep). Set up the best study environment possible: good lighting and a comfortable work area. If background music helps you focus, you may want to turn it on, but otherwise keep the room quiet. If you are using a computer to take notes, be sure you don't have any other windows open, especially applications like social media, games, or anything else that could distract you. Silence your phone and turn off notifications. Be sure to keep water close by so you stay hydrated while you study (but avoid unhealthy drinks and snacks).

Also, take into account the best time of day to study. Are you freshest first thing in the morning? Try to set aside some time then to work through the material. Is your mind clearer in the afternoon or evening? Schedule your study session then. Another method is to study at the same time of day that you will take the test, so that your brain gets used to working on the material at that time and will be ready to focus at test time.

STEP 5: STUDY!

Once you have done all the study preparation, it's time to settle into the actual studying. Sit down, take a few moments to settle your mind so you can focus, and begin to follow your study plan. Don't give in to distractions or let yourself procrastinate. This is your time to prepare so you'll be ready to fearlessly approach the test. Make the most of the time and stay focused.

Of course, you don't want to burn out. If you study too long you may find that you're not retaining the information very well. Take regular study breaks. For example, taking five minutes out of every hour to walk briskly, breathing deeply and swinging your arms, can help your mind stay fresh.

As you get to the end of each chapter or section, it's a good idea to do a quick review. Remind yourself of what you learned and work on any difficult parts. When you feel that you've mastered the material, move on to the next part. At the end of your study session, briefly skim through your notes again.

But while review is helpful, cramming last minute is NOT. If at all possible, work ahead so that you won't need to fit all your study into the last day. Cramming overloads your brain with more information than it can process and retain, and your tired mind may struggle to recall even previously learned information when it is overwhelmed with last-minute study. Also, the urgent nature of cramming and the stress placed on your brain contribute to anxiety. You'll be more likely to go to the test feeling unprepared and having trouble thinking clearly.

So don't cram, and don't stay up late before the test, even just to review your notes at a leisurely pace. Your brain needs rest more than it needs to go over the information again. In fact, plan to finish your studies by noon or early afternoon the day before the test. Give your brain the rest of the day to relax or focus on other things, and get a good night's sleep. Then you will be fresh for the test and better able to recall what you've studied.

Step 6: Take a Practice Test

Many courses offer sample tests, either online or in the study materials. This is an excellent resource to check whether you have mastered the material, as well as to prepare for the test format and environment.

Check the test format ahead of time: the number of questions, the type (multiple choice, free response, etc.), and the time limit. Then create a plan for working through them. For example, if you have 30 minutes to take a 60-question test, your limit is 30 seconds per question. Spend less time on the questions you know well so that you can take more time on the difficult ones.

If you have time to take several practice tests, take the first one open book, with no time limit. Work through the questions at your own pace and make sure you fully understand them. Gradually work up to taking a test under test conditions: sit at a desk with all study materials put away and set a timer. Pace yourself to make sure you finish the test with time to spare and go back to check your answers if you have time.

After each test, check your answers. On the questions you missed, be sure you understand why you missed them. Did you misread the question (tests can use tricky wording)? Did you forget the information? Or was it something you hadn't learned? Go back and study any shaky areas that the practice tests reveal.

Taking these tests not only helps with your grade, but also aids in combating test anxiety. If you're already used to the test conditions, you're less likely to worry about it, and working through tests until you're scoring well gives you a confidence boost. Go through the practice tests until you feel comfortable, and then you can go into the test knowing that you're ready for it.

Test Tips

On test day, you should be confident, knowing that you've prepared well and are ready to answer the questions. But aside from preparation, there are several test day strategies you can employ to maximize your performance.

First, as stated before, get a good night's sleep the night before the test (and for several nights before that, if possible). Go into the test with a fresh, alert mind rather than staying up late to study.

Try not to change too much about your normal routine on the day of the test. It's important to eat a nutritious breakfast, but if you normally don't eat breakfast at all, consider eating just a protein bar. If you're a coffee drinker, go ahead and have your normal coffee. Just make sure you time it so that the caffeine doesn't wear off right in the middle of your test. Avoid sugary beverages, and drink enough water to stay hydrated but not so much that you need a restroom break 10 minutes into the test. If your test isn't first thing in the morning, consider going for a walk or doing a light workout before the test to get your blood flowing.

Allow yourself enough time to get ready, and leave for the test with plenty of time to spare so you won't have the anxiety of scrambling to arrive in time. Another reason to be early is to select a good seat. It's helpful to sit away from doors and windows, which can be distracting. Find a good seat, get out your supplies, and settle your mind before the test begins.

When the test begins, start by going over the instructions carefully, even if you already know what to expect. Make sure you avoid any careless mistakes by following the directions.

Then begin working through the questions, pacing yourself as you've practiced. If you're not sure on an answer, don't spend too much time on it, and don't let it shake your confidence. Either skip it and come back later, or eliminate as many wrong answers as possible and guess among the remaining ones. Don't dwell on these questions as you continue—put them out of your mind and focus on what lies ahead.

Be sure to read all of the answer choices, even if you're sure the first one is the right answer. Sometimes you'll find a better one if you keep reading. But don't second-guess yourself if you do immediately know the answer. Your gut instinct is usually right. Don't let test anxiety rob you of the information you know.

If you have time at the end of the test (and if the test format allows), go back and review your answers. Be cautious about changing any, since your first instinct tends to be correct, but make sure you didn't misread any of the questions or accidentally mark the wrong answer choice. Look over any you skipped and make an educated guess.

At the end, leave the test feeling confident. You've done your best, so don't waste time worrying about your performance or wishing you could change anything. Instead, celebrate the successful completion of this test. And finally, use this test to learn how to deal with anxiety even better next time.

Review Video: Test Anxiety
Visit mometrix.com/academy and enter code: 100340

Important Qualification

Not all anxiety is created equal. If your test anxiety is causing major issues in your life beyond the classroom or testing center, or if you are experiencing troubling physical symptoms related to your anxiety, it may be a sign of a serious physiological or psychological condition. If this sounds like your situation, we strongly encourage you to seek professional help.

Online Resources

Due to our efforts to try to keep this book to a manageable length, we've created a link that will give you access to all of your online resources:

mometrix.com/resources719/nbptslibmecya

It's Your Moment, Let's Celebrate It!

Share your story @mometrixtestpreparation